A HISTORY OF
KOREA

D'YOUVILLE COLLEGE
LIBRARY

A HISTORY OF
KOREA

Roger Tennant

Kegan Paul International
London and New York

First published in 1996 by
Kegan Paul International
UK: P.O. Box 256, London WC1B 3SW, England
Tel: (0171) 580 5511 Fax: (0171) 436 0899
E-mail: books@keganpau.demon.co.uk
Internet: http://www.demon.co.uk/keganpaul/
USA: 562 West 113th Street, New York, NY 10025, USA
Tel: (212) 666 1000 Fax: (212) 316 3100

Distributed by

John Wiley & Sons Ltd
Southern Cross Trading Estate
1 Oldlands Way, Bognor Regis
West Sussex, PO22 9SA, England
Tel: (01243) 779 777 Fax: (01243) 820 250

Columbia University Press
562 West 113th Street
New York, NY 10025, USA
Tel: (212) 666 1000 Fax: (212) 316 3100

© Roger Tennant 1996

Set in 11 on 12 pt Garamond
by Intype, London

Printed in Great Britain by TJ Press, Padstow, Cornwall

All rights reserved. No part of this book may be reprinted
or reproduced or utilized in any form or by any electronic,
mechanical or other means, now known or hereafter invented,
including photocopying and recording, or in any information
storage or retrieval system, without permission in writing
from the publishers.

ISBN 0–7103–0532–X

British Library Cataloguing in Publication Data
Tennant, Roger
History of Korea
I. Title
951.9

ISBN 0–7103–0532–X

US Library of Congress Cataloging in Publication Data
Tennant, Charles Roger, 1919–
A history of Korea / Roger Tennant.
310pp. 19cm.
Includes bibliographical references and index.
ISBN 0–7103–0532–X
1. Korea – History. I. Title.
DS 907.18.T46 1996
951.9—dc20   95–43488
                                                   CIP

DS 907.18
.T46
1996

For Charlotte and Leo
– the other half of your story

CONTENTS

LIST OF MAPS

AUTHOR'S NOTE

THE romanization of Korean follows the McCune-Reischauer
system except for a few people such as Kim Young Sam or
places such as Seoul or Pyongyang that are already familiar in other
forms. For Chinese, the Pinyin system is used and for Japanese the
Hepburn.

For the sake of simplicity I have called Kings by titles that were
not awarded until after their deaths, and where the names of places
have changed I have used those that can be found on modern maps.

The Far East

INTRODUCTION

HILLS AND RIVERS

Always there are hills in the distance, backed by mountains, wreathed in mist, and always the sound of water. These are the things that have inspired the country's poets and artists and haunt the dreams of its exiles. An eastern backbone of sharp mountains has ribs that run westward and from these wooded hills flow the water that trickles through the rice fields. Climatic maps show it to be at the centre of a small area that is almost unique in its combination of cold dry winters and hot rainy summers. Most of its plants and animals are common to the temperate zone of the Northern Hemisphere but they are tested almost to destruction by seasonal alternations of Siberian cold and summer monsoons. In May the brown desert of winter begins to shimmer in a delicate veil of green which grows into a summer jungle and dies with glory in a long warm autumn of red and gold.

About 600 miles in length and 150–200 miles wide, it reaches out from the mainland like an oriental Italy, with China embracing it to the north and west and Japan only 100 miles away to the south and east. The northern border with Manchuria is marked by the deep valleys of two rivers that flow from the opposite sides of Paektusan, highest of the 'Long White Mountains', a snow-capped volcanic range. One, the Tumen, twists north and eastwards towards a short border with the Maritime Provinces of Russia while the Yalu goes south-west towards the Yellow Sea where its banks level off to provide a pathway to Beijing.

On the eastern coast the mountains are near and the sea is deep, while on the west alluvial plains slope down to shallow waters with countless islands, 3,000 of them large enough to be named on the map, while others come and go with the 20-foot tides of the Yellow Sea. At the south-east corner an arctic current meets warmer waters from the south to provide rich fishing grounds.

I

This unique combination of climate and terrain, mountainous, with the rivers full only in the summer and the death of vegetation in the winter, set its inhabitants certain problems for which they produced a series of elegant and interconnected solutions, a way of life that established in its essentials by the end of the Iron Age, would for its peasant farmers, change little over the centuries and in the country areas would survive until the period of rapid industraliz- ation that began in the 1960s.

It would be based on small villages built on the southern slopes of the hills, with terraced rice fields below and barley or vegetable patches on the higher ground. Timber-framed houses with earthen walls and thatched roofs provided insulation from both heat and cold. From as early as neolithic times there is evidence of the *ondol* system, the use of the kitchen fire to heat the living room by flues that pass between the floor stones. It would be found in every home, even the poorest, and made possible the continuation of a comfortable and civilized life through the period of bitter cold between January and March. It would serve to keep the rooms largely free of furniture other than mats or mattresses and also ensure that everyone took their shoes off before they came in. In the summer the doors could be thrown open and wooden verandahs provided a cool place to sit. In the nineteenth century the King would have one of these traditional houses built in the palace grounds so that he and his consort could retreat there from the comfortless rooms of the palace.

Village houses would huddle close, but each with its own walled backyard. In the background were the successively steeper wooded hills where dwelt tigers, bears, deer and a myriad birds and lesser creatures, notably foxes (which sometimes changed into wicked women) and magpies (a more honest variety than those of the West), which brought luck. Among a wealth of migrant birds the geese were the ones which carried messages to or from loved ones who were at war or in exile. The hills could be a base for bandits, or a refuge for escaping slaves or prisoners who might become pro- fessional hunters or slash-and-burn farmers. On the lower slopes there would be long potters' kilns or in a glade by a mountain stream a rambling monastery. Each mountain had its own spirit whose deep cry would occasionally be heard, benevolent but easily offended and in need of placatory offerings.

With little tillable land to spare and no winter pasture the only domestic animals would be poultry, pigs fed on household scraps, and oxen of a docile breed, rarely more than one per family, kept under cover in winter and fed with warm gruel. These animals, indispensable for ploughing the paddies, were never bred for meat, nor was their milk thought suitable for human consumption. Dogs, as barely tolerated survivors from prehistoric times, were chiefly valued for *posint'ang*, a medicinal soup that preserved one's health through the hottest days of summer.

Burdens were mostly carried by women on their heads, and heavier ones, such as firewood, by men with a *chi'ge* or A-frame, a wooden frame with shoulder straps on which heavy loads could be carried with the body tilted forward to keep the centre of gravity over the feet. It suited the narrow banks between rice fields and the steep paths over the hills, where men were faster than horses. When the farmer took his ox to the paddy he carried the plough on his own back.

Their early culture was shared with the other Tungusic tribes of north-east Asia, as evidenced by the 'spirit poles' that still stand outside many villages and their still pervasive shamanistic beliefs, but from the second century BC onwards they were drawn ever deeper into the intricate web of a Chinese culture that, despite its periodic upheavals, had already amassed a dazzling array of political theories, philosophical insights, technical skills and stylized art. The peasant farmers who made up the majority of the population may not have been greatly affected by a culture that was for them locked up in mysterious ideograms but for their rulers it would provide the pattern for the growth of a sophisticated bureaucracy and prescribe the codes and fashions in every aspect of social life. It gave them a rich inheritance but it was a Faustian deal that would cost them half of their own souls. The adoption of Chinese as virtually the only form of written communication would curtail for another 2,000 years the growth of a vernacular literature. Not until the fifteenth century AD would an adequate alphabet be produced for their own language and even then the Confucianist elite, with all their intellectual capital invested in ideograms, would largely ignore it.

The language itself, thought to be of Ural-Altaic origins, does not appear to have suffered any significant change in its grammar or style from the influence of Chinese as the two are so utterly unlike, but there was a great influx of Chinese words, so much so that they take up more than half the space in a modern dictionary. In many cases the Korean equivalents have dropped out of use, but often, as with the Anglo-Saxon and Latin elements in English, the original language prevails in everyday speech while terms of Chinese origin provide synonyms and shades that are valued by bureaucrats and scholars. The way Koreans pronounce them is no longer generally intelligible to the Chinese.

Something of the gap between the two cultures can be sensed from the awkward juxtaposition of the nation's alternative foundation myths. The earliest written versions are found in a history by the monk Iryŏn in the thirteenth century AD, quoting older sources. The first tells of Hwan Ung, a younger son of the Heavenly King, who came down on Paektusan, where he found in a cave a bear and a tiger which had been praying that they might be transformed into human beings. He gave them a stalk of wormwood and 20 cloves of garlic and told them to hibernate for 100 days. The tiger, being restless, wandered out but the bear remained and emerged as a woman who subsequently bore to Ung a son. Tan'gun, who became the founder of the nation. In the fiftieth year of the Chinese emperor Yao (2333 BC) he established his capital at Pyongyang and called his kingdom 'Chosŏn'.

Although this version has been fitted into a Chinese chronology and Hwan Ung demoted to a *younger* Son of Heaven, Paektusan was beyond the ken of ancient China, the tiger and the bear, who like the shaman can fast and dream, are Siberian animals and the difference in their habits of hibernation is accurately depicted.

The alternative founder is Qizi (pronounced 'Kija' in Korean), a Chinese nobleman of the thirteenth century BC who was exiled for refusing to recognize an Emperor who had usurped the throne. The Korean story, which has no support from Chinese sources, credits him with arriving there in 1122 BC to teach the people the fundamentals of civilized life. This legend cannot be traced back before the first century BC and the earliest Chinese reference to the cult of Qizi in Korea comes in the seventh century AD. A shrine for him in Pyongyang dates back only to the twelfth century, which was the period when Neo-Confucianism began to flourish and the scholarly elite were eager both to counter the influence of Buddhism and to persuade the Chinese to see them not as 'northern barbarians' but as the inheritors of an ancient civilization that had long followed the *Dao*, 'The Way'.

In Iryŏn's history the two accounts are reconciled by explaining that on the arrival of Kija, Tan'gun, having ruled for 1,500 years, agreed to abdicate, and returned to Paektusan to resume his former role as a mountain god. Here he would be left in peace for another twice times 1,500 years until in 1886 Sir Francis Younghusband, chiefly famed for driving the Dalai Lama out of Lhasa, became the first Westerner to plant his country's flag above the holy lake in its crater. In more recent times it has been a favourite spot for photo calls by the ruling dynasty of the People's Republic.

Before the Iron-Age settlements in the north came into regular contact with Chinese culture they reflected that of the Central Asian horsemen who founded or, more often, conquered them. As their descendants moved southwards to impose themselves on the inhabitants of the valleys and eventually to be absorbed by them, horses would become increasingly irrelevant. The hills and rivers were virtually impassable for wheeled vehicles while the shortage of grassland and the lack of winter fodder made the animals an expensive luxury. Apart from the cavalry horses needed for defence the only common breed would be the tiny pack-horses developed by the mountain tribes of the north and known to the Chinese as *kwahama*, 'under the fruit horses', because you could ride one under the branches of a fruit tree. Quarrelsome, but shapely and surefooted, they were not strong enough to plough the wet fields or carry heavy loads and would play no part in village life, but merchants would use strings of them for long-distance haulage. They had to be provided with hot meals every night at the inns on the way and in later times the expense and the stubborn behaviour of both the ponies and their grooms would exasperate Victorian visitors. Indeed, the first professional explorer, Angus Hamilton, FRGS, ended up using his whip on his head groom, which started a punch-up in the courtyard of the inn and almost cost him his life. There were few roads wide enough for carts, and it would not be until the age of the railway and the car that the Koreans would find much use for the wheel.

Only the large island of Cheju, which lies in warmer waters to the south, and has thousands of acres of grass, is still the kingdom of the horse, and was developed as a breeding centre by the Mongols, some of whose terms and customs still survive. Its three ruling families of Yang, Ko and Pu claim descent from spirits that came from one of its great lava-tube caves. The Ko family's successes in the civil service examinations often won them official appointments in the capital. One of them served in the palace guards, and after an acquaintance had come back from an official visit to the island he asked him whether he had been to see the cave from which his ancestors came and was told, 'Yes, and I pissed in it'.

In the nineteenth-century a visitor would need several ponies to carry the strings of metal coins that served as currency. The weight of coins required to buy anything, even an egg, was a source of grievance, even of tragedy, for when the British Navy occupied a south-coast island in the 1880s and a Japanese entrepreneur brought some girls to an island nearby, a young sailor who fell out of the boat on his way over to them went straight to the bottom. In fact, money was another invention that they did not take to. For short periods – in the last days of Tang-dynasty China in the nineth century, the last days of the Yuan in the fourteenth, and the early days of the Qing in the eighteenth – there would be short-lived bursts of trade, travel and money, but, generally speaking, if coins had any intrinsic value they were hoarded and if they did not they were not trusted, so either way it was hard to make them circulate – a general distaste for trade was part of the Confucian way of life. Up to the 1880s taxes and government salaries were paid in rice or rolls of cloth and even as late as the 1950s it was common for village people to take rice or eggs to market for the few manufactured goods that they needed.

Glass was another development in which they would show little interest. An attempt to set up a glass works in the 1890s suffered financial failure. Glass beads they had worn since the second century BC but for windows they preferred the privacy and insulation afforded by their translucent paper, which had been from early times an important export to China. It would not be until the seventeenth century that the Chinese discovered the trick of it, which was to use the inner bark of the mulberry tree. A waxed version provided an ideal fume-proof covering for their hot floors and was also used for conical throw-away umbrellas that could be placed on top of one's hat. A twelfth-century Chinese visitor noted their use of it for disposable tablecloths. They were slow to copy the Chinese idea of paper money, though by the seventh century they were using letters of credit, valued in ounces of silver, to finance students going to study in China.

There can be little doubt that woodblock printing began in China but, perhaps because of the quality of their paper, the world's oldest extant examples are Buddhist scriptures discovered in the base of a Korean pagoda that was completed in 751. They were probably the first to develop movable metal type, which they were using at the time of the thirteenth-century Mongol invasion. Paper was used not only for art, literature and insulation, but also as armour – the pen may be mightier than the sword, but 15–20 thicknesses of paper sown into a leather garment could resist the bullets from sixteenth-century muskets. It was also employed in kites, which had their military use as signals and later as wings for airborne troops, first used by General Ch'o Yŏng in an attack that drove the Mongols out of Cheju Island in 1374. The island is renowned for its high winds which served to lift them into the enemy's last cliff-top refuge.

Court dress began to conform to that of Tang China from the sixth century but the clothes used in everyday life would change little through the ages, beginning with the simple wide-sleeved hempen costumes common to that area of north-eastern Asia but modified in the thirteenth century when the marriage of Korean crown princes to the daughters of the Mongol dynasty in China led to their adopting the short jackets and voluminous skirts or baggy trousers of their allies, and these garments, are still known by their Mongol names.

The introduction of cotton at about the same time would change the texture but not the form, and in the summer months hemp would still be preferred for its coolness, while cotton padding provided winter warmth. The hair-style for men which required a boy's pigtail to be wound up into a topknot only when he married was common to much of the Far East but in later centuries would seem strange to visitors from China where it had been forbidden by their Manchu conquerors. This custom was deeply rooted in the Korean psyche and an attempt to enforce a Short Hair Edict in 1894 met such violent resistance that it would be quickly repealed and only an obsession with Westernization since 1945 has caused it to disappear. To match it came a distinctive hat, woven from bamboo or horsehair, in two pieces, an inner one to cover the topknot and an outer section with a large circular brim.

The peninsula is well endowed with harbours and islands and its waters with fish, but the élite, perhaps because of their Central Asian background and the influence of the Chinese, who preferred the calmer waters of their canals, never really took to the sea. Coastal defences were on a provincial basis with no separate naval ranks for officers – they were appointed indifferently to land or sea. There were one or two who appear to have been highly competent on both, notably Silla's seventh-century 'King of the Yellow Sea', Chang Po-go, the tenth-century 'Lord of the Hundred Ships', Wang Kŏn, who founded the Koryŏ dynasty, and General Yi Sun-sin, with his 'Turtle Boats', at the time of the sixteenth-century invasion by Japan.

Apart from fishermen and coastal defenders, the only people to have adventures at sea were those accidentally blown out there in the course of their duties. One famous example is Ch'oe Pu, who in the fifteenth century was caught in a storm while being ferried home from the island of Cheju, and after some days was washed up on the shores of China, where they found his insistence on the finer points of Confucian etiquette quite exasperating and were glad to send him back to Seoul. Two hundred years later, Yi Chi-hang, sailing up the east coast from Pusan, was blown as far as Sakhalin, and after adventures among the hairy Ainu came home via Tokyo, Osaka and Tsushima.

That Korean culture did not become entirely Sinified, despite the apparent victory of Kija and Confucius, may owe much to the counter-influence of Buddhism. Even though it was introduced largely through the medium of Chinese ideograms it first came to Korea from Central Asia as an essentially anti-Chinese ideology. In China itself Buddhism was taken up by warlords, Emperors' widows and sometimes even by the Emperors themselves, but it never won over the Confucian intellectuals and consequently rarely attracted the deepest thinkers or the greatest poets and artists. In Korea, by contrast, from the fifth or sixth centuries AD until the close of the thirteenth, it was the state religion, and in the seventh and eighth centuries, when the dominant state of Silla was singularly united in fervent devotion, scholars were sent to explore its sources in India as well as to consult the leading monasteries of China, resulting in sophisticated works of Buddhist philosophy as well as magnificent murals and sculpture.

The area around what was then the capital of Silla, Kyŏngju, became thickly populated with Buddhist institutions. The most impressive of those that survive is Pulguksa, a complex of temples and pagodas built on stone terraces and containing two eighth-century buddhas, one representing Amita and the other Vairocana, heavenly powers of whom the Gotama was the fullest earthly emanation. Between this temple and the sea lie hills that look east towards Japan. In 1909, while climbing a narrow path across them to take letters to a village on the coast, a postman was caught by a thunderstorm and noticing what appeared to be a cave, crept inside. As his eyes became accustomed to the darkness he began to discern a great stone buddha looming over him, while on the walls around were other shadowy figures. Thus was rediscovered, after decades of neglect, the Sŏkku-ram, an artificial grotto built in the eighth century to house what is perhaps the world's finest example of Buddhist art.

The central seated figure, ten feet high and carved from a single block of granite, has great simplicity and grace, while the figures in relief on the surrounding walls, chiefly 11 delicate bodhisattvas and ten muscular and earthy disciples, show the influence of their Indian and Central Asian sources with a combination of boldness and delicacy that is distinctively Korean.

The nation was unified from three kingdoms to one by Silla about 1,000 years ago, after which two more dynasties of roughly 500 years apiece, Koryŏ and Chosŏn, would carry it through to modern times. Despite incursions by the Mongols, the Manchus and the Japanese, the famines that a drought can bring to those who depend on rice, occasional epidemics and a too-rigid class system, with obsessive eccentricities of the kind that arise from geographical isolation, there grew up in these fertile valleys a complex scholarly culture. Their typical representatives can be seen as the farmer who as the sun goes down on a late summer evening sits cross-legged on his verandah listening to the chorus of the frogs and gazing with deep content on his terraces of golden rice and the scholar-official with a taste for

8

poetry, chess and wine, dressed in a long white coat and loose trousers tied at the ankles, a circular black hat perched on his topknot, and a fan to cool him as he sets off for the capital on a tiny horse led by a servant who chides him ironically in highly respectful language – an exemplar of elegance and virtue for almost 1,000 years, welcomed in China as the most literate and courteous of the Northern Barbarians, respected in Japan as one who could instruct them in the ways of civilization, but destined suddenly to wither under the cruel laughter of the nineteenth-century Westerner.

One of the more sympathetic of these superior visitants was the American astronomer Percy Lowell. He is chiefly famed for predicting the discovery of the planet Pluto, but as a young man he lived for a time in Japan and then went on to Korea, about which he wrote a book that begins by asking the reader to 'go with me to a land whose life for ages has been a mystery, a land which from time unknown has kept aloof ... whose people might have been denizens of another planet'. Perhaps it was this experience that would make him so ready to believe that the 'canals' he observed on Mars were the marks of an 'intelligent but dying race'. The canals did not survive closer scrutiny while the Koreans would continue to escape it and seemed doomed to fulfil their predicted role as a dying race. Submerged under the colonial rule of the Japanese from the turn of the century until 1945, they were then divided and occupied by the rival powers of the Cold War and pulverized by their tanks and bombers in the 1950s, but they have a proverb that says that even if the sky falls in there will still be a crack to crawl through. They demonstrated it by surviving to produce in the 1970s an economic miracle, after which, in the 80s they hosted the Olympic Games with style and charm and in 1991 they avenged 20 years of *MASH* by sending a medical unit to succour the American casualties of the Gulf War: by the end of the century they can expect to be one of the leaders in a rapidly developing area.

In a longer perspective it is a return to the world stage rather than a debut, for by the end of the fourth century AD their northern kingdom of Koguryŏ controlled much of north-east Asia and went on in the seventh century to outwit the largest army ever assembled by the Chinese, while to the south, Paekche took Buddhism to Japan. In the next century the third kingdom, Silla, came to dominate the commerce of the Yellow Sea and as far away as the Middle East people learned of this legendary land of hills and rivers from which, it was said, no traveller ever wished to return.

In the thirteenth century they were, of all the peoples overrun by the Mongols, the only ones never to be completely subdued, though their sufferings were such that after they had been followed by the Japanese and then the Manchus, they tended to see themselves as an endangered enclave with nothing but darkness beyond: the one thing needful was to keep the barbarians at bay. As yet the Western ones had not troubled them and they were hardly aware of their existence. It may be that a few Frankish mercenaries were there towards the end of the thirteenth century when Kubilai Khan set up his Field Headquarters for the Chastisement of Japan, and certainly Franciscans at the Mongol court took notice of the Korean diplomats because their dress reminded them of mass vestments and bishop's mitres.

Early in the sixteenth century the Portuguese established regular trade with Japan but it was not until 1577 that one of their ships, driven off course in a storm, caught a first glimpse of Korea. Fifteen years later, when a largely Catholic Japanese army was engaged in invading it, a Portuguese priest visited their bases on the south coast and among numerous Korean orphans taken back to be baptized in Japan a few were enrolled in the Jesuit college and some subsequently became martyrs. When the Italian merchant-explorer Francesco Carletti arrived in Nagasaki in 1597, on his way round the world, the persecution of the Catholics had just begun and he was taken outside the city to view the spectacle of 26 Christians, Western, Japanese and Korean, crucified upside down. He purchased five Korean boys, whom he set free in Goa, and one of them, baptized as Anthony, went back with him to Florence, the first of his countrymen known to have reached Europe.

Hideyoshi had once offered to make China a Catholic country if the Jesuits could provide him with enough Portuguese warships to defend the invading fleet, but the proposal was rejected, and after his successors had become more aware of what had happened to the native populations of the Philippines and Peru under Catholic rule they allowed only the Dutch to continue trading. On two occasions in the seventeenth century Dutch voyagers were washed ashore in Korea. The first provided the country with a technician who modernized their artillery, and the second involved a larger group, most of whom eventually escaped to give the West its first detailed account of the country. They included one Scotsman, Alexander Bosquet.

By the beginning of the nineteenth century ships from Europe and America were frequenting the Pacific but few of them touched Korea and as the names that appear on early maps seem to testify – Deception Bay, Insult Island or False River – not often with happy results. As the century wore on the Koreans were increasingly shocked by the treatment that the Chinese were receiving at the hands of the Western pirates and resolutely dismissed requests for trade.

In the last two decades of the century, under a strong-willed but backward-looking regent, the Koreans tried on the one hand to shut out the West and on the other to imitate its technology, with larger cannons in their forts and amateurish efforts to build a steamship and even a bird-winged seaplane. They banned Catholicism and were surprisingly successful in beating off punitive expeditions from France and America, but they had no answer to the ruthless efficiency of the new Japan, which having defeated China in 1895 and Russia in 1904 found itself in control of the peninsula it had used as a convenient bridge for its mainland victories. Japan was now a Great Power, 'the only one in the Far East, and attractive as an ally to both Britain and America. They had no grounds for criticizing its annexation of Korea, and the appeals of its King, with whom both of them had recently signed treaties of friendship, went unheard.

By the 1930s, as they pursued their conquest of China, the Japanese came to see the peninsula as the natural site for the administrative capital of their future empire, and by enforcing their language on the Koreans, giving them Japanese names and preparing for them to be represented in the Japanese parliament, they hoped eventually to turn them into loyal citizens – what greater blessing could there be? By 1943 many leading Koreans who had suffered torture and imprisonment as patriots began reluctantly to cooperate with the Japanese in the hope that at least their children might find some happiness in 'Asian Co-prosperity', only to find themselves, two years later, again on the wrong side.

The story is a fascinating one, but how does one tell it in a mere 300 pages? Some attempts, understandably, have dealt briefly with earlier times and concentrated on the last 200 years, but mindful of Burckhardt's dictum that for the historian all generations are equidistant from eternity I have tried to give the earlier ages their due, though for the earliest, of course, the sources are scanty. It may be that in stone-age politics also, a week was a long time, but when only the stones remain whole millennia recede like distant galaxies, while with more recent events the choice of focus is, inevitably, highly subjective. My method has been to slow the pace a little for what seem to be decisive events – such as the Tang alliance with Silla that led to the country's unification, the Mongol incursions of the thirteenth century, the Japanese invasion at the end of the sixteenth, and the early exchanges with the Western powers – and every now and again to provide a closer glimpse of an influential figure, or recall one of

those trivial incidents that can convey the flavour of an age and give
the abstractions of 'history' a local habitation and a name.

PART I

THE THREE KINGDOMS

CHAPTER ONE

BEGINNINGS

KOREANS like to boast of 'five thousand years of history', calculated from the birth of a legendary ancestor, born of a bear in 2333 BC. Much of their real prehistory still awaits the spades of the archaeologists. The earliest relics of *Homo erectus* to be found in the area are those of Lantian man who lived in the north Chinese province of Shaanxi about a million years ago. It was then warmer than today and there was forest and grassland that supported tigers, bears, elephants, deer and horses. The bones of 'Ryonggok man', thought to date from 400,000–500,000 years ago were found near Pyongyang in the 1980s. In the same area the bones of 'modern man' have been found in layers said to be from 40,000–50,000 years ago, along with a wide variety of animals. Fluctuations in climate and sea level must have affected these people and much of the area was inundated, but it escaped glaciation so that some continuity of the population is not impossible.

As the ice receded and warmer water rose to form the Yellow Sea, it shaped the coastline of the peninsula, isolating Japan and submerging the high ground that ran north-east from the south of China until at the other end it became the south-west of Korea, thus storing up for their potters the clay with which they would someday rival the Yue celadon of China. Although the sea did not reach its present level until about 5000 BC, there is evidence of both paleolithic and early neolithic groups from long before – hunters and gatherers moving through the wooded valleys of the larger rivers and, later, settling in pit houses near the seashore, where shellfish were plentiful. They have been linked with the Jomon people of Japan and like them they were making pots at least 10,000 years ago, which implies, if not agriculture, at least a settled life and cooked meals.

From about 6000 BC early villages with the incised pottery known as 'combware' are found and the rising sea-level may have provided the stimulus to build boats, to venture out after larger fish, and to establish colonial settlements. By about 2000 BC villages with walled houses begin to appear on higher ground. They domesticated pigs, dogs and chickens and on fields below grew millet and other grains and eventually rice which, whether across the Yellow Sea or through Manchuria, presumably came from the south of China. They made, and broke, many pots, the changing styles of which may reflect local invention, migratory movements or primitive trade.

At this time new migrations across the now drying steppes were beginning – people who were accomplished horsemen and who probably came as aggressors demanding tribute from the sedentary settlements. They brought with them the skills and weapons of the militaristic semi-barbarian culture that spread from the fringes of the early civilizations in the Middle East. These cultures, identified with the painted pottery of what is known as the Lower Xiajiadian, appear first in Manchuria and seem to have spread south to Shang dynasty China. Pottery with similar patterns is found in North Korea, as are also the bronze daggers and mirrors of the Upper Xiajiadian culture of about 1500 BC.

This is the period in which the early Chinese states of Xia, Shang and Zhou were established and Chinese settlers would gradually extend their cultivation into Manchuria, but their earliest influence seems to have been across the Yellow Sea to the south-western side of the peninsula. The oldest bronze-age items are found in the north, but the quantity of tools, pottery and monuments from sites in the south suggests that for most of the last millennium BC the river valleys of these warmer areas were more prosperous and thickly populated. We find new styles of pottery and evidence of weaving and specialized craftsmen in wood and stone. Similar styles found in the Shandong Peninsula and on the south island of Japan indicate trade, and perhaps migrations, by sea, and there is anthropological and linguistic evidence to suggest, at some stage, a Polynesian influx. These southern tribes, who came to be known generically as 'the Han' (not in any way connected with the Chinese dynasty of that name) presumably provided the basic genetic pool of the Korean people, reflected in their retention through the ages of their self-identity as 'the People of the Han'.

Protected by natural barriers, they were not compelled to build walls, though villages had palisades as a guard against wild animals, forest maurauders or pirates, and these would still be used as outer defences even after they had grown to towns, which in the north at least, would need ever bulkier stamped-earth walls to resist the iron weapons of horsemen with chariots and compound bows. Stone was still used for the majority of implements, but arrowheads and spears were of bronze, the weapons of the intruders.

From about 2000 BC, all over the settled valleys of the peninsula, the graves of the élite begin to be marked by dolmens with heavy capstones, often brought from distant sites, at great expense in labour. It appears to have been an indigenous development, presumably a kind of territorial marker or hieratic status symbol, which spread into the fringes of Manchuria, but can hardly have any connection, other than a similarity of social psychology, with the rather similar outbreaks that occurred in ancient Britain and other distant parts of Europe or Asia. In the peninsula something like 100,000 of them were erected over a period of about 1,500 years, associated with stone coffins or burial chambers and varied grave goods, few of which have survived, and the bones of sacrificial victims.

From about 600 BC the practice of erecting dolmens began to decline in the north, to be replaced by carefully constructed stone chambers with more elaborate grave goods, and covered by mounds or stone pyramids, probably indicating a new wave of bronze-age conquerors from Siberia, but perhaps only a new generation of enterprising funeral directors. From this period come vigorous Scytho-Siberian animal figures and belt clasps featuring tigers, deer and horses and over the next few hundred years these would be reshaped into forms that combine simplicity and realism in a distinctively Korean style.

This continuing influx of bronze-age invaders and immigrants and the resulting battles and alliances between tribal rulers in the north resulted in five distinctive areas mentioned in Chinese records of the fourth century BC: Puyǒ, Yemaek, Imdun, Chinbǒn and Chosǒn. The archaeological evidence suggests a ruling caste with walled settlements sometimes of a considerable extent, and no doubt, as in early Europe, the question of whether the walls were used to shelter those who tilled the land outside or as a protection against them will have varied from place to place and from one age to another.

Of these groups the only one to have much historical substance is Chosǒn, which by the end of the third century BC seems to have had a rudimentary bureaucracy controlling, or at least exacting tribute from, most of the area from the mouth of the Yalu across to the east coast. It is referred to by China as a *guo* or 'dynasty', ruled by a *wang*, the title conferred on Kings who paid tribute to the Emperor. Kibu, the first to receive the title, claimed supernatural status as a descendant of the legendary Kija referred to above. Even after Chosǒn itself had fallen, its name would still be used, not only by the Chinese, but by the ruling classes over much of the peninsula itself, to describe their origins. The Chinese represented it by two ideograms, *chao-xian*, literally, 'morning fresh', presumably chosen to express both the sound of an indigenous name and its geographical relation to China's position as the centre of the earth in the same way that Japan would be given the title of *nippon* or 'sun source'. Whatever their origins, the Japanese as the people of the 'Rising Sun' and Korea as the 'Land of Morning Calm' are phrases too firmly fixed in the minds of journalists and travel agents ever to be in danger of decline.

As the dominant power in the area, Chosŏn was able to control the peninsula's trade with the adjacent Chinese state of Yan, one of the warring states that followed the break-up of the Zhou empire and had its heartland north of the Yellow River where Beijing now stands. The extent of this trade is testified by the Zhou dynasty knife-money, weapons and implements found at numerous sites in the north of the peninsula. Although Chosŏn eventually established its capital on the Taedong River close to what is now Pyongyang it appears to have had most of its territory in Manchuria, and it was on its western marches along the Liao river that it came into contact with the Yan who wrote of them as 'arrogant and cruel'. Soon after this Yan temporarily succumbed to the Qin who were gobbling up states 'like silk worms eating mulberry leaves', while at the same time the next wave of mounted bowmen from the steppe, the Turkic confederation of the Xiongnu, were also driving refugees into Chosŏn.

With the collapse of the Qin in 207 BC Yan was re-established as a self-governing fief of their successors, the Han, but the whole region was increasingly threatened from the north and the west by the Xiongnu who were stretching their destructive power across the steppe from Europe to Manchuria, sending more refugees into the northern parts of the peninsula and forcing the rulers of Yan to become their allies.

Retaliation by the Han then brought in refugees from Yan, the most notable of whom was a war lord, Weiman ('Wiman' in Korean), who somewhere about 200 BC led his followers into the territory held by Chosŏn. According to Chinese sources, he adopted the local 'topknot' hairstyle and was appointed by King Kibu's successor, Kijun, as commander of their border defences. His success subsequently encouraged him to march on the capital and usurp the throne, and Kijun is said to have fled with his court to settle on the west coast south of the River Han. Over the next century Wiman's successors expanded to the north and to the east and as far south as the River Han, building fortified settlements to consolidate their territory, so that his grandson, King Ugo, was able to control

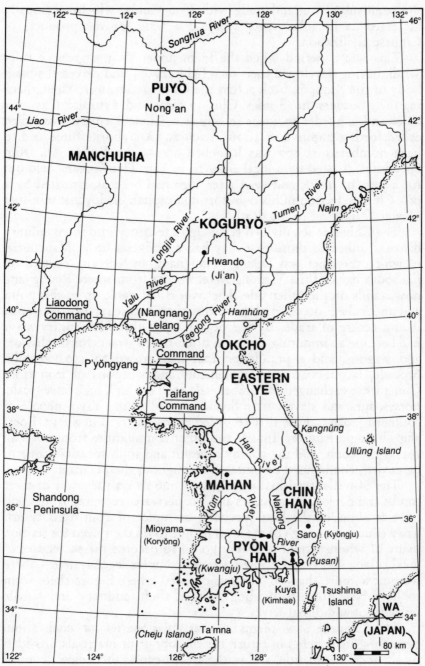

Chinese Territories and the Tribes
(Second Century AD)

the peninsula's overland trade with Han China, which continually increased as its inhabitants acquired a taste for the products of Chinese civilization.

This was a period when the Han, under their aggressive ruler Wudi, having developed their own light cavalry and driven the main body of the Xiongnu back across the Gobi Desert, were strengthening their borders on all sides. Chosŏn came under suspicion as their allies and a border incident in which a Chinese envoy was killed called forth a punitive invasion in 109 BC. A seaborne force said to have numbered 50,000 was launched across the Yellow Sea from Shandong, assisted by a local army from Yan. The Koreans held out for a year or more, and even after Ugo had been assassinated by a pro-Chinese faction in his own fortified capital, his loyalist minister, Sŏnggi, fought on to the death.

The Chinese then divided King Ugo's territory into three military districts linked to those that they had already set up in Manchuria, of which the chief was Lelang ('Nangnang' in Korean), centred on the south bank of the Taedong River not far from where Pyongyang now stands on the other side. The river is navigable up to this point and under the protection of their army the Chinese rapidly developed it as a centre of trade. By the beginning of the first century AD it had become an imposing city with brick-paved streets for its chariots and wagons, and a population that had grown to 350,000. Silk, brocade, lacquerware and implements and weapons of iron from China were exchanged for timber, salt, iron ore and, on a lesser scale, horses, furs and slaves. Its influence spread to the Yayoi people of southern Japan, whose first recorded envoys arrived in AD 57. Local ships brought iron ore, timber and other commodities from ports all round the coast, and the colony's wealth and sophistication came to be envied, condemned or imitated throughout the peninsula.

The officials lived luxuriously, and murals on the walls of their tombs and personal ornaments and lacquerware recovered from them provide some of the best surviving examples of Han dynasty art. They educated enough of the local people to fill their need for scribes, many of whom would probably go on to become the secretaries of local rulers, and they imposed a more complex legal system – there were now more than 60 'commandments' where before there seem to have been four, forbidding murder, theft, adultery and female jealousy of additional wives.

The Chinese saw themselves as missionaries of civilization, bestowing its benefits in return for the labour or materials provided by the local population, and in the areas beyond their direct control they won the support of the native leaders by awarding trade concessions and honorary titles and regalia. To this end, all business was done within the formality of offering tribute to the Han Emperor, and vestments were kept at the border posts for visiting tribal leaders to put on before they entered Chinese territory. It was under the Han that in China Confucianism flourished, paper was developed, and the first great historians arose. Its refining influences would blend with the more militaristic Scythian traditions of the area to produce a distinctive local culture. The first historical records date from this period and Chinese ideograms are still referred to as 'Han writing', there being no evidence of an earlier indigenous script.

The natives did not always respond in the way one would have hoped and the Chinese record occasional raiding parties from the south, sometimes on a scale that threatened their very existence. The varied effects of Chinese culture and iron-age invaders and refugees on the social organization of the agricultural communities south of the River Han are difficult to assess and the interpretation of the archaeological evidence is still in dispute. They are thought to have formed three large tribal federations, traditionally known as Mahan in the west, Chinhan in the east and Pyŏnhan to the south.

In the northern areas conflict with China provides more in the way of historical records, and from this point of view the most prominent of the tribes in Manchuria were the Puyŏ. They were former nomads who had settled in the arable land on either side of the Songhua River without abandoning their horses or their weapons, and they were valued by the Chinese as allies against further incursions from the steppe.

The people of Koguryŏ who occupied the mountains to the south of them as far as the Yalu were more warlike, and often in conflict with them and their Chinese allies. Koguryŏ's foundation myths refer to ancestors from Puyŏ and describe their state as founded in 37 BC by Chumong, born of an egg sent down from Heaven. As Chumong would also be worshipped as ancestral spirit by the rulers of Paekche, a state yet to be founded on the banks of the Han by migrants from Puyŏ, the Chumong myth presumably originated there. Other dynasties in the area also acquired a family tree that went back a few generations to a supernatural ancestor from an egg, all of them dating from this period. It may be connected with the fact that this was about the time when they first acquired scribes and began to keep records in Chinese, though none of them survives other than in the versions edited by Kim Pu-sik for his twelfth-century *History of the Three Kingdoms*, or less reliably in Iryŏn's *Tales*.

The Koguryŏ myths also refer to war with the Malgal tribes who were the earlier Tungusic occupants of the area and would, after many centuries as vassals, foot-soldiers or slaves, organize themselves as the Ruzhen and extend their own rule over half of China. The Koguryŏ used their horses and weapons to protect and exploit these earlier semi-nomadic settlements, including those of the Okchŏ who occupied the arable land towards the east coast of the peninsula. Using their captives to build defensive walls, they set up a string of fortified settlements and in the third century AD established their capital on the middle reaches of the Yalu near the modern Chinese town of Ji'an, calling it 'Hwando'.

By developing both their iron weapons and their political organization, they had reached a stage where in the turmoil that accompanied the break-up of the Han empire they were able to threaten the Chinese colonies, now under the nominal control of the Wei. In 242, under King Tongch'ŏn, they attacked a Chinese fortress near the mouth of the Yalu in an attempt to cut the land route across Liao, in return for which the Wei invaded them in 244 and sacked Hwando.

Soon after, the Wei fell to the Jin and Koguryŏ grew stronger, until in 313 they finally succeeded in occupying Lelang and bringing to an end the 400 years of China's presence in the peninsula, a period sufficient to ensure that for the next 1,500 it would remain firmly within the sphere of its culture. After the fall of the Jin in 316, the proto-Mongol Xianbei occupied the North of China, of which the Murong clan took the Shandong area, moved up to the Liao, and in 341 sacked and burned the Koguryŏ capital at Hwando. They took away some thousands of prisoners to provide cheap labour to build more walls of their own, and in 346 went on to wreak even greater destruction on Puyŏ, hastening what seems to have been a continuing migration of its people into the north-eastern area of the peninsula, but Koguryŏ, though temporarily weakened, would soon rebuild its walls and continue to expand.

CHAPTER TWO

THE THREE KINGDOMS
AND KAYA

I N MANCHURIA the fall of their Chinese allies, the Jin, had left
Puyŏ too isolated to survive on the plains. The attack by the
Murong in 346 was followed by further harassment by the Malgal,
and eventually the remainder of the Puyŏ élite, with their weapons
and their horses, crossed the mountains to seek refuge with their kin
in Koguryŏ. Some of them may have settled on the coastal plains of
the north-east where the Okchŏ tribe were tributaries of Koguryŏ
but the main body appear to have moved on down the northern
branch of the Han to build a walled settlement, Wiryesŏng, on the
north bank of the river in the area now occupied by Seoul. Here
they were still liable to attacks from Malgal tribesmen and moved
across the broad river to build the walls of 'Hansŏng'. This was
traditionally associated with the impressive fortress of Namhansan-
sŏng, later used as a refuge by Yi dynasty Kings, but there are other
older sites now thought to be more probable.

Here they founded the state of Paekche, presumably, by imposing
themselves on the Mahan, who occupied the land to the south, and
as well-armed horsemen they would have been difficult to dislodge,
or even contain. There are other more complex views of Paekche
origins, that involve a migration from Liaodong, as well as the long-
accepted claim of the twelfth-century historian, Kim Pu-sik, that it
grew out of an earlier kingdom founded in 18 BC by Onjo, a son of
the Puyŏ founding father, Chumong. So far, the archaeological evidence seems more in favour of the fourth-century date. Chinese
sources indicate that by the end of the fourth century it had established a bureaucracy with six departments, the heads of which were
replaced every three years – presumably a concession to earlier tribal
customs rather than an anticipation of modern ones – along with an
academy in which they could be trained.

By 370 they controlled the land to the north of the Han up to the Imjin River and in the following year, under their warrior King, Kŭn Ch'o-go, they struck further north in an attempt to wrest control of the former Chinese capital from Koguryŏ. In the course of the campaign the Koguryŏ king was killed by an arrow and Pyongyang was temporarily occupied, but politically this was not a serious loss as their main territories were to the north and the east. Paekche looked mainly to the south and to trade by sea, developing relations with Japan and with the Jin, who, forced out by the Xianbei, had retreated southwards across the Yellow River to set up their capital at Nanjing where they would survive for another hundred years.

The tribes occupying the fertile south-eastern corner of the peninsula, the Chinhan, had by the third century AD developed into a third state known as Saro or Silla. According to Kim Pu-sik, himself of Sillan descent, its founders were six migrant families from Chosŏn, and this is consistent with some of the bronze items discovered in the area, but they were obviously not its original inhabitants. Sometime in the last century BC the leaders of these six clans, worried by the threat of external enemies, including raids from Japan, met by the side of a stream at the site of what would become its capital, Kyŏngju, and elected one of their number, Pak Hyŏkkŏse, as their first ruler.

They had a sophisticated culture with highly specialized workers, probably slaves, in a variety of crafts, based on an ascetic form of shamanism and totemic worship of the horse. That they would continue to worship and, under strict state control, to breed horses suggests that they must once have imposed themselves on an already well-established agricultural community. This is supported by the way in which Kim Pu-sik claims that after the arrival of the migrants from Chosŏn a winged horse had, in 57 BC, delivered an egg containing the child, Pak Hyŏkkŏse, who was to be their King. His clan was allied by marriage to the Sŏk, and the later emergence of the Sŏk clan as rulers led to a development of the myth by which another egg had arrived by sea in 4 BC.

It was 250 years later that the crowing of a cock in the wood adjoining the palace announced the arrival of a golden box containing the ancestor of the Kim (gold) clan which, after sharing the succession with the Sŏk from AD 262 would eventually become the ruling dynasty, and Kyerim, 'Cock Wood', would be another name for 'Silla'. This ruling caste inherited their spiritual authority not through their 'blood' but through the quality of their bones – only they were the possessors of *sŏngkol*, 'holy bones', probably in the first place, through maternal inheritance. In the seventh century, when male inheritance through the Kim clan had become the norm, it would be replaced by the concept of *chinkol*, 'true bones'.

Koguryŏ had lost its King in the attack by Paekche in 371, but under his successor Sosurim it found powerful allies in the latest wave of horsemen to arrive on their borders, the proto-Tibetan dynasty of Earlier Qin which, under its ruler Fu Qian, sought their assistance in driving the Xianbei out of the Liao peninsula. Fu Qian was an ardent Buddhist and relied on the spiritual powers of the monks to aid him in the conquest of China where, as he put it, 'the Buddha himself is a barbarian god'. Buddhism served to unify the tribal loyalties of his horsemen and would prove almost equally appealing to his Chinese subjects at a time when their own leaders had apparently lost the Mandate of Heaven. His diplomatic mission to Koguryŏ in 372 included a monk, Sundo, who presented Sosurim with scriptures translated into Chinese and images of bodhisattvas. He was joined two years later by another monk, Ado, the son of a Korean woman who had returned from Liao after the death of her indigenous husband, and temples were built for them.

Fu Qian's eventual attack on the Jin with an army said to have numbered 900,000 was the largest yet mounted by a nomad invader but it had to rely on reluctant peasants for its foot-soldiers and it disintegrated before it had reached the Yangzi leaving a vacuum in Manchuria that Sosurim would hasten to fill. Before his death in 384 he had adopted Buddhism as the state religion and also established a centralized government with a Confucian academy to train its officials.

Their shamanistic inheritance made them receptive to the idea of extreme asceticism as a source of spiritual power and Mahayana Buddhism, with its grandiose cosmic philosophy, could build on this foundation to promise protection against all those incalculable forces that threaten either the individual or the state, including the stars, disease and the weather, as well as evil spirits. As the animal species, sex, and social status into which one was born had been decided by the quality of one's previous lives there were no grounds for discontent, and every incentive to do better. It encouraged the martial arts as a necessary defence against evil enemies, but insisted that killing, when necessary, should be done with compassion.

When Sosurim's nephew Kwanggaet'o came to the throne in 391 at the age of 18 he would be able, like an oriental Alexander, to conduct a series of campaigns that by the time of his death at 39 would leave his son Chang-su with the prospect of making Koguryŏ a power second only to China. His title of 'Kwanggaet'o', posthumously awarded in Chinese fashion, means 'Opener of Wide Lands'

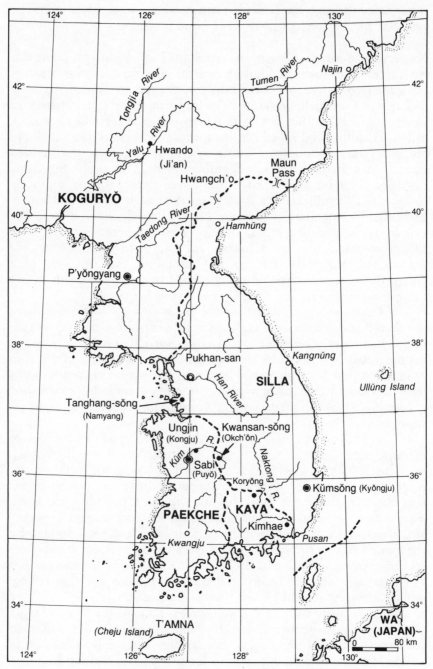

The Three Kingdoms in the Sixth Century

and it was said that the whole earth echoed to the battle cries and the thundering hooves of his cavalry. A 22-foot stone pillar erected beside his grave still stands in Ji'an, which is now in the Chinese province of Jilin. It is the earliest surviving record of purely Korean origin and tells, in 1,800 ideograms, how Kwanggaet'o captured, in all, 64 walled cities and 1,400 towns and villages, expanding northwards as far as the Songhua River and southwards through Silla to repel the Japanese. At this point there has been some defacement of the stone for which the Japanese, during their colonial period, are commonly blamed. His son Changsu moved their capital from Ji'an on the Yalu to the old Chosŏn capital at Pyongyang on the fertile plains of the Taedong River. Already involved in the politics of Silla, they would now show more interest in the peninsula to the south of them but the defence of their Manchurian borders would continue to absorb most of their resources.

After the move to the Pyongyang area, the royal tombs are built on a grander scale, presumably reflecting a stronger economy and further centralization of power. The stone burial chambers, covered by great mounds, have long since been robbed but their vivid murals survive. Those from the fifth century show lively scenes from palace life, such as dancing girls or the annual hunt, with galloping horsemen and fleeing tigers and deer, while later ones take up more sophisticated mythological themes.

Between Silla in the south-east and Paekche on the west lay Kaya, another group of six tribes, which developed into two wealthy chiefdoms occupying the fertile area between the lower reaches of the Nakdong River and its western tributary, the Nam. Their origins lay in the Pyŏnhan tribes of earlier times and their culture closely resembled that of Silla. They had strong trading links with the Yamato kingdom of Japan, which maintained a settlement on the coast known as 'Mimana'. The extent of this area as marked on Japanese historical maps is probably rather exaggerated, but as the founders of Yamato are said to have emigrated from the southern island of Kyushu there are also theories that they themselves were people of Korean origin who pushed out the original Ainic tribesmen. It certainly appears that Yamato, because of its strength, regarded Kaya as a 'tributary', but the recognition of this kind of pecking order was the standard diplomacy of the time and should not be confused with Western-style 'colonialism'.

Recent archaeological finds indicate that by the fourth century AD there was plenty of Chinese money about in both Old Kaya, centred on the ports in the delta, and Great Kaya in the hinterland, the result of extensive trade which included exporting iron ore to the

Chinese colonies in the north-west, to Koguryŏ ports on the east coast, and to Japan, and importing iron utensils and weapons and Chinese luxuries. The discovery of iron body armour of Japanese design as well as their own styles amongst the goods in fourth and fifth century Kaya graves has added another intriguing element to the puzzle of their relationship with Yamato.

As in Silla, the upper classes rode horses and they developed high standards in music, pottery and weaving, the status of their rulers being attested by their elaborate burial mounds. Towards the end of the fourth century they joined with Paekche and Yamato in the direct attack on Silla that, as we have seen, forced them to call on the mighty Kwanggaet'o of Koguryŏ who, as described on his stele, sent down a force of 50,000 to drive out the attackers, in return for which he regarded Silla as a tributary.

Buddhism was now rapidly extending its influence in China, and in Nanjing Indian monks were employed in translating the sutras. It was here that a Paekche diplomat was introduced to one of them, Malananda, who returned with him to Paekche, where he was welcomed and provided with a shrine, and other monks followed. Their continuing success would now be assured by Paekche's alliance with the Toba, a Sinified clan of the Xianbei, also followers of the Mahayana, who had flooded into Shanxi after the collapse of Fu Qian. By allying themselves with the Chinese landlords they were able to establish a more stable regime under the revived dynastic title of 'Wei'. They would rule the northern half of China for the next 200 years, establishing links with the West and creating a great wealth of Buddhist art.

Extending eastwards towards the Liao delta they found themselves confronted by Koguryŏ and were ready to make an alliance with Paekche, to whom they were friends in need, as Koguryŏ, under Changsu, was now ready, after many minor battles, to deal them a crushing blow. His posthumous title of 'Changsu' means 'long life' and it was in the sixty-third year of his reign that, before any assistance from their allies in Liao, Silla or Japan could reach them, he drove them out of their stronghold on the Han, beheaded King Kaero, and forced the survivors to retreat to a mountain fortress at Kongju about 75 miles to the south. It was on the Kŭm River, which gave them a safer outlet to the sea, but it would be early in the sixth century before they ventured to move their capital down to the more hospitable lower reaches of the river, where they gave it their ancient dynastic title of 'Puyŏ'.

As an insurance against further aggression from Koguryŏ or Silla they became tributaries of Japan, sending the King's eldest son there as a surety against betrayal. As a result of these ties they supplied the Japanese with a constant stream of learned monks and craftsmen to set up Buddhist institutions and provide them with scriptures, icons and murals, so that although they would later receive important contributions from Silla and from the east-coast monasteries of Koguryŏ, Paekche was the primary source and more of its art survives there than in its homeland.

Another Paekche monk, Kyŏmik, travelled as far as India to study and bring back scriptures for translation. The fourth-century Indian monk Kumarajiva who had been captured in the Tarim basin by the Chinese and put to work on this task likened it to 'feeding a man with rice that has already been chewed by someone else', and in Korea the instruction of the common people involved a further oral conversion of the ideograms into their own language. Popular worship centred simply on 'the Lord Buddha' though later it would be divided amongst various cults, chiefly Amit'a-bul, the Lord of the Western Paradise, and some of the bodhisvattas who had postponed their attainment of buddhahood in order to assist their suffering brethren. Of these it would be Avalokitesvara, 'The One Who Views with Mercy' who received the greatest devotion. Translated into Chinese as Guanyin, pronounced in Korea as 'Kwanŭm', he came to be thought of as essentially feminine, though the lack of gender distinctions in Korean or Chinese has served to give the virtual sex-change a continuing ambiguity.

In Koguryŏ, Kwanggaet'o had secured their borders with the Toba Wei along the line of the Liao River, and Changsu, after moving his capital to Pyongyang in 425, had hung on to the line of forts that commanded its eastern bank, paying tribute to the Wei but also sending envoys by sea to the southern dynasty at Nanjing, which the Wei tried to intercept. In 466 the Queen Mother of Wei informed Changsu that there was a vacancy in one of the Emperor's five palaces for subsidiary wives, so would he like to offer one of his daughters? He offered them one of his nieces and the Wei's immediate acceptance of this aroused suspicion. Perhaps it was a trick by which they would spy out and undermine the country's defences? He told them that the niece had unfortunately died. At this point they were saved further embarrassment by the death of the Emperor himself but the relationship remained uneasy, the Wei fearing that they were conspiring against them with the Southern dynasty while Koguryŏ naturally suspected that the Wei were planning to regain their lost territory up to the Yalu, the peasant population of which was largely Chinese.

CHAPTER THREE

THE LAND OF THE BUDDHAS

S ILLA, in the south-east, was the furthest from the Chinese
colonies and though it had traded with them, its culture
developed in a way that showed much less of their influence. Their
own shamanistic beliefs had reached high levels of artistic expression,
with graceful flying horses as their angels and fantastic masks, crowns
and ornaments of gold and jade for their royal priesthood. The ruler
was known as the *isagum* or 'successor prince', and the succession
was not yet from father to son, but in an earlier style still based on
consensus and qualities of leadership so that it more often went to
brothers, nephews or cousins than to sons. Once chosen from two,
or three, clans, after the time of Naemul, who reigned from 356 to
402 and had been responsible for calling in Koguryǒ's Kwanggaet'o
against Paekche, the title was changed to *maripkan* and became the
hereditary privilege of the Kim family. After his death the office
went to a mature relative rather than to his young son Nulchi but
in 417 Koguryǒ intervened to put Nulchi on the throne. From this
point, as in Koguryǒ, a father to son succession was formalized, but
the Kims were required to take their queens from the still powerful
holy-bone family of Pak.

Early in the fifth century Ado, one of the two monks responsible
for establishing Buddhism in Koguryǒ, came to Silla with three
companions and settled in a valley at Sǒnsan, where they had some
local success but failed to arouse much interest in the capital. Gradually their numbers would grow and miraculous cures, pregnancies
for barren wives and other answers to prayer would spread their
influence as far as the women of the court, but in regard to
their aspirations to replace the national religion it would be more
than a hundred years before they were able to overcome strong
opposition from the heads of the holy-bone families, who saw it as

an ideology that subverted family ties and favoured the growth of an autocratic monarchy.

This almost inevitable movement towards centralization was accompanied by the increasing use of Chinese as the essential tool of its bureaucracy. It is from this period that the clans began to adopt one-syllable Chinese names such as Kim or Pak. At first they were used alongside the multi-syllabic native names but from the sixth century onwards the King would adopt the Chinese title of *wang* in place of *maripkan*, preceded by one-syllable ideograms for his personal name. This practice would spread to the aristocracy and eventually to everyone so that the vernacular names disappeared, and later, to enforce the new system, place names would also be changed to Chinese, though for local use the old names would long survive.

Control of the Chinese-style ministries that were now established in Silla were, perhaps even more than in the other two kingdoms, limited to a small élite. The top five grades in the ministries were only for holy-bone royals, who wore purple, while posts in the remaining ranks, from a total of 17, though open to able men from three successively lower groups, were in practice usually filled by people from the ever-proliferating holy-bone families. Also at about this time control of the country's half-dozen provinces was taken over by governors who were royal relatives rather than local men and would normally reside in Kyŏngju, then known as 'Sŏrabŏl'.

The archaeological evidence indicates that Silla was never forced to build walled cities but from early times there are records of incidents and minor battles with intruders from the other two kingdoms at the forts that had been built at mountain passes or river fords on their respective boundaries. In this way, as the three kingdoms grew in strength and sophistication they were bound to become rivals for the control of the whole peninsula. The crucial area was the fertile basin of the great Han River where already Paekche and Silla were pushing northwards against sporadic retaliation by Koguryŏ, which could muster the Yemaek and Malgal tribesmen who still occupied the hills of the north-east. It encouraged Paekche and Silla, temporarily at least, to become allies and they assisted each other in defending the forts they had established at points such as Ch'ungju and Wŏnju.

Each of Silla's six provinces had its own troops and the governors seem to have been able to provide about 3,000 men when required. In the time of Nulchi's son Chabi there were also at least two large-scale attacks by Japanese maurauders, and fleets of galleys were provided for coastal defences.

His successor, Soji, was concerned with improving the country's roads and in 487 he instituted a post-horse system with stations on the main routes, and three years later the first public market was set up in the capital. It is said that a drought in the spring and summer of the year 492 caused him to spend some time in self-examination and fasting for, as in China, from ancient times, the behaviour of the Heavens was seen as a commentary on the worthiness of the ruler, and the records are filled with eclipses, falling stars, freak storms and the like, all of which required some self-examination on the part of the ruler. They also prompted frequent pardons for prisoners as unjust imprisonment also caused anger in Heaven.

There was, in Soji's time, a country gentleman at Yŏngju whose 16-year-old daughter was said to be the loveliest in the land. He had her dressed in satin and put in a cart which was swathed in silk and sent to the King, who was visiting that area. When the parcel was opened, the King, expecting it to be a gift of provisions, was shocked and sent her home, but when he returned to the palace he could not forget her and took advantage of the improved roads to make frequent trips to Yŏngju. A widow at whose house he stayed on the way said to him, 'People say that your majesty is a saint but if this is how saints behave we must all be saints!' The King took the point and had the girl brought to the palace and given an apartment as a proper subsidiary wife. Even so, he had no children and after his death in 500 he was succeeded by Chijung, a grandson of Nulchi and the first King to adopt the Chinese title of *wang*.

He is said to have presided over improvements in agriculture, including the use of oxen for ploughing the paddies and new systems of irrigation. He was also the first to provide the palace with cellars where blocks of winter ice could be stored for use in the summer.

Silla now held the east coast at least as far as the port of Kangnŭng and in 512 the Military Governor there, Isabu, was ordered to subjugate the large and beautiful island of Ullŭng which lies about 150 miles out to sea. Knowing the islanders to be fierce but unsophisticated, he had his fleet provided with wooden lions of menacing appearance and ensured an immediate surrender by threatening to put them ashore. Tigers, being more familiar, and greatly valued for their skins, were not as fearsome as the mythical Chinese lion.

The Koryŏ historian Kim Pu-sik, who provides this story, also says that King Chijung was a man of great size and strength, but it is Kim's monkish successor, Iryŏn, who has delighted generations of Korean schoolboys by adding that his 'tool', to use their term, measured more than a foot. Messengers were sent to all parts of the land to find a Cinderella of matching proportions. Two of them, coming upon a golden turd of great size, followed the path through the woods to the home of a young lady six feet tall and the King sent a carriage, with two horses, to bring her to the palace where she became his Queen.

It was under Chijung's son Pŏphŭng that Silla finally came to adopt Buddhism as the state religion. He is said to have been attracted by it from his youth, but there was still strong opposition from the conservatives. The turning-point seems to have been the coincidence over a period between 520 and 530 of influences from both inside the court and from the Liang dynasty in Southern China, whose founder, Wudi, though a military strong-man, was also a great patron of the arts and a generous benefactor of Buddhism. It was under him that the first translation of the whole Buddhist canon, the Tripitaka, was completed and it was to his court that the Indian monk Bodhidharma first brought those mystical paradoxes that would so captivate the Far Eastern soul as to bring forth within the next few years a radical form of Daoistic Buddhism that would take the ideogram for 'meditation' as its logo – pronounced 'chan' in China, 'sŏn' in Korea and 'zen' in Japan.

Liang had diplomatic exchanges with Koguryŏ and Paekche as well as with Silla and contributed to the development of all three. Pŏphŭng sent them envoys in 521 and Wudi responded by dispatching a Buddhist mission with scriptures. After this, the turning-point seems to have been the martyrdom of Ich'adon, a young holy-bone aristocrat said to have been of great charm and courage. The facts of his story have been buried under a great weight of legend and hagiography but it appears that after being sent to Koguryŏ as an exile, diplomat or spy, he was converted to Buddhism, returned as a monk, and was accused by the conservative nobles of being a traitor. His execution, which he is said to have invited as a sign, was followed by a miraculous flow of white blood from his veins.

However it might be, the King, the Queen and a sufficient proportion of their relatives were now ready to embrace the new ideology with great enthusiasm, and on his deathbed, in 540, the King himself was ordained as a monk and his Queen a nun. She now became regent, as his cousin, Chinhŭng, who succeeded him, was only seven. In accordance with the 'Laws of Buddha' the slaughter of domestic animals was restricted, monasteries were built, and young people were allowed to leave their families to enter them. A group of novices was sent to Liang to study and when, in 549, the first of them, Kakdŏk, returned with some holy relics the young King and all his ministers turned out to greet them. As it would be later in medieval Europe, religious devotion was closely linked with ideals of military valour and intensified loyalty to an absolute monarch and Silla's adoption of Buddhism was followed by the growth of newly recruited regiments based on the capital so that the court became less dependent on the forces controlled by the regional governors.

Paekche, where Buddhism had been established for 150 years or more, also valued its contacts with Liang. In 541, at the request of King Sŏng, they were supplied with craftsmen, artists, scriptures and a visiting professor of poetry and these influences would also be passed on to their Yamato allies in Japan. New insights into the artistic riches of Paekche were provided in 1971 with the discovery at Kongju of the burial mound of Sŏng's father, Muryŏng, and his Queen, the last rulers before the move to Puyŏ. The Paekche royal tombs, unlike those of Silla, had entrance tunnels that made them easy to loot, but Muryŏng's had escaped the vandals and yielded exquisite golden crowns and hundreds of other well-wrought items. In contrast to the Scytho-Siberian styles of Silla, they show the influence of their continuing contacts with the kingdoms of southern China.

These were still troubled times in China and when the envoys from Paekche arrived at Nanjing in the autumn of 549 they found the walls broken down and the palace in ruins. As they wept before the palace gates others joined them, with the result that the rebel forces came and arrested them, but soon after the city was retaken and they were able to go home, though the dynasty would not long survive the death of Wudi in the following year.

In 551, while Koguryŏ was preoccupied with repelling an incursion from the Steppe by Turkic nomads, Silla managed to capture another ten fortified settlements along the upper reaches of the Han River and Paekche also regained its former territory up to its southern bank. If the court records of Silla, as given in Kim Pu-sik's *History*, are to be trusted, these acquisitions were not regarded as the main event of the year, they are mentioned only briefly after an account of how the famous court musician of Great Kaya, Urŭk, and his disciple Imun were tempted to cross to Silla's north-west frontier city of Ch'ŏngju, where their performance on the 12-stringed zither, the *kayagŭm*, so captivated the King that he sent three students to be taught by them. When they performed at the court a year later the King cried, 'That is the very sound that I heard at Ch'ŏngju!' and generously rewarded them. It is still a much-loved instrument.

Silla now began to expand its territory westwards along the River Han and despite the long alliance with Paekche that had been cemented by the marriage of one of Soji's nieces to King Sŏng's grandfather and more recently by the gift of one of Sŏng's own daughters as bride for Chinhŭng, Silla forced them out of all their recently acquired territory on the southern side of the river right up to the coast. Sŏng was determined on revenge and in the summer of 554, with the support of Great Kaya, he led his army directly east-wards across the hills to invade Silla at Okch'ŏn, a point not far from Taejŏn. Silla's forces were rapidly mobilized, Sŏng and four of his ministers were killed in a mountain ambush, and, according to Silla records, his whole force of 30,000 were slain or captured and not even one horse escaped. This disastrous campaign also marked the virtual end of Great Kaya and soon afterwards it was peacefully absorbed by Silla.

Silla continued to develop its civil service and new departments were set up to deal with shipping, land transport, finance and the arts. At the same time it was also deepening its Buddhist culture and building up its army. Its inheritance of artistic skills evidenced in the spectacular golden crowns with their mobile decorations found in their early burial mounds was put to new uses as they absorbed the Indian and Central Asian influences that had come with Buddhism. In 574 a great Buddha was set up in the Hwangnyong Monastery made, it is said, from 20 tons of copper and covered with 300 ounces of gilding, and when, in the following summer, there was a serious drought, tears flowed from its eyes.

In this period, or perhaps even earlier, came the setting up of the Hwarang, the Flower Corps, a youth organization that would enrol and mould the most gifted sons of the aristocracy to provide an élite force of scholars and soldiers. According to legend, its founders, in the hope of attracting the best type of young men, began by choosing from holy-bone families the two young women whom the King judged to be the finest from the point of view of both their beauty and their talent for music and dance. These two, Nammo and Chun-jŏng, were nominated as 'Source Flowers', and a group of about 300 young men was formed around them. Unfortunately these two pin-ups or holy damsels – presumably the two concepts were not then as mutually exclusive as in later times – grew jealous of each other. Chunjŏng invited Nammo round to her place for a drink and after doctoring it, had her pushed into the river, for which she herself was subsequently executed.

Whatever its origins, the Hwarang was by the sixth century attracting, or perhaps conscripting, brave and talented young men. Its beliefs reflected the country's already fairly sophisticated form of shamanism – they worshipped the 'godlight of heaven and earth', dragon-kings, holy hills and ancestral spirits. As lovers of mountains, flowers and music they enhanced their own beauty through the use of powder and make-up. Early in the seventh century under Chinhŭng's successor Chinp'yŏng they would be given a more Bud-dhist-oriented code by their chaplain-general, the monk Wŏn'gwang, and encouraged to think of themselves as *mirŭk*, buddhas of the future.

This seems to have been part of a general campaign under Wŏn'g-wang's superior, Chajang, by which the monks, having succeeded in establishing the King and his cabinet as responsible for administering the 'Laws of Buddha', concentrated on bringing the populace into the fold, not by contradicting their earlier beliefs and customs, but by incorporating them. Midwinter darkness would be dispelled by the Yŏndŭnghoe, the Festival of Lanterns, and the late-autumn harvest celebrations grow into the Pa'lgwanhoe, or Festival of the Eight Vows, both of which would become state occasions with royal subsidies.

It was boldly claimed that Silla had already been 'The Land of Buddhas' in ancient times and its mountains the abode of countless bodhisvattas. Mt Odae, in Kangwŏn Province, where Chajang saw visions and built a temple, had once, he claimed, been populated by 10,000 of them. In this way the more Confucian-oriented education developed in Koguryŏ and Paekche was to some extent pre-empted by Buddhist institutions, and although they would become increasingly Sinified and encourage Confucian attitudes towards women, family and the King, it would be another hundred years before Silla had the benefit of a fully authorized Confucian university.

In 587 another new note appears: two boys, Taisae and Kuch'il, one of them a cousin of the King, felt that if they had to spend their lives within the confines of Silla's hills and valleys they would be like fish in a lily pond or birds in a cage – they would run away to sea. They boarded a ship for China and were never seen again, but in the future there would be ever-increasing opportunities for young men to study in China, and in the case of monks, to go as far as India, where the great Buddhist university of Nalanda was attracting students from every corner of Asia.

Silla continued to extend its territory northwards along the east coast, pushing past Wŏnsan into the former Okchŏ lands, but its main concern was the fertile area up to the mouth of the Han, where Koguryŏ still threatened the estuary, so that after crossing the river to stake their claim to the mountains around the present site of Seoul, they moved back to build a fort south of the estuary at Inch'ŏn and a larger one on the shores of Namyang Bay, to the west of Osan, which they developed as their port for China. Paekche and Koguryŏ now joined forces against them, and Koguryŏ sent an army under their legendary hero Ondal, the son of a beggar who by his success in the annual hunt by which military prowess was judged, had become a general and married King P'yŏng'wŏn's daughter, but he was slain by a Sillan arrow and failed to drive them out.

The whole situation was now about to be changed by the rise to power in China of the north-western dynasty of the Sui, who in 589 went on to defeat the southern kingdom of the Chen, so that for the first time in 200 years China would be united and once more present a serious threat to Koguryŏ's Manchurian territories.

CHAPTER FOUR

KOGURYŎ'S WARS WITH CHINA

As we have seen, Koguryŏ had cultivated its relations with the southern dynasties of China to balance the threat across the Liao from the northern ones, so that when in 589 they heard that in the south the Chen had fallen to the Sui they closed their frontiers and began to prepare for war. This earned them a strong rebuke from the Sui emperor Wendi, to which King Yŏngyang responded with a humble apology and was granted the vassal's title of 'Duke', after which he applied again in 591, with tribute, and was invested as 'King'. In fact there was little chance of harmony, for the Sui wanted to regain control of Manchuria, whilst Koguryŏ regarded its Malgal tribesmen as their own vassals and employed them as their infantry.

In the five years that followed they sent tribute only twice and in the early summer of 598 they crossed the Liao with a force of about 10,000 Malgal. The Sui sent a great army, said to have numbered 30,000 to drive them out but the Chinese were hampered by floods, which cut off their food supplies, and subsequent disease, whilst a simultaneous seaborne assault on Pyongyang was hit by a typhoon and lost many of its ships. Even so, the Korean army was almost wiped out and at the end of the summer Yŏngyang sued for peace and the border was restored as before.

Paekche, fearful of both Koguryŏ and Silla, was quick to seek the support of the Sui. During their final battles with the Chen a Sui warship had been washed up on Cheju Island, then a minor kingdom that paid tribute to Paekche. The ship, along with its crew, was rescued and repaired by Paekche and sent home with generous supplies. The Emperor congratulated them on this 'beautiful action' but it had less aesthetic appeal for Koguryŏ who responded with a raid on Paekche in which they took 2,000 prisoners.

At this time, perhaps in the hope of improving its fortunes,

Paekche deepened its public commitment to Buddhism. New monasteries were built and in 599 they followed Silla in limiting the slaughter of animals, decreeing that hawks and falcons should be freed and fishing nets burned, though the rule on nets does not appear to have been strictly enforced, probably because too much food and too many livelihoods were involved.

In 607, in sending tribute to the Sui, King Mu requested a punitive expedition against Koguryŏ, which was still making raids on them, and in 608 Silla's King Chinp'yŏng, faced with similar attacks, also appealed to the Emperor. When Chinp'yŏng's secretary, the monk Wŏn'gwang, was told to draft the petition, he said, 'How can I, as a man of religion, ask for other people's lives to be sacrificed to save my own? Yet as one who lives safely in your land and eats your food, how can I refuse?' The question still awaits an answer.

The new Sui Emperor, Yangdi, had no intention of leaving the fiasco of 598 unavenged and welcomed Paekche and Silla as prospective allies, though the magnitude of his own preparations made their possible contributions seem almost irrelevant. Early in 611 he began to assemble what was perhaps the largest armed force the world has ever seen, said to have totalled 1,133,800. They were divided into six armies, each of their divisions being made up of four battalions of cavalry and eight battalions of infantry. At the beginning of 612 he issued a decree listing the many evil deeds of Koguryŏ under King Yŏngyang and the heavenly omens that presaged his downfall, and as spring approached the armies were marched off at regular intervals, each battalion with its flags, trumpets and drums so that the whole force, with its continuous martial din, is said to have stretched for 250 miles and to have taken 40 days to pass a given point.

These figures, whether or not they be exaggerated, seem to be generally consistent with the scale on which Yangdi and his father Wendi had provided employment for their 60 million subjects – they had used two million in rebuilding their capital at Louyang and in 607 had sent off about a million and half to repair the Great Wall, of whom about half survived, while more than five million were used to build canals.

In April the vanguard of the army reached the waters of the Liao, now in full flow, and the Emperor himself came to observe their progress. His engineers built a floating bridge in three sections which were intended, when linked together, to span the river, but turned out to be about 12 feet short so that the soldiers had to struggle through the water to reach the bank and a fierce Korean attack caused them such continuing losses that they had to pull back the bridge. Two days later, when it had been lengthened, they were able to pour across in such numbers that the defenders were overwhelmed and suffered heavy casualties. The Chinese were then able to cross a second smaller river, the Hun, and lay siege to Liaoyang, a fortified city of about 40,000 that dominated the area.

Encircled by the Emperor's armies, the well-stocked city held out for week after week, while the Chinese, hampered by bad weather, threw away their men in fruitless attempts to breach its walls. The Emperor intended to stay with them and the court was set up in six mobile palaces just out of range. Meanwhile the Chinese fleet intended to form the other half of a pincer movement on Pyongyang had already reached the Taedong River. They overran the defences at its mouth and decided to attempt an immediate attack on the city but their land forces were ambushed from a deserted monastery outside the city wall and they had to retreat and set up a camp on the coast.

One of Yangdi's ministers told him that he was being made a fool of by a paltry band of barbarians and advised him to abandon the whole thing, but he decided instead to make a direct march on Pyongyang, sending a force of about 100,000 under two generals, You Wensu and You Zhongwen, of whom Wensu was the superior, to converge on the mouth of the Yalu by several different paths. Most of the tracks were through barren country and each man, in addition to his equipment, was made to carry such a crippling weight of grain that despite the death penalty for anyone found wasting it, they are said to have dug holes in the floors of their tents at night and buried much of it.

When they reached the Yalu, Yŏngyang sent his minister, Ŭlchi Mundŏk, to parley with them, a man noted equally for his calm courage and his literary wit. He went ostensibly to discuss terms of surrender, but really to assess the state of the enemy's forces. When he returned with their proposals he had seen enough to convince him that they were weary and short of food – his aim now would be to make them a little more so. He let them cross the Yalu and fight a battle which they won, and gave them a whole series of minor victories until they had been tempted to cross the Ch'ŏngch'ŏn, the last river, and that night, with their supplies virtually exhausted, they camped seven miles from Pyongyang. He sent the Chinese general a poem, the Daoist undertones of which would not have been lost on him:

> Your godlike plans reached to the heavens
> Your subtle reckoning spanned the earth.
> You have won the battles and made your name:
> Why not be content and withdraw?
>
> (translated by Kim Jŏng-gil)

It was accompanied by a promise that he would escort the King to the Emperor's camp when the roads were clear. You Wensu must have known that the offer could hardly be taken at its face value, but he had seen Pyongyang's formidable defences and had little choice. He directed his men into defensive square formations and began the retreat. The Koguryŏ forces harried them all the way and killed thousands at the Ch'ŏngch'ŏn river crossing. It is said that only 2,700 finally reached Liaoyang, where the Emperor lifted the siege and went home, with You Wensu in chains, a tragic loss that is recounted in one of China's classic folksongs.

The following year Yangdi led another attack on the fortifications at Liaoyang, but rebellions at home, precursors of the dynasty's downfall, forced him to withdraw and one of his ministers was captured. He made a final attempt in 614 but troubles at home forced him to make peace and by 618 his rule would have given way to another family from the north-west of China, the Tang.

While the Sui had still been preparing their campaign, King Mu of Paekche had been sending envoys between Puyŏ and Louyang to prepare for their part in the war and their army had been on the alert ready to cross the frontier as soon as their allies appeared, but as they never did they managed to avoid any involvement, while Silla took the chance to add a little more to the land it had already wrested from Koguryŏ.

In Paekche, King Mu, said to have possessed extraordinary powers and a majestic air, still sent his generals off to make spasmodic attacks on Silla but he seems to have been more concerned with dreams of beauty and splendour. He built new palaces, lakes and gardens, said to have rivalled those of the Chinese capital, and a great temple, Wanghŭngsa, for the protection of the state. In his later years, while passing a lake in the Iksan district, to the south of the river, he was granted a religious vision in response to which he built a set of great temples to house three embodied emanations of the *mirŭk*, the Buddha of the future, apparently in the belief that it would thus become the capital of a messianic kingdom.

It had not come about, however, before his death in 641, and his son Ŭija, being more interested in military expeditions against their old enemies in Silla, the temples rapidly decayed leaving only the ruins of a massive stone pagoda, the country's oldest and largest. Years of excavation in the 1980s have revealed that it was one of a pair and that the whole complex covered hundreds of acres and must have been the largest ever built. Ŭija had great success against Silla, and was evidently a virile warrior for in the seventeenth year of his reign there was a special ceremony at which 41 of his *sŏja*, sons from subsidiary wives, were enrolled in the highest rank of the aristocracy and granted feudal estates.

The Tang were established in Chang'an (Xi'an) by 618 and in the following year King Yŏngnyu of Koguryŏ sent them tribute. Their diligence in dealing with the nomadic tribes on their borders encouraged him to treat them with respect, while the new Emperor was well aware of the heavy losses the Sui had suffered at the hands of Koguryŏ and in 622 he wrote to say that he had ordered all the prisoners taken by the Sui to be sent home, and asked that in a spirit of mutual forgiveness the prisoners taken by Koguryŏ should be returned. As a result of this some tens of thousands of Chinese went home, though many who had settled in Manchuria preferred to stay.

In 624 Koguryŏ's tributary status was formalized by accepting the Tang calendar, and an official was sent to invest Yŏngnyu as Duke of Liao and King of Koguryŏ, a distinction that implicitly sustained China's claims to the east bank of the Liao. The Emperor also sent a Daoist sage to give lectures at the court, for although the Tang were tolerant of other religions and would establish a multi-racial society as successful as any the world has yet seen, they had adopted Daoism as their own faith, and under their patronage it would seek to become, for the first time, an organized religion, a kind of 'own brand' Buddhism.

By 631, with peace established along their northern borders, the Chinese sent officials to inter the bones of their war dead, giving them the chance to see the impressive 'Great Wall' that Koguryŏ had just completed, a continuous line of defence running for 200 miles or more from the former Puyŏ territory on the Songhua River to the estuary of the Liao. It had taken them 16 years to build and was studded with well-stocked fortified towns.

In 640 Yŏngnyu sent the crown prince to Chang'an as a student, a guarantee of peace to which the Emperor responded by dispatching a high official to make a ceremonial tour of Koguryŏ, distributing gifts to the towns he visited and receiving an enthusiastic welcome from the Chinese residents in the western areas. The Koreans subsequently came to see it as a means of gaining military intelligence and reviving Chinese loyalties, for it soon became clear that the vigorous and talented Taizong, who had replaced his father as Emperor in 626, was critical of the Sui's failure to recover the whole of the Liaodong and confident that he could do better.

The all-important command of Koguryŏ's Western Wall was in 642 given to the politically ambitious General Yŏn Kaesomun and he soon became involved in a coup that led to the death of the King and his leading ministers. The King was replaced by his nephew, Pojang, with Yŏn as his chief minister. It was a militaristic state in which, under the King, the chief minister, the *kuksang*, had always controlled both the army and the civil service, but Yŏn was given the new and hereditary title of *makriji*, which made the King no more than a kind of constitutional monarch in the manner of the later Japanese shogunate. Yŏn did his best to placate the Tang, issuing an edict in favour of Daoism and requesting that more doctors of philosophy be sent to educate them in the Way. The Emperor, biding his time, sent them a party of eight Daoist sages, for whose benefit Yŏn emptied one of the city's Buddhist monasteries, but now, with a legitimate Koguryŏ crown prince in his hands, Taizong had the pretext he needed to prepare for war.

He set up bases in the Shandong peninsula where a force of 40,000 men and 500 ships were prepared for an amphibious attack on Pyongyang while he himself went to join the main army of 170,000 assembled in Hebei. He would ride at the head of his staff with a bow and quiver over his shoulder and a raincoat strapped behind his saddle. They moved quickly and while one army crossed the Liao on floating bridges another one moved enough soil to make a path through marshes to the south. At this point King Pojang left Pyongyang at the head of an army of 40,000 to go to the relief of Liaoyang and in what seemed like almost a reversal of Ulchi Mundŏk's victory the cavalry of the Chinese advance guard, after waiting until they had marched far enough to become weary, made a surprise attack that inflicted about a thousand casualties and turned them back.

As soon as his troops had crossed the river to face the walls of Liaoyang they were set to work filling the moat, and the Emperor and his staff used their own horses to help with the bags of soil. The town was now encircled by ring after ring of soldiers, and for 12 days and 12 nights the walls rang with their drums and war cries, but they were defied by the voice of Chumong, Koguryŏ's legendary founder, who spoke from his shrine within the walls through the mouth of his shaman priest. The Chinese had numerous towers and scaling ladders, and catapults that could hurl rocks for 300 yards, making gaps in the battlements which the Koreans mended with ropes and planks. The Chinese had also a secret weapon provided some years before by Paekche, armour polished with the resin of a tree grown on Cheju Island, *textoria morbifera*, which reflected the sun so brilliantly that opponents were dazzled. Finally, taking advantage of a strong southerly wind, they managed to send some agile men up a scaling tower on the southern side with enough incendiary material to start a blaze under cover of which they poured over the parapet and overwhelmed the defenders.

After this the only serious obstacle on the road to Pyongyang was the smaller fortress of Anshi, near the mouth of the Liao. It was built on a steep hill and so difficult to take that although its commander, Yang Man-ch'un, had refused to acknowledge Yŏn Kaesomun's usurpation, he had been left in command of it because there was no way of dislodging him. Everything now depended on holding Anshi and as the Chinese approached it a reorganized Korean army, said to have numbered, with its Malgal auxiliaries, about 150,000, marched north to relieve it. The commander set up camp a few miles short of the scene of the siege and wondered whether to make an immediate attack or wait for colder weather and shortages of food to weaken the Chinese force. Taizong, his army's morale high, knew that he needed a quick result, and with a skilful attack he overran their headquarters so that the Korean high command and about 40,000 of their men were forced to surrender. He separated the officers and told the rest of them to find their own way home.

He was now minded to march directly on Pyongyang but his generals persuaded him that if they did not first take Anshi it would threaten their supply lines so he set about besieging it, but the Koreans not only held out, but planned a counter-attack. One night several hundred of the defenders slid down the walls on ropes for what they hoped would be a surprise assault, but the Chinese, having heard the squeals of pigs and chickens during the day, guessed that someone was being given a good meal in preparation for a sortie, and were on the alert, so that none of the commandos survived.

Taizong then set 50,000 men to work raising an artificial hill which after 60 days was high enough for them to shoot down into the fort from an armoured stockade on the top, but it was built so close to the walls that part of it collapsed against them and broke the battlements. This happened at a moment when the officer commanding it was not on duty and a few hundred Koreans were able to run along the walls and capture it. The Emperor had the officer executed and spent three days in a vain attempt to get his men up there again. Winter set in earlier than usual and as the grass dried up and the streams began to freeze he decided to go home. As a tribute to the courage and tenacity of the defenders he sent Yang Man-ch'un a parting gift of a hundred rolls of silk.

He did not abandon his hopes of subduing Koguryŏ but the logistic problems involved in sustaining great armies in Manchuria led him to favour a seaborne invasion, so that while he kept up the pressure on Koguryŏ's north-western frontier with local campaigns in 647, he was busily building ships. In the following year he made a raid on the west coast, and later in the year, with a larger force, captured a fortress at the mouth of the Yalu. At this point the whole situation began to change, first through a fateful visit from the Silla diplomat Kim Ch'un Ch'u and then through his own death, which would leave the Tang in the hands of a less decisive successor.

CHAPTER FIVE

THE SILLA-TANG ALLIANCE

I N SILLA, Chinp'yŏng's 53-year reign ended with his death in 632, after which, having no male heir, he was succeeded, at his own insistence, by his wise and talented daughter, Sŏndŏk, Silla's first woman ruler. When she had been a small child her father had received a gift of peony seeds from the Tang emperor, along with a painting of the plant. She had noticed that there were no bees or butterflies in the picture and had rightly deduced that it would have no scent. She must have been well aware of Chinese antipathy to the idea of a woman ruler, but she nevertheless encouraged the spread of Tang culture and it was probably under the influence of Daoist science that in 634 she built the elegant and mysterious bottle-shaped Ch'ŏmsŏngdae, 'Star Observation Tower', the world's oldest surviving observatory. Constructed from exactly 365 great stones, it still stands complete in Kyŏngju, evidence of the vital role that was played, in their world, by the stars in their courses.

It was also during her reign that, under the direction of the Paekche architect Abiji, there was built in the grounds of their largest temple, Hwangnyongsa, a great nine-storey wooden pagoda that was seen as a sign that they would someday receive tribute from the nine nations or tribes that had attacked them in the past. Far from fulfilling the Chinese adage that when the hen crows, the kingdom falls, she seems to have had an Elizabethan quality that enabled her to inspire the graduates of the Hwarang in the manner that the original Source Flowers had failed to achieve.

The time of her accession was indeed a time of peril for Silla as the aggressive Ŭija of Paekche was determined to destroy it and regain his lost Han River territories, while, in between its massive struggles with China, Koguryŏ was also a threat. Sŏndŏk was fortunate in having at her service men gifted at both war and diplomacy. The great soldier was Kim Yu-sin, descended from the old royal

46

house of Kaya. For some years he would hardly spend a night at home for after repelling an attack at one end of the long frontier with Paekche he would be galloping his cavalry to the relief of a besieged fortress at the other. The diplomat was Kim Ch'un-ch'u of the Silla royal family, and as both Sŏndŏk and her cousin Chindŏk, who would succeed her, were childless, he would eventually inherit the throne himself as King Muyŏl. His partnership with Kim Yu-sin was further cemented by his marriage to Yu-sin's younger sister, a love affair said to have begun when she was called to sew up a tear in his tunic while he was visiting her brother.

At this time Yu-sin's great love was for a courtesan, Ch'un'gwan, which distressed his mother so much that she made him promise never to see her again, but one evening, when weary, he dozed off in the saddle and his horse followed its accustomed path. Somebody had to pay for the breaking of his vow, so the horse was slain, while Ch'un'gwan, accepting the final separation, endowed a convent to which she retired. Yu-sin subsequently married one of Ch'un-ch'u's daughters.

In 642, just after Yŏn Kaesomun had been made *makriji* in Koguryŏ, Paekche succeeded in seizing 40 Silla forts along the frontier, pushing it back to the line of the Nakdong River, and then with aid from Koguryŏ they took the vital Yellow Sea port of Namyang. It was at this point that in desperation Kim Ch'un-ch'u went to Koguryŏ to see if he could persuade them to change sides. He was told that first of all Silla must give back all the land along the Han River that it had occupied a century before, and indeed that he would be kept in prison until they did so, and it was only when Kim Yu-sin marched an army to their border that he was allowed to return. Silla's hopes now lay with the Tang, who until now had avoided taking sides in quarrels between the three states. This was just the moment at which Taizong was about to launch his attack on Koguryŏ, and apart from adding Silla's grievances to his accusations against them, he was not inclined to do any more.

Silla was now holding its own against Paekche but suffering raids from Japan and in 647 Kim Ch'un-ch'u embarked on another adventurous and, in this case, successful mission to the Yamato court. In the following year he went to make the first of two personal visits to Taizong, again with great success. Apart from an evident mutual attraction, the Emperor must have realized the advantages of opening a second front against Koguryŏ, and Paekche's failure to do this, along with their aggression against Silla, provided a pretext. His death in 649 delayed the process, but Silla continued to cultivate China's friendship and in 650 Queen Chindŏk sent Kim Ch'un-ch'u's son Pŏpmin to deliver to the new Emperor, Gaozong, a personally embroidered scroll with a twenty-line psalm in praise of the blessings that would flow from his reign. The Emperor, said to be greatly pleased, gave Pŏpmin an honorary peerage.

It was at about this time that two young Silla monks, Ŭisang and Wŏnhyo, set out on foot to study in China. On their way north they were forced to pass a night in a hillside cave. During the night Wŏnhyo woke up feeling thirsty, and stretching out his hand in the darkness came on a bowl of cool water from which he drank. In the morning he discovered that the water had collected in a human skull. This experience aroused in him thoughts of such profundity that he felt no inclination to travel any further and left Ŭisang to go on alone.

Many are the legends concerning the scholarly and charismatic Wŏnhyo, some of them bawdy and others over-pious. He wrote many volumes of scripture, the best known being his 'Harmonization of the Ten Schools', a pioneering attempt at a synthesis, but the role of Thomas Aquinas was not enough – he would also foreshadow those of Abelard and Francis of Assisi. After an affair with a widowed princess, through which he fathered the famous scholar Sŏl Ch'ong, he expiated his fall by leaving the monastery to become a mendicant preacher, dancing singing, and persuading the common people to call on the saving name of Amita.

Ŭisang distinguished himself in China and returned to set up, under royal patronage, ten great temples to propagate the doctrines of Hwaŏm (Avatamsaka), which would become the most influential Buddhist school. Another seventh-century monk who went to China was Wŏnch'uk, who became a leading exponent of the Hwaŏm, but as he was also the Empress Wu's favourite preacher he was not allowed to return and the pagoda that contains his ashes still stands near Xi'an.

Later in the seventh century another Silla monk, Musang, having persuaded a Chinese master of Zen to accept him by burning off one of his own fingers, became himself one of its great sages. He also never returned to Silla but this radical sect would soon arrive, one of its early centres being Sinhŭngsa, near the east coast in what is now the Sŏraksan National Park. It was dedicated to Zen after being rebuilt by the monk Ŭisang in 701 and here one can see the bell-shaped stupas that house the ashes of early monks and a mural that shows an aspirant offering his severed arm to Poridalma (Bodhidharma).

When, in 654, Queen Chindŏk died without issue, Kim Ch'un-ch'u, who was a cousin, was crowned as Muyŏl, and from this time his successors would take their queens from their own clan, strengthening their authority over the others. He had as his representative at the Tang court his second son Kim In-mun, who had already spent some years there as a student and acquired a considerable reputation as a scholar, musician and calligrapher. In response to new appeals for assistance against Paekche, preparations began for a combined attack which would be followed by a renewed offensive against Koguryŏ.

Early in 660 Gaozong appointed Su Dingfang as supreme commander of an army of 130,000 men, with Kim In-mun as his deputy. They set off from various harbours on the Shandong Peninsula at the end of June and made for Tŏkchokdo, a large island about 50 miles south-west of Inch'ŏn. Here they were met by a fleet of a hundred warships from Silla led by the crown prince, Pŏpmin, and dates were fixed for an attack by Silla's land forces across the mountains to coincide with a Chinese landing at the mouth of the Kŭm River, the gateway to the Paekche capital of Puyŏ, where they were scheduled to meet on the tenth day of the seventh moon.

Paekche's King Ŭija, a military hero in his younger days, was now an old man. With his successive victories against Silla, his alliance with Koguryŏ, and his links with Japan to protect his coast, he must have felt secure and the sudden news of an impending Chinese invasion seems to have thrown his court into confusion. His ministers were still arguing about what to do when the Tang fleet overwhelmed the forts at the mouth of the river and news came of Silla's attack across the hills just east of Taejŏn. An élite force of 5,000 under the Paekche commander Kyebaek set off to stop them. They went knowingly as a 'suicide squad', for the Silla forces outnumbered them by ten to one and Kyebaek killed his family by his own hand before he left. They were too late to reach the mountain pass at Tanhyŏn before Kim Yu-sin's forces had crossed it and had to face them on the level ground at Yŏnsan where in four desperate battles they managed to delay them for a day.

Meanwhile, the Chinese galleys had come up the river with their drums beating and set up camp on the opposite bank from the fortified capital. After inflicting heavy losses on the Paekche forces they surrounded the city and that night the King and the crown Prince were smuggled out and taken to the fortress at the old capital of Kongju, further up the river. At Puyŏ the next morning came the legendary 'falling flowers', as from a cliff with a pavilion at its edge the women of the court, dutifully putting death before dishonour, plunged into the river below. The city then opened its gates to surrender.

When the Silla army arrived, after heavy losses on the way, Su Dingfang accused them of being late and wanted the Silla general Kim Mun-yŏng to be executed at the gate of the camp as an appropriate penalty. Kim Yu-sin is said to have been so angry that his hair stood on end and his sword began, of its own accord, to rise out of his scabbard. He replied that if they were going to face senseless charges like that they would settle accounts with the Tang first before they dealt with Paekche, at which the Chinese deputy commander stepped forward and persuaded Su to change the subject.

At Kongju, the King was soon forced to surrender and he and his chief ministers and their families, a party of 93, were shipped off to China, soon to be followed by 12,000 others. On arrival they were reprimanded by the Emperor and then forgiven and provided with accommodation. Ŭija did not long survive and his son Yung was given ducal rank and kept in store.

The forces led by Paekche's famous general Hŭkch'i Sangji took part in the general surrender that followed the fall of the capital and the capture of the King, but when the general saw the Chinese imprison the elderly King and join the Silla soldiers in ravaging the surrounding countryside he changed his mind. He escaped with about ten of his commanders and collecting a band of followers they established themselves in a fortress to the north-west of Yesan where their numbers grew to about 30,000 and they succeeded in recovering most of the fortified towns in the area. At the same time, Poksin, a cousin of the King who had served as an envoy to China, and Toch'im, a martial monk, along with other ministers who had fled from Puyŏ, set up a loyalist administration at the Churyu fortress on the south-west coast where they had similar success.

Thus, although Chinese administrators were nominally in control of the local government in each province, the country was far from pacified. Meanwhile, Su Dingfang, having failed to dislodge Hŭkch'i Sangji, left to take charge of a seaborne attack on Pyongyang, taking with him most of the Chinese troops. This meant that Silla under the now elderly Muyŏl, as well as trying to keep control of Paekche, was expected to support China's assault on Koguryŏ.

In the autumn of 660 the Tang Emperor sent an embassy to Silla with gifts to express his gratitude but during the ceremony the King collapsed, and although he was sufficiently recovered to go out with the army again against the Paekche rebels, he died in the early summer of 661. Water in the well at Taikwan temple turned red like blood and at Chang'an the Emperor, on hearing the news, went to the gates to mourn. Pŏpmin succeeded him as King Munmu and confirmed his ever-vigorous uncle and brother-in-law Kin Yu-sin as commander-in-chief of the army.

In the spring of 661 a Chinese army of 40,000, assembled from the northern provinces, invaded Koguryŏ through the Liao peninsula, again in the presence of their Emperor. This time, to avoid their earlier misfortunes, they marched straight down the east bank of the Liao to cross the Yalu, and by August they had surrounded Pyongyang, but in September a force led by Yŏn Kaesomun's son Namsaeng managed to regain control of the Yalu crossing, so that as winter came on their supplies were cut off and it seemed that only grain from Silla could save them.

That winter, which was severe, Silla had to send men and grain across the frozen hills to Kongju, where the Chinese were under siege from Paekche loyalists, and they also took warm clothes for the Tang soldiers, donated by the public, but their greatest task was to answer the appeals from Pyongyang. Kim Yu-sin took charge of this operation, which involved moving about 1,500 tons of grain from one end of the peninsula to the other and crossing its highest mountain range in the worst winter weather. Nine generals were involved and 2,000 carts, which could not get very far before the loads had to be transferred to the backs of oxen, mules or horses. They struggled northwards through heavy snow and under attack from Koguryŏ.

By the beginning of February they were across the mountains and finally set up camp about 20 miles from Pyongyang. The Chinese, having taken delivery of the supplies, abandoned the siege and left Kim Yu-sin's men to fight their own way back. They were short of food, their hands and feet were crippled with frostbite, and it is said that countless bodies were left frozen by the wayside, a tragedy that would be repeated in the same hills in the bitter winter of 1951 as the UN forces retreated before the Chinese assault.

Meanwhile in Paekche the loyalists still held a number of more or less impregnable forts and as well as their local support they were now receiving aid from their Japanese allies who sent a fleet of ships to accompany the return of P'ung, the Paekche prince who had been the diplomatic hostage at their court. He was delivered to Poksin's headquarters at Fort Churyu on the Pyŏnsan Peninsula, where he was proclaimed as King and headed another popular uprising that led to Puyŏ and Kongju again being besieged. In 663 another Tang fleet sailed out to relieve them bringing with them their own Paekche prince, P'ung's elder brother Yung. The Japanese fleet attacked them at the mouth of the Kŭm but the Chinese beat them off and the capital was relieved. There was now dissension in the loyalist camp where the arrival of P'ung seems to have aroused the jealousy of his uncle Poksin, who, after executing Toch'im, planned his asassination, but P'ung, forewarned, struck first.

The Tang general at Puyŏ, rather than risk a march through largely hostile territory, planned an amphibious assault on the loyalist stronghold at Churyu. The Chinese ships, under the nominal command of Yung, who had been proclaimed as King, were brought down the river, and after taking on board a combined force of Tang and Silla troops they set off for the Pyonsan Peninsula, but the Japanese fleet, with their rival ruler, P'ung, were waiting for them at the mouth of the river. Four battles were fought and the Chinese won, probably through the use of their recently acquired pyrotechnical skills, for it is said that 400 Japanese ships were burned, covering the sky with smoke and reddening the water with reflected flame. P'ung fled, his final fate unknown, but his two sons were captured, along with the fort, and this marked the virtual end of Paekche resistance.

Hŭkch'i Sangji still held out at Imjŏnsŏng but the Chinese commander, who had a high regard for him, persuaded him to surrender on favourable terms and he emigrated to China, where he would become one of the Tang's great generals, winning a series of victories against the Turks and the Mongols on the north-west frontier.

CHAPTER SIX

UNIFICATION UNDER SILLA

K ING YUNG of Paekche now set up his court in the old walled capital of Kongju, where the Chinese governor had resided. The establishment included a Chinese orchestra and in 664 Silla sent 28 musicians there to be trained. Silla had already adopted the Tang calendar, and its style of dress for officials, and this was now extended to women's clothes. This enthusiasm for Chinese culture would be fostered by an increasing flow of students to the Chinese capital and by the influence of the King's brother, Kim In-mun, who had spent most of his life in China and had won the trust and friendship of the Emperor to a degree that would enable Silla to pursue its own secret agenda for gaining control of the peninsula without ever finally breaking off diplomatic relations.

With Paekche and Koguryŏ apparently pacified, the Emperor now hoped to inaugurate a new era of peace for the whole of the Far East. In the autumn of 665 his representative called a reluctant King Munmu of Silla to join the newly appointed Yung of Paekche on a hilltop near Kongju where Daoist priests sacrificed a white horse to the spirits of earth and heaven and the spirits of the hills and rivers. The two kings then touched its blood to their lips and swore, under the peril of an everlasting curse, to keep an everlasting peace. King Yung was then taken back across the Yellow Sea, along with representatives from Japan and Tamna, as the island of Cheju was then known, to the sacred mountain of Taishan on the Shandong Peninsula, where they were joined by Poknam, the crown prince of Koguryŏ, Kin In-mun of Silla and finally by the Emperor himself. They all ascended the mountain and took part in another sacrifice and an international pledge of peace.

That a representative of Koguryŏ was able to be present was because after the retreat of Su Dingfang from Pyongyang in 662, Yŏn Kaesomun was given a few years of respite and by 665 diplomatic relations with the Tang had been restored, but the situation was soon destabilized by Yŏn's death in 666. He was succeeded as *makriji* by his son Namsaeng, but as soon as he left on a tour of inspection his younger brother Namgŏn seized control of the court, aided by a third brother, Namsan. Namsaeng, afraid to return to Pyongyang, appealed to the Tang, who with the support of Silla decided to further the era of everlasting peace by finally subduing Koguryŏ.

Namsaeng appears to have had widespread support outside the capital, including that of his uncle Yŏn Chŏngt'o who held an area on the southern border and was able to join the Silla forces with about 3,500 men. On the Manchurian side, however, the defenders of the Western Wall and their Malgal allies seem to have been as ready as ever to resist the Chinese. They failed to reach the Yalu before the autumn of 667 so that it was not until the summer of the following year that the Chinese general, Li Ji, was able to join the Silla forces in surrounding Pyongyang. The city was divided in its loyalties, with the King in favour of peace, so after they had endured a month of siege the monk Sinsŏng was able to negotiate a surrender, and the King, the crown prince, Namgŏn, who had tried to kill himself, and some thousands of its citizens were taken back to China by Li Ji.

The now elderly Kim Yu-sin had been appointed to lead the Silla forces, and although an illness described as *p'ungbyŏng*, probably leprosy, had forced him to stay behind in Kyŏngju, he, along with Muyŏl and Munmu, must be seen as the chief protagonists in a long campaign of war and diplomacy through which Silla, once the weakest of the three states, was now in a position of dominance.

China's intention for the peninsula, reflected in the peace pledge on Taishan in 666, was for the three states, along with the offshore kingdoms of Tamna and Japan, to retire within their respective boundaries and as dutiful tributaries of the Emperor turn their swords into ploughshares. This had often been the theme of letters to them from the Tang emperors – their concern that the men in their conscripted armies should be sent home to plough their fields and gather their mulberry leaves. As soon as Koguryŏ had fallen the Tang set up at Pyongyang a Bureau for the Preservation of Peace in the East, putting it under the control of their famous general Xue Rengui, who as governor-general would rule directly over the parts of Manchuria where there was a Chinese peasant population, while the rulers of a truncated Koguryŏ and the two southern kingdoms were expected to accept his mediatorial supervision.

This was not acceptable to Silla. It had emerged as the eventual victor after centuries of struggle and regarded itself as entitled to the spoils of war. It had cooperated in the peace-plan only in so far as it served to hasten the departure of the Chinese and now attempts by the residual Chinese troops to protect Paekche and Koguryŏ from further encroachments by Silla would soon lead to coolness, and eventually hostility, between the former allies. In Koguryŏ the Silla armies continued to attack the Malgal across the Yalu until the Chinese had to change sides and force them back, after which Silla supported a former Koguryŏ official, Kŏm Mo-jam, who led a rebellion against the Chinese in the name of Ansung, a youthful nephew of Yŏn Kaesomun, whom he set up as pretender to the throne. In 670 Ansung had to flee to Silla where he was welcomed as a King in exile and with his followers was settled at Iksan, south of Puyŏ, in Paekche, an act that the Chinese saw as a direct provocation.

Continued plundering of Paekche by Silla's army of occupation had already led to the restoration of a Chinese governor and in 669 he arrested and deported to China two Silla generals, Hŭm Sun and Yang To, the former of whom was released in the following year, but Yang To, who had been one of Kim Yu-sin's two deputies in the relief of the Chinese at Pyongyang in the winter of 661–2, would be left to die in a Chinese prison.

The Chinese brought Malgal troops down from the north to help them in Paekche, where Silla continued to plunder it, and there was an exchange of letters between the Governor-General and King Munmu. The Chinese letter recounts how when Silla was threatened by its enemies Munmu's aged father had crossed the sea to appeal to the Emperor, and the Emperor, though he had nothing to gain from it, had expended his men and his treasure in saving Silla, only to be rewarded now by Munmu's opportunistic betrayal of their trust and friendship, even to the extent of making an alliance with the anti-Tang pretender to the throne of Koguryŏ.

In his reply Munmu recalls in detail all that Silla has done to assist and feed the Tang armies through the past nine years, mentioning in particular the countless soldiers who froze to death in the winter of 661 and the major part they played in the final attack on Pyongyang, and he then goes on to claim that in 648 the former Emperor had promised his father that after the war, as he himself had no desire for more land or wealth, all the territory south of Pyongyang would be handed over to Silla. Whether or not such a promise was ever made, it certainly reflects Silla's intentions and expresses the presuppositions of its policy.

Silla went on to occupy the Paekche capital, taking the Chinese governor back to Kyŏngju, designating the area as a province, and appointing a governor of their own. The Chinese repaired the defences of Pyongyang and began to ferry an army across the Yellow

Sea, and although on one occasion about 70 of their transports were sunk by a warfleet from Silla, they were eventually ready to set out from Pyongyang for the northern borders of Silla. This, combined with the news of further reinforcements pouring into Paekche, and their public condemnation by the Emperor, seems to have caused something of a panic in the Silla capital. Munmu hastily sent back the former Paekche governor, along with 170 other Chinese hostages, adding also quantities of gold, silver, copper and silk, and an abject letter of apology.

It was only a bid for time, as Silla's strength was steadily growing. Their generous treatment of any Paekche or Koguryŏ leaders who supported them against the Chinese helped to foster an increasing sense of the peninsula's common identity even though it was para-doxically largely based on their shared Chinese culture, to which Silla still increasingly attempted to conform. They built new forts and repaired old ones, they raised new regiments, smartly uniformed, made up of recruits from Paekche, Koguryŏ and Malgal tribesmen, with collars of different colours to distinguish them.

They soon resumed their attacks on the Tang forces, in response to which the Emperor deposed the King and appointed his younger brother Kim In-mun to replace him, but before the ship that was bringing him back from China had arrived Munmu, having just lost a battle with Chinese forces from Pyongyang at the Imjin River, staged another repentance and offering of gifts, and was again for-given and restored.

In 673 Silla defeated an attack from the north by Tang troops with Malgal and Qidan auxiliaries and in the following year they again went on the offensive, extending their grip on Paekche and crossing the Han to occupy another province of Koguryŏ. General Xue Rengui now prepared a large army to march south from Pyong-yang, and decided on a tactic that would later be used, in reverse as it were, by General MacArthur in 1950, an amphibious assault to establish a bridgehead at the mouth of the Han. Guided by a Silla student whose father had been executed for treason while he was studying in China, they came ashore at a point on the northern bank of the estuary close to where the Yesong River flows into it and surrounded a nearby fort. Silla was quick to respond and before the Chinese had taken the fort they had to make a hasty retreat, leaving behind 40 ships and about a thousand horses.

A couple of weeks later the main Tang army of about 20,000 was met and defeated just north of the river near Ŭijŏngbu. A few months later the Chinese made another landing further down the coast and over the next year there were frequent battles in the Han River basin and south as far as Puyŏ, with heavy losses on both sides. Xue

Rengui evidently had a good press in Chang'an as he became one of China's legendary heroes and a fictional account of his exploits in Korea is a Tang dynasty classic, though the Korean records incline them to see him more as an early example of a paper tiger.

Through all these battles Korean scholars, monks and diplomats had continued to travel to and from China, Kim In-mun had stayed at the Emperor's side, and there had never been any formal break in the tributary exchanges. By this time the Chinese appear to have decided to accept the situation on Silla's terms. They removed the headquarters of the Bureau for the Preservation of Peace in the East to Shenyang in Manchuria and made no more armed interventions to the south, although it would be another 50 years before they formally acknowledged Silla's title to the whole area.

CHAPTER SEVEN

SILLA AND PARHAE

W ITH SILLA now in control of all the land south of a line
that ran from Pyongyang on the eastern side to Wŏnsan
on the west, they divided it into nine provinces, three of which were
in what had been Paekche and three in regions taken from Koguryŏ.
The commanders of the occupying forces were replaced by governors
appointed from true-bone families and they retained a military garrison that could be used to round up thieves and bandits and, when
necessary, enforce the collection of taxes. Under them, local grandees
were given ranks that reflected their former status and allowed a
degree of regional self-rule, but they were required to send one
member of the family to the capital as *ki'in*, literally, 'that person', a
kind of liaison officer who was in effect a hostage.

There were some forced movements of population in sensitive
border areas and it seems that this, along with the upheavals of war,
had reduced great numbers of people to the condition of vagrants or
slaves. At the same time, in their rather remote capital in Kyŏngju
there would be continuing friction between the increasingly autocratic rulers and their numerous true-bone relatives. Over the past
century or more the development of a Chinese-style bureaucracy
and a centralized army had steadily eroded the status of the many
true-bone relatives who made up the Hwabaek, the council that had
once been responsible for choosing the ruler.

The two chief officers of state were the *sangdaedŭng*, who presided over the Hwabaek and had traditionally been the King's chief
adviser, and the *chungsi*, an official originally concerned with petitions to the court, but since 651, as the head of the Chipsabu, the
office which coordinated the six ministries and conveyed to them
the King's wishes, he seems to have become in effect the chief execu-
tive or 'prime minister'. To this, King Munmu now added a further
touch of Confucian sophistication, a Board of Censors, whose duty

it was to watch over the conduct of officials and criticize their performance.

In the mean time, Japanese raids on Silla were again reaching dangerous proportions, and Munmu came to believe that if his body was cremated in 'the Indian manner', as recommended by Buddhist sages, and buried in an undersea tomb, he would become a dragon-spirit of the Eastern Sea to defend his country from them. He died in 681 and his tomb, in a calm pool between the rocks of a small island just off the coast, is still marked by two great stone pagodas which are all that remain of Kamunsa, a temple on the shore that had been built with an open chamber below the floor to allow the dragon-spirit of the King to come in with the tide.

The kind of Confucian administration established by Munmu required efficient educational institutions to train its officials and in 682 his successor, Sinmun, established a new Dynastic College, the Kukhak, which in addition to teaching the Chinese Classics, had departments for art and handicrafts. It was open to young people between the ages of 9 and 30 and was only for those whose families were below true-bone rank. Most of the students of the classics are thought to have been from Head Rank Six, what might be called 'the gentry', while the technical subjects were open to the lower ranks. It would serve to increase the numbers of the literati, socially inferior to the ruling caste, but often more able and better educated. They would favour more authority for the court, while the true-bone families would continue to fight for what they regarded as the ancient traditions of Silla as opposed to foreign innovations. Their resistance led to various executions for treason which culminated in an abortive coup in the first year of Sinmun's reign, followed by a purge in which he sentenced to death not only his father-in-law who had led it but the *sangdaedŭng* who was alleged to have connived in it, and a number of others.

Sinmun died in 692 and his son, who succeeded him, died childless ten years later, to be followed by his younger brother Sŏndŏk. In 714 he sent one of his sons to study in China, where he was welcomed by Emperor Xuanzong, whose reign marked the Golden Age of Tang culture. When he returned to Silla three years later he brought with him portraits of Confucius, the Ten Philosophers, and the Seventy-two Disciples, which were set up in a hall at the Kukhak, where the full cult could now be practised, and its title was changed to that of 'T'aehak', after the Chinese original on which it was modelled.

To the north, the Tang tried to keep their hold on Liaodong, but survivors of the Koguryŏ aristocracy still controlled the Malgal tribes to the north-east as far as the Songhua, and were able to hold on to the land on either side of the Yalu, giving them an outlet on the Yellow Sea, as well as the ports on the north-east coast of the peninsula from which they traded with Japan. This successor state to Koguryŏ was ruled by a former general, Tae Cho-yong, who eventually took the dynastic title of 'Parhae'. Silla had hoped to push its boundaries northwards as far as the Yalu, and for this purpose sustained a Koguryŏ government in exile at Kyŏngju, but Tae Cho-yong's son, King Mu, proved so aggressive that in 721 Silla had to build a defensive wall across the eastern coastal plain to the north of Kangnŭng.

Parhae formed a defensive alliance with the Japanese, who renewed their seaborne attacks on Silla and it is recorded that in 731, perhaps with the aid of Munmu in his sea-dragon mode, Silla repelled a Japanese war fleet 300 strong. Two years later, Parhae, having won control of the south coast of Liao as far as Dalian, attempted to gain a foothold on the Shandong Peninsula. The Tang called on Silla to assist them by marching north, but by this time it was winter and with snow blocking the mountain passes more than half the Silla force was lost without achieving any result. The extent to which they dominated the Yellow Sea can be judged from the fact that even today one approaches Beijing through the Strait of 'Parhae', pronounced as 'Bohai' in modern Chinese, and crosses the Gulf of Bohai to the estuary of the Yellow River on the Bay of Bohai.

Over the next two centuries Parhae made peace with both China and Japan, extending its trade and developing a sophisticated Buddhist culture. Their capital at what is now the city of Dunhua in Jilin Province was built on a grand scale and excavations have recovered attractive murals, stone lanterns, buddhas and lotus patterned tiles, along with *ondol* hot floors. Their greatest period was probably under King Sŏn who from 818 to 830 ruled over an area that stretched from North Korea and Liaodong as far as the Amur River, with five provincial capitals. Nevertheless, as an ethnic minority with no secure natural frontiers to the west, their alliances with the nomads of Central Asia were, by their nature, unstable and by the tenth century they would be overrun by the Qidan and leave virtually no traces other than the walls of their ruined cities and their name writ large on the waters of the Yellow Sea.

Among the increasing numbers who went to study in China was the monk Hyech'o, who in 724, at the age of 20, met there an Indian monk and sailed home with him via Sumatra and the Nicobar Islands to land at Calcutta. He followed the course of the Ganges to visit the holy places associated with Sakyamuni and then went on through most of the kingdoms of Central Asia and westward to Iran and the borders of Europe before he turned east again to walk back towards China, writing a detailed account of it all, a copy of which was rediscovered in a Chinese monastery in 1908. It provides the earliest known descriptions of these areas and also includes poems that express his longing for his homeland, which he would never see again, for after his return to China he would be employed as a translator of sanscrit sutras and die there in 787 at the age of 83.

Returning eastwards along the Silk Road he may have been forced aside by the cavalry escorting another wandering Korean, Ko Sŏn-ji, known in China as 'Gao Xianzi'. His father, exiled from Koguryŏ, served in the Tang army, where he became the commander of a line of desert forts on the western edge of Mongolia, and Sŏn-ji, brought up in this area, became a general while still in his twenties. In 747, to outflank the Tibetans, he led an army of 10,000 over 'the roof of the world', the icy, snow-bound passes of the Pamirs, which the archaeologist Sir Aurel Stein, who retracted his steps in the 1920s, described as a greater feat than Napoleon's crossing of the Alps. On another expedition he took Tashkent, capital of what is now Uzbekistan, and extended Chinese rule further than ever before, only to be forced back from Samarkand a year later by the rising tide of Arab power. It is said to be from Chinese prisoners taken here that the Arabs learnt the art of paper making, though it would be another 300 years before it reached Europe. Ko Sŏn-ji would die five years later in the rebellion of An Lushan that temporarily toppled the Emperor.

As well as many monks, a few students from gentry families were sent to study the classics at the Tang capital, usually with a joint sponsorship under which they paid for their travel and books while the Chinese provided tuition and lodgings. After taking special examinations administered for foreigners they could be enrolled as officers in the Tang Army or awarded posts in the civil service. For students who were not of true-bone birth, service with the Tang offered much better prospects than anything in their own country. The first of them to be recorded was Sŏl Ke-du, who had left in 621 and entered the Tang Army, where he rose to high rank, and in Taizong's invasion of Koguryŏ he had died in battle so bravely that the Emperor had posthumously awarded him the rank of full general. At least 60 others are known to have served the Tang, though probably more returned home where the now steadily burgeoning bureaucracy was able to offer, at least in the lower ranks, plenty of places.

Hardly any written documents survive from this period but in 1933 part of a Silla census register, believed to date from 755, turned up in Japan. It indicates that surveys, made every three years, were as detailed as the later Norman Domesday Book, recording not only the human population in six age groups, on which depended their liability for army service or local public works, but every ox, horse, or fruit-bearing tree. There were also communities in which large numbers of landless peasants, rebels or prisoners of war worked in virtual slavery, though continued orderly behaviour apparently entitled them to achieve regular village status.

The second half of the eighth century from the accession of Kyŏngdŏk in 742 probably represented the golden age of Silla's culture: it was in this period that Pulguksa and the Sŏkkuram grotto were completed and the greatest temple bells were made, including the beautifully decorated 'Emille', eleven feet high, which still survives in Kyŏngju. The nickname reflects the sound it makes, suggestive of a child railing against its mother, heard, it is said, on a still day, up to 40 miles away. The legend is that, as an offering to Buddha, a mother gave her child to be thrown into the 20 tons of molten metal from which it was cast.

Kyŏngdŏk also initiated further centralization, enforcing the use of two-syllable ideograms for local place names throughout his territories and trying to establish the Chinese system of governing the regions through competent officials appointed by the court rather than leaving them at the mercy of local grandees, but it inevitably aroused wide opposition and does not seem to have been generally implemented before his death in 765. His one son, Hyegong, was only 7 when his father died, which meant that his mother was nominally the regent. Such occasions frequently resulted in power struggles, and in this case, although the mother was the daughter of a former *chungsi*, which implies that she came of a powerful family, she had been only a subsidiary wife, while the boy himself was apparently a transvestite whose taste for feminine clothes was regarded as immoral. The conservatives saw this as their opportunity to gain control of the court and annul his father's reforms.

Unrest continued for three years, with repeated rebellions and palace plots from which the eventual winner was Kim Yang-sang, a son of the late King's elder sister. He had been *chungsi* at the time of Kyŏngdŏk's death, and had himself appointed as *sangdaedŭng* in 774, after which he acted as regent and repealed most of Kyŏngdŏk's reforms. An attempt to restore power to the now 15-year-old King by Kim Chi-jŏng in 779 led to a civil war in the course of which the King and his mother were assassinated and at the end of it Kim Yang-sang usurped the throne, basing his claim on descent from the fourth-century *maripkan* Naemul. After this his health declined, and seeing a succession of bad harvests as a judgement he apologized to the people before his death in 785, and ordered his body to be cremated and the ashes scattered on the Eastern Sea. Those who had brought him to the throne hastened to install his chief henchman, the *sangdaedŭng*, also a descendant of Naemul, as King Wŏnsŏng, while his opponents had supported Chu-mong, a descendant of the original line through Muyŏl, and his son would later lead an extensive rebellion.

Through all this period increasing trade and cultural exchanges with the Tang were having a profound influence on every aspect of life, and although the aristocracy may have resisted changes that threatened their power or wealth they could not put the clock back, and in this respect Wŏnsŏng was no reactionary. In 788 his government introduced Civil Service Examinations, in three grades, although the level of knowledge of the classics required even for the highest does not appear to have been very rigorous and in any case it did not open the way to the higher ranks for those who lacked true bones. Nevertheless, it was a further step towards a meritocracy and men of Head-rank Six, or even lower, began to receive the King's affection and to exert their influence in various ways.

Notable among them was Wŏnhyo's son, Sŏl Ch'ong, who in contrast to his fervently Buddhist father devoted himself to bringing to the people the Nine Classics of Confucianism. He used a system of phonetic symbols known as *kugyŏl*, based on simplified ideograms, which enabled Chinese to be read out in the native language and would also be adapted for the recording of hymns and folk-songs. Later forms, known as *hyangch'al* or *idu*, would change and develop, partly through a large-scale adoption of Chinese words in everyday speech and also through a simplification and ordering of the symbols to form a basic syllabary. As *idu*, it would continue to be used until the introduction of the modern alphabet in the fifteenth century and provided the pattern for the similar script still used in Japan.

By the time that Wŏnsŏng died in 798 both his sons were already dead and his grandson who succeeded him died two years later leaving the throne to a 12-year-old great-grandson, Aejang. His uncle Onsŭng, who had served as an envoy to the Tang, acted as regent and his policy of restricting expenditure on Buddhist temples and icons reflects a contemporary Confucian attitude. He was also active in establishing a reconciliation with Japan. By 809, when the King had reached the age of 20 and was entitled to assume power himself, his uncle, who also held the office of *sangdaedŭng* led a coup in which the King was killed and he took the throne himself as Hŏndŏk.

He was given instant recognition by the Tang Emperor, who needed help in quelling one of the many rebellions that marked the last years of the dynasty and Hŏndŏk sent a force of 30,000, by sea, from the south-western provinces. It was also a time of increasing unrest in Silla, made worse by several years of famine. In 822, perhaps in the hope of easing the succession, he appointed his younger brother to the newly created post of Assistant King, with a palace of his own. It was immediately followed by a rebellion in the south-west led by Kim Hŏn-ch'ang, Governor of Kongju, who was the son of the Chu-mong, the descendant of Muyŏl whose legitimate claim to the throne had been usurped by Wŏnsŏng. He carried with him the provinces of what had been Paekche and proclaimed a new dynasty of 'Chang'an'. The civil war ended with his defeat, and after holding out for a time in his fortress at Kongju he killed himself, and more than 200 of his family and followers were executed. Hŏndŏk died in 826 and was succeeded by his brother, Hŭngdŏk.

Despite the perils of pirates and storms, which took a heavy toll, traffic across the Yellow Sea steadily increased, with the initiative appearing to come mainly from Silla. The ships operating from their west-coast ports grew continually in size and number providing also transport for goods and passengers between China and Japan, where the seeds of Tang culture were about to produce another flowering. A reference in the records of Silla to about 170 people who at a time of local famine in 816 emigrated to the province of Zhejiang, south of the Yangtze delta, indicates the relative ease of movement across the water.

Unfortunately this growth of traffic was accompanied by a corresponding increase in the pirate fleets that preyed on it, mostly from Japan. A constant demand for slaves in China meant that the crews and passengers were as valuable as their cargoes and coastal villages were also raided for slaves. The man who tackled this problem was Chang Po-go, who would be listed by the twelfth-century historian Kim Pu-sik along with Ŭlch'i Mundok and Kim Yu-sin as one of the country's three great saviours. Little is known of his origins but he is thought to have have come from a gentry family in the area that would provide his base, the island-studded south-west corner, and the fact that his closest friend, Chŏng Yŏn, was said to have been able to swim under water for a mile provides a clue to their provenance.

As young men they had crossed the sea together to train as officers for the Chinese Army. After retiring with the rank of major-general, Chang Po-go returned to Silla while Chŏng Yŏn, also a general, having quarrelled with him, chose to stay in Shandong. Chang had been deeply moved by the misery of the many Korean slaves he had seen in China and he sought an audience with the King and won his support for the establishment of a new force that would be primarily concerned with policing the Yellow Sea. He took as his base the naval garrison at Wando, a group of islands that huddles close to the shore at the south-western tip of Chŏlla, the strategic point for controlling the eastern approaches to the Yellow Sea, not far from the smaller group, Komundo, that would, for similar reasons, be chosen by the British Navy a thousand years later and temporarily renamed as 'Port Hamilton'.

It was only one of three such garrisons on the west coast, but as it controlled the sea route to the Silla capital it became the largest, and the fact that the number of men under Chang Po-go's command is said to have reached ten thousand is some indication of the magnitude of his task and the extent to which trade between the three countries had grown – greater than at any other time until the close of the nineteenth century. Substantial Korean communities grew up in the Chinese ports and on the island of Tsushima, with their own Buddhist shrines at which offerings were made for safe journeys. It is known that at Penglai, the main port for Chang'an, a temple set up by Chang Po-go was provided with enough rice fields to support a community of about 30 monks and nuns, while in Silla there are references to Chinese merchants even in inland cities and Chinese coins seem to have circulated freely.

Meanwhile, the ambitions of the rival clans who contested the succession were a cause of continuing instability. After the death of Hŭngdŏk in 836 there were several deaths before Hŭigang, a great-grandson of Wŏnsŏng, became King, whilst Kim U-jing, the son of his assassinated rival, fled to Wando to take refuge with Chang Po-go. Two years later Hŭigang was assassinated and his cousin Minae who had been involved in the death of his own father in the struggle to put Hŭigang on the throne, took his place. Kim Yang, who had been *sangdaedŭng* under Hŭigang, then led an army out of Kyŏngju to join U-jing at Wando where he appealed to Chang Po-go to avenge the murder of the King.

Chang had been joined at Wando by his boyhood companion and fellow general Chong Yŏn, whom he now put in charge of 5,000 men to support Kim Yang in a march on the capital. They were met at Naju by a force loyal to Minae, which they defeated, and moved on to win a decisive battle at Taegu. After this they reached Kyŏngju so quickly that the King, with his ministers, was under a large tree outside the city when they arrived. Slain on the spot, he was replaced by Kim U-jing, to be known as King Sinmu. A few months later, soon after he had ordered the execution of Kim I-hŭng, the chief supporter of Minae, he woke from a dream in which I-hŭng had shot him in the back with an arrow. The pain was caused by a poisoned abscess from which he died a few days later and was succeeded by his son Munsŏng.

Before his death, Sinmu had given Chang Po-go a special military rank and an official residence in the capital, and Munsŏng wanted to take one of his daughters as his second wife – the legend is that they had fallen in love while gazing out to sea from the walls of the castle at Wando – but he was persuaded that it would be improper for him to take a wife who lacked true bones. Her father took her back to his base at Wando where he was thought to be plotting rebellion. To forestall it, the court pretended to expel a well-known warrior, Yŏm Jang, who had been at Wando with Kim Yang, ensuring him a welcome there, which he used to assassinate Chang.

Even after his death the Wando garrison remained a refuge for opponents of the group that dominated the court, and in 851 it was closed and the civilian population moved to the Kunsan area about a hundred miles to the north. This brought to an end Silla's dominance of the Yellow Sea – it would return to its state as a haunt of pirates and remain so until modern times. Even so, there were still several other active ports at the mouth of the Han and further down the west coast and there would soon be other regional leaders ready to revive old loyalties and defy the inbred oligarchy in Kyŏngju.

The ninth century saw an increasing enthusiasm for Zen, reflecting its success in China, where in line with the Buddhist creation myth of nine holy mountains with eight seas between them, nine patriarchs had come to preside over nine separate mountain communities. A number of student monks from Silla found their way to one or the other of them to fast, meditate and be beaten by their staves until they reached that state of *kong*, void, empty sky, beyond words, beyond thought, that brought 'awakening'. A few of them received the *sim'in*, 'heart-seal', of mastership and returned to plant similar monastic families in the hills, where their opposition to the 'establishment' would win them favour with dissident provincial landlords.

The first and fiercest was Toŭi, who went to Mt Kaji in south Cholla in 821, followed through the century by six others, including Muyŏm, who, sent to study the Hwaŏm at the age of 9, suffered shipwreck on the way and survived by clinging to the wreckage for 14 days, and Toyun, pupil of the famous Nanquan, who after a discussion as to whether or not his kitten had the Buddha-nature, ended it by cutting off its head. The last, Yiŏm, would return from the dying days of the Tang in the tenth century to find Silla in its final decline and accept an invitation to establish a holy hill beyond its borders at Haeju in the new northern state of Koryŏ.

CHAPTER EIGHT

THE LATER THREE KINGDOMS

I N T H E autumn of 857 the Silla King, Munsŏng, was laid up with a serious illness feeling, as he put it, as if he were treading on thin ice at the edge of a deep lake, and, having no son, he appointed his uncle, the *sangdaedŭng*, as regent. He died a few days later and the uncle became King Hŏnan. Within three years he also died, without a male heir, but he left two daughters, of whom the elder was married to a 15-year-old first cousin who became King Kyŏngmun. He had studied in China and was considered to be able and wise.

He also would die young, but not before sowing seeds of future discord, for when after three years his wife had not produced a son he took her sister, but neither did she, and after he had turned to another lady of the court who did, the sisters plotted the death of the mother and her son. The mother was assassinated but the child, Kungye, was smuggled away by his wet nurse and handed over to a monastery, losing one eye in the process. There is an alternative version of the story which makes him the son of Hŏnan – either way, the one-eyed prince would have cause for grievance when he eventually learned of his parentage.

Meanwhile, before the death of Kyŏngmun in 875, at the age of 28, another consort had provided him with another son, who succeeded him as Hŏn'gang, and he would for 11 years or so preside over an Indian summer in which even while its economic base was being eroded by regional disaffections, the capital reached the pinnacle of its conspicuous consumption. In his day, it is said, every house within the city walls had a tiled roof, and no woodsmoke obscured the sky, as only charcoal was used. One evening in 880, as the King and his two chief ministers gazed out over the glistening tiles and listened to the music that rose from the courtyards below, the *chungsi* said, 'From the time that your majesty began to reign over us, yin and yang have been in harmony, and the weather always seasonable, with bumper crops year by year. All our borders are peaceful and the people rejoice in the streets. All this is thanks to your majesty's virtue.' The King replied that it was due rather to the efforts of his ministers.

In the provinces, however, unrest was increasing and thieves and bandits are said to have swarmed like insects. To resist them, large landowners increased their private armies and sent excuses rather than taxation rice to the capital. The great monasteries were extending their rice-lands and they also had their warrior monks and paid no taxes.

In 885 there returned from China the most distinguished of the many scholars who had served in the Tang administration, Ch'oe Ch'i-wŏn. His father, an official of Head Rank Six, had sent him to study there at the age of 11 and six years later, in 874, he had entered the civil service where he had won rapid promotion, bringing him to the attention of the Emperor, and when Huang Chao's rebellion broke out he was appointed as secretary to the commander-in-chief of the army. The rebellion spread ever wider, forcing the court to flee, but when finally the Emperor was able to return, he allowed Ch'oe, then 28 to go back to his native land. He bequeathed to China a classic collection of essays that is still extant. Two other unusually talented men returned at about the same time, Ch'oe On-wi and Ch'oe Sung-u, so that they became known as 'The Three Ch'oes', but the caste system that had caused them to emigrate ensured that they could now be offered nothing better than minor posts.

Hŏn'gang died, without a son, in 886 and was succeeded by his younger brother, who also died within the year to be followed by a younger sister, Queen Chinsŏng. She is said to have been of manly build and appears to have been something of a free spirit. She allowed the Prime Minister, Kim Wi-hŭng, to move into the palace where they reigned jointly and together edited a collection of folk-songs in *idu*. After his death later in the same year she posthumously promoted him to kingly rank, and then brought into the palace several pretty young men and gave them important posts in which they were said to have taken bribes and given unjust decisions. Someone hung up an anonymous protest outside the palace, but the constabulary were unable to find the culprit. Eventually, on a tip-off, they arrested a well-known scholar and he wrote a poem on the wall of his cell appealing to Heaven. That night there was a storm with thunder and lightning and he was hastily released.

There was further evidence of divine displeasure in a severe drought that summer and several provinces could send no taxation grain. An attempt to enforce collection by troops from the capital led to a series of rebellions in which two famous names first came to the fore, Kungye, the one-eyed prince referred to above, now full-grown, who in alliance with a bandit leader, Yanggil, was in control of ten counties to the north-east of the capital, and Kyŏnhwŏn, the son of a farm worker from Sangju who after enlisting in the army had received rapid promotion to become a local commander in Chŏlla province and then the leader of a peasant army. The fact that both would soon win control of large areas implies a failure on the part of Silla's true-bone oligarchy to gain the loyalty of these regions.

Silla had lost control of the sea routes to China, while Parhae and, later, the Qidan, blocked the land route, and in any case the decline of the Tang meant that they no longer had a reliable ally there. The last recorded Silla envoy to the Tang was lost at sea in 893. In the following year Ch'oe Ch'i-wŏn was awarded a sixth-grade post after he had submitted to the court ten proposals on current affairs, but he immediately resigned. Of the other two Ch'oes, On-wi would eventually serve the kingdom of Koryŏ, which would develop from the rebellion of Kungye, while Sŭng-u would join Kyŏnhwŏn in a revival of Paekche.

For Ch'oe Ch'i-wŏn, who had tasted so young the elegance of the Emperor's court and the adventures of war, it seems that only the higher realms of art and mysticism remained. He made his home by the tumbling stream at the Haein Monastery on Mt Kaya, where he would write inscriptions for memorials to some of the leading masters of Zen, along with a few more essays and poems:

> The autumn wind intones a bitter song;
> Few my friends on life's way.
> Outside drips the midnight rain;
> Under the lamplight my thoughts travel far.

In 892 Kyŏnhwŏn took the city of Kwangju with a peasant army of about 5,000 and Queen Chinsŏng, being unable to oust him, recognized him as the de facto ruler and gave him the title of Duke of the South-West. He then came to an agreement with the forces of Yanggil and Kungye and gave them titles as local rulers, Yanggil remaining in charge of an area to the south of the Han while Kungye, with an army of about 3,500, extended his rule to the north and east. A devoted Buddhist, he was revered by his men and is said to have shared their hardships and divided things equally among them.

The Queen's health was now declining and the provision of an heir became an urgent problem. Kungye had put himself beyond the pale so a boy called Yŏ was brought forward, the child of a village girl whom Hŏn'gang had made pregnant on a hunting trip. The Queen, after feeling the shape of his shoulder blades, declared him to be her brother's son and in 897, when he reached the age of 14, she resigned in his favour, and he became King Hyogong. When Kungye found his portrait on the wall of an outlying monastery at which he called he shredded it with his sword.

Kungye and Kyŏnhwŏn had both been born within the original confines of Silla but they would fulfil their ambitions by appealing to the ancient loyalties of the areas in which, by chance, they found themselves. Kyŏnhwŏn, having familiarized himself with the history of Paekche, proclaimed himself the King of a reborn version of it, Later Paekche. With Chŏnju as his capital, he began to harass the borders of Silla to avenge the death in exile of its former King, Ŭija. In the north Kungye became aware that Pyongyang, the once-proud capital of Koguryŏ, was now a waste of weeds, and promised to bring vengeance on those who had destroyed it. He set up his capital at Kaesŏng, a fortified town to the north of the Han estuary, where he had won the support of its ruling clan, the Wang, a seafaring family who through their bases at the mouth of the Yesŏng River and on the nearby island of Kanghua were now the chief traders of the west coast. In 901, with their backing, Kungye was enthroned as the King of Later Koguryŏ.

With its control of the fertile Han River basin and what must have been a considerable flow of trade, the wealth and power of Later Koguryŏ continually increased, but Kungye seems to have lost his mental balance. Proclaiming himself as a living Buddha, with a supernatural knowledge of what was in other people's minds, he set about building a grandiloquent new capital at Ch'orwŏn in the hills of Kangwŏn Province, and filled it with temples. It was sited on the trade route that wound its way through interconnected valleys to the north-east and surrounded by mountain peaks such as were thought to be the dwelling place of bodhisvattas, so that it combined the best of both worlds. The slaughter of any living thing was forbidden and he moved amongst the people on a be-ribboned white horse, wearing a golden crown and a purple robe, with bands of children carrying flags, parasols, flowers and incense to go before and a choir of 200 monks to follow behind.

His political success was largely due to the vigour and enterprise of the elder son of the Wang family, Wang Kŏn, whose naval domination of the west coast enabled Kungye both to isolate Silla and to harass his chief rival for control of the peninsula, Later Paekche, threatening their links with China and Japan by occupying the fortress at Naju and the large island of Chindo at the south-west corner of Cholla. As the years passed Kungye became increasingly paranoiac, his psychic powers enabling him to detect adultery on the part of his wife, who was executed in 915, and later his two sons, whom he had declared to be bodhisvattas, were also condemned to death, along with many others. Finally, in 918, his chief ministers decided that he must be replaced by the Lord of the Hundred Ships, Wang Kŏn, who was reluctant to rebel and is said to have been finally persuaded only by his wife Sinhye, who fetched his armour and made him put it on.

He moved the capital back to Kaesŏng, which was the established centre of the region as well as his own home base, and named the new dynasty 'Koryŏ', an abbreviated form of Koguryŏ. To give himself breathing space, he abandoned Kungye's hostile attitude to Silla and accepted a diplomatic exchange with Kyŏnhwŏn, without, it would seem, abandoning his hopes of eventually reuniting the three kingdoms.

In Silla, Hyogong had died, childless, in 912 and the succession had passed to the husband of his half-sister, who became King Sindŏk. He was not even a member of the ruling clan of Kim, but of the old holy-bone family of Pak, a descendant of Successor-Prince Adalla who had died in 184. He was followed in 917 by his son Kyŏngmyŏng, who established friendly relations with the new ruler of Koryŏ, Wang Kŏn, and called for his help in 920 when Kyŏnhwŏn attacked them with a force of about 10,000. The invaders had to withdraw, as they did also after another attempt in 924, but in 927 Kyŏnhwŏn himself headed a lightning attack which reached Kyŏngju before Wang Kŏn could intervene. The King, who was having a picnic in the Posŏk Pavilion with the Queen and the ladies of the court, was slain on the spot and the women raped.

It was said of Kyŏnhwŏn that as a baby he had been left in the shade of the trees while his mother weeded the fields, so that his cries attracted the attention of a tigress which came and suckled him, evidence of a ferocity that was felt to need some special explanation. Certainly, it made a deep impression on the people of Kyŏngju, and although he made a bid for the favour of those who supported the house of Kim by replacing Sindŏk by a descendant of Munsŏng, the new King, Kyŏngsun, turned even more enthusiastically to his northern rival, Wang Kŏn. On this occasion Kyŏnhwŏn fought off a counter-attack by Koryŏ, after which both of them continued to eat away at the borders of Silla by forcing local fortified towns or bandit leaders to change sides.

After the final collapse of the Tang in 907, Later Paekche, Silla and Koryŏ all maintained contact with the Later Liang and Later Tang dynasties in the south, while the north became a battleground for conflicting nomad forces, out of which the Qidan would forge an empire based on the Liao peninsula. One of the avowed aims of Kungye had been the restoration of Pyongyang, and this was given added urgency by the threat from the north. Wang Kŏn had already established a garrison there in 918 under his cousin Wang Sing-nyŏm and from 922 he began to repopulate it. In 926 Parhae's resistance to the Qidan collapsed and a large body of the aristocracy, led by their crown prince, fled southwards. They were warmly welcomed as kinsmen by Wang Kŏn, who provided their prince with a ducal palace in Kaesŏng. Thus, when the Indian monk Samchang Mahura went on from south China to visit Koryŏ in 929 it was probably by then the only safe port of call north of the Yangtze.

In 930 the greatest battle yet between Koryŏ and Later Paekche was fought at Andong and won by Wang. As a result of this, there was now a continuous border between Koryŏ and what remained of Silla on its northern side and Wang Kŏn was welcomed in Kyŏngju as the 'Father' who would protect them from the 'Tiger'. In 935 the Silla King and his ministers finally decided to entrust him with the care of their kingdom. Only the crown prince opposed the plan – 'How can you decide in one morning to end a dynasty of a thousand years?' He refused to accept the decision and left to spend the rest of his days in the northern mountains clothed in hemp and eating wild herbs, affectionately remembered as 'Maŭi T'aeja', the Sackcloth Prince. It is said that he was loved by Wang Kŏn's eldest daughter, the Nangnang princess, named for the ancient Chinese city that Koguryŏ had inherited, and whom he had been intended to marry. There is a legendary tale that she visited him in the hills but failed to persuade him to return: history records only that Wang Kŏn gave her, instead, to the Prince's father, Kyŏngsun.

To strengthen further the legitimacy of his claim to all the former territories of Silla Wang Kŏn himself took a Queen from its royal family, one of the many marriages through which he tried to ensure the continuing loyalty of the magnates who had submitted to him. He gave Kyŏngsun a palace in Kaesŏng with a title that ranked him above that of the Koryŏ crown prince and invited many of Silla's scholar-officials to serve in his administration. In November, watched tearfully by the populace, the King and his court left for their new home in a procession of palanquins, carts and horsemen that stretched for eight miles.

Even before Kyŏngsun arrived in Kaesŏng, Kyŏnhwŏn of Paekche had also taken refuge there. The favouritism that he had recently been showing towards his fourth son, Kŭmgang, had so alarmed his ministers and his two elder sons, Sin'gŏm and Yanggom, that they had shut up the old man in a monastery, killed Kŭmgang, and proclaimed Sin'gŏm as King. Kyŏnhwŏn had subsequently managed to escape to the west coast where he had been picked up by one of Wang Kŏn's ships and brought to Kaesŏng, where he also was given a royal welcome and provided with another ducal palace.

In the following year, 936, he rode at the head of Koryŏ troops to defeat his sons and win for Wang Kŏn the last battle. It meant that Wang, later to be known as 'T'aejo', the traditional Chinese title for the founder of a dynasty, had now, by an extraordinary combination of statesmanship, military success and good fortune, not only restored the lost kingdom of Koguryŏ, but had in contented residence in his capital the former rulers of Silla, Parhae and Paekche, giving him legitimate claims to the whole peninsula up to the Yalu and the Tumen, and even beyond. The disorder generated by the decline of Silla and the growing strength of the Qidan, and after them, of the Ruzhen would, nevertheless, delay, for several centuries, any permanent advance up to these rivers, and it is only the confidence engendered by their recent industrial success that has, in the last decade of the twentieth century, inspired chauvinistic dreams of reclaiming the larger areas once ruled by Koguryŏ.

PART II
KORYŎ

PART II

KORYŎ

CHAPTER NINE

THE FOUNDING OF A
DYNASTY

WITH the fall of Later Paekche in 936 T'aejo had won control of the peninsula, but the fragile unity once imposed by the royal house of Silla had long since broken down and to secure and stabilize his authority would be no easy task. In the same year one of his closest associates, the leader of his horsemen, General Hwan Sŏn-gil, attempted a rebellion, followed by a further plot by another cavalry general, and apart from these dangers, most of the outlying areas were still ruled by warlords with their own private armies.

By giving his cousin Wang Sing-nyŏm the task of rebuilding Pyongyang, encouraging the refugees from Parhae to settle in the area, and bringing in discharged veterans from Paekche, he created a loyal force in the north and, for the rest, he built up an extraordinary network of kinship ties by accepting as wives daughters from the heads of all the more powerful clans, giving them what was the traditional high status of a royal father-in-law. In this way he would have taken, by the time of his death, 29 wives, of whom six ranked as Queens. At the same time, to avoid unduly ambitious sons-in-law, he married all of his daughters, apart from the Nangnang Princess and one of her younger sisters given to Kyŏngsun, to one of their many half-brothers. It must have done much to restore the sense of national identity that had grown up in the 200 years of unity under Silla, though it did bring in a few powerful men with ambitions to put their grandsons on the throne.

By 936 the Qidan, fully established in the area that still bears their dynastic title of 'Liao', and ready to move into China, hoped to win the support of T'aejo, but for him they were the barbarians who had expelled his kinsmen from Parhae, and when, in 942, they sent envoys, bringing with them a small herd of camels as an exotic gift, he had the diplomats detained on an offshore island while the 50 camels were left to starve under the Manbu bridge. He increased the size of the garrison at Pyongyang and prepared to defend the line of the Ch'ŏngch'ŏn River, but the Qidan, more interested in the wealth of China, were for the moment content to ignore him.

T'aejo had no surviving children from his first wife Sinhye, and his second Queen, Changhwa, was the mother of his eldest son and designated successor, Hyejong. As she had come from the relatively insignificant O family of Naju, he appointed as Hyejong's guardian Pak Sur-hŭi, one of the chief warlords of the south-east, with a large army under his control, and after T'aejo's death in 943 Pak succeeded in establishing him on the throne, but rival contenders made the situation far from secure.

Wang Kyu, the head of a powerful clan based on Kwangju, the chief city of the south-west, had been one of the last to make peace with T'aejo so that when they had exchanged daughters, two from Wang Kyu became only the fifteenth and sixteenth of his wives, but after one of them had produced a son, the Prince of Kwangju, Wang Kyu further strengthened his foothold in the court by providing a second wife for Hyejong, and the military strength of his father made the Prince a much-feared contender for the throne. Wang Kyu tried to stir up trouble between Hyejong and his two younger half-brothers who were next in line, as well as plotting his assassination.

Hyejong had good reason to suspect the elder of his half-brothers, Chŏngjong, as his mother was the daughter of Pak Yong-kyu, one of T'aejo's best-loved and most able generals who had strong support both within the court and outside, including that of Wang Sing-nyŏm, the powerful cousin who controlled the north from his base in Pyongyang. In these unhappy circumstances, after two years and two attempted assassinations, Hyejong took ill and died. Wang Sing-nyŏm then intervened to eliminate Wang Kyu and ensure the succession of Chŏngjong, but he also could not feel secure in Kaesŏng and attempted, unsuccessfully, to have the court removed to Pyongyang. Instead, four years later, in 949, he and Wang Sing-nyŏm both disappeared in unrecorded circumstances.

T'aejo's third son, Kwangjong, who now came to power, appears to have been a stronger character, with two influential wives, one the daughter of his own father by a different mother, from the powerful Hwangju family of Hwangbo, and the other the daughter of his elder half-brother Hyejong by his first wife, of the Im clan of Chinju. This, by later standards, rather incestuous concentration of power from both within the court and without enabled him to purge his opponents and begin a whole series of political reforms that would enormously strengthen the power of the throne. Royal relatives or former friends of his father who opposed him were steadily exiled or imprisoned until the prisons overflowed and new ones had to be built. He then began a series of reforms that would bring nearer the ideal of a meritocratic bureaucracy.

During the wars that accompanied the decline of Silla a great many refugees, prisoners of war and ruined peasants had been forced into slavery. One of his first moves was a Slave Review Act by which all those who had not been born as slaves were to be freed. It aroused some controversy but it had the support of the Buddhist clergy as although those born into slavery were thought to be expiating the karma of their former lives, those forced into it by others were clearly the victims of injustice. It had the effect of reducing the power of the large estates and their private armies while at the same time increasing the number of those who could be taxed.

There was a detailed survey of the country's rice-land, followed by restrictions on the size of private holdings, and large areas of it were set apart to provide income for the holders of official posts. The tenants were to pay a quarter of their crop for this purpose, compared with the half-share traditionally demanded by landlords, so that this in itself created a vested interest in the new system. Similar arrangements were made for the payment of soldiers for a strong central army, and of local government officials, and rice-land was also set aside to provide for the expenses of the palace and of the government offices.

Medical centres known as Taebiwŏn, or Houses of Mercy, pre-sumably based on Chinese patterns, were set up in Kaesŏng and Pyongyang, and later, as the Hyemin'guk, or Public Health Depart-ment, would open branches in the provinces. T'aejo had provided regional granaries, ŭich'ang, first developed in China by the Sui, to provide relief in times of drought, and Kwangjong added chewibo, stores which charged interest on loans of grain, using the profits for poor relief. These would later be supplemented by sangp'yongch'ang, 'ever-normal granaries', a Han dynasty invention by which grain was stored at harvest time and later sold at controlled prices to counteract free-market profiteering.

These complex schemes for the production, transport, storage and distribution of vast quantities of rice must have involved leakages, but nevertheless they worked, and in modified forms would keep on working for the next 900 years. The areas under cultivation would grow and the methods improve, with reservoirs providing more and more wet fields, thus keeping pace with the growth of population. Whatever the degree of local corruption, theft or mismanagement, all of it had to be eaten by someone – there are certain advantages in keeping the national currency in a perishable form.

In 957 the short-lived Chinese dynasty of Later Zhou sent a

distinguished scholar, Shuang Ji, as envoy to Koryŏ, and after its fall he elected to stay on as an adviser to Kwangjong. Under his guidance the *kwagŏ*, the standard civil service entrance examination in the Chinese Classics, was set up, open in theory to all the free-born, though only sons of the gentry were likely to gain the necessary education, while royal relatives of the five highest ranks would still be exempt. With North China in the hands of the Qidan and the Song in retreat, Kwangjong further strengthened his authority by declaring his country to be an independent 'empire' of its own, and promoting his provincial cities to 'capitals'.

After his death in 975 he was succeeded briefly by his son Kyŏngjong, with some restoration of those he had 'purged', and then by his nephew Sŏngjong, under whom the influence of those whose origins lay in Silla seems to have further increased. Already in T'aejo's time colleges had been established at Kaesŏng and also at Pyongyang, now known as the 'Western Capital', but the new system set up under Shuang Ji had increased the demand and in 992 they were replaced by a National University, very similar in principle to that of Silla, with degrees in the classics for the upper classes, divided into two or three separate colleges according to their rank, and technical colleges in which those of lower rank could study law, calligraphy or accountancy.

The most influential thinker of this period was Ch'oe Sŭng-no, the son of one of the Head Rank Six officials who had gone to Kaesŏng with Kyŏngsun. He was not against centralization, but strongly opposed to the kind of unfettered autocracy imposed by Kwangjong and he feared that an examination system that promoted on merit the sons of provincial gentlemen with no power base at the court would increase the danger of this. He therefore persuaded Sŏngjong to aim rather for a well-educated élite from which to choose his ministers. The privileges of the nobility were to be protected by the provision of special schools through which they could enter the government at their own inherited level, though not without competition from their peers.

Thus, among the five higher ranks, one member of the family was always entitled to receive an official post, and the rice-land that provided the income was hereditary. In the next century, under Mungjong, this principle would be extended to officials of all ranks, giving the whole society a high degree of stability but very little upward mobility. Also, in his time, to avoid serious miscarriages of justice, the law was amended so that in cases of murder the accused could not be convicted on his own confession, but only after three independent investigations had reported to the King.

Provincial administrators and officials were appointed under rules that prevented them from going to their own home areas and gave them fixed terms of office. At the same time an inspector-general whose home was in that area was appointed to safeguard local interests and as in earlier times leading families were required to send a son to reside in the capital. Even so, officials from the centre would rarely succeed in subduing the more powerful of the local landowners. To guard the capital and the northern frontier a large conscript army was maintained, its officers being provided by hereditary military families, to each of which land was allocated.

Despite the the freeing of those enslaved during the wars, there was still a large class of hereditary slaves who were kept not only on upper-class estates but also in special areas of the capital where they worked in factories that supplied the court and the government offices. The daughters of government slaves, if attractive, were sent to special schools to be educated as professional entertainers, *kisaeng*. As civil servants, they would be graded according to their talents and appointed to the palace, where a large dancing troupe was kept, to the ministries, as official entertainers, or to local government offices, but they still ranked as slaves, and whether willing or not were commonly made the mistresses of the officials in charge. Poor people with good-looking daughters could also sell them for this purpose.

CHAPTER TEN

WAR WITH THE QIDAN

DESPITE the strength of Confucianism, Koryŏ had been founded as a Buddhist state and T'aejo, in the first of ten precepts that he left for the guidance of his successors, had insisted that their security would always depend on the protective power of Buddha. They were to support both the Zen and the traditional scripture-based communities and appoint the abbots who led them. Under these provisions monastic institutions continued to grow in size and wealth and the great temples, of which Kaesŏng had 75, and the major festivals, held at government expense, involved the whole nation. When, under Confucian influence, official examinations were set up for monks, there were separate forms according to whether they were of the textual or the Zen persuasion, a paradox that might have amused some of the original Masters of Zen for whom it had cost, if not an arm and a leg, at least a finger.

This close association of church and state had been welcomed by Kwangjong as an aid in his struggle to subdue the local magnates, and he had enlisted Kyunyŏ, the Abbot of Haeinsa, to promote popular teaching on Buddhism as the protector of the state. It was conceived in terms of invisible forces that provided visible results – it was generally believed that holy monks could halt an army with a blizzard in a mountain pass or freeze the sea round an invading fleet, and reinforced by popular hymns, *hyangga*, in Silla style, of which Kyunyŏ's works are the last extant examples. He also attempted to make peace between the Zen and textual schools but in this he did not have much success beyond the confines of his own monastery.

After the collapse of the Tang northern China was ruled by a succession of military dictatorships culminating in the Later Zhou, who had provided Kwangjong with his educational adviser, Shuang Ji. Their rule came to an end in 960 when the Emperor died with only a child to succeed him and the commander of their army, Zhao

Kuangyin, on his way to repel the Qidan was, like a Roman Emperor, empowered by his obedient soldiers and returned to found a new dynasty, the Song. He went on to organize a peaceful reunion with the southern states that involved, temporarily at least, abandoning to the Qidan not only the mountains of Manchuria, but the northern plains as far as the Yellow River.

Koryŏ continued to improve its northern defences. Already in T'aejo's time they had restored the walls of Pyongyang and pushed their border up to the Ch'ŏngch'ŏn River, and under Kwangjong they had moved further towards the Yalu. This area was occupied by the Ruzhen and some of the Parhae families who had remained there managed for a while to establish on the middle reaches of the river the small buffer state of Ting'an, hoping for support from the Chinese.

Koryŏ had sent their first envoys to the Song in 962, but they were anxious not to provoke the Qidan kingdom of Liao and were slow to respond when in 985 the Song, having launched an attack on Liao, called for their assistance. When finally a Korean force crossed the Yalu they were too late to save the Chinese and now had to expect a Qidan reprisal. This came in 993 with a force said to have numbered 800,000, and the Song, in turn, now declined to help. The Koreans were well prepared, with defences in depth all the way back to the Ch'ŏngch'ŏn River but when the Liao General, Xiao Sunning, reached its northern bank Sŏngjong sent Sŏ Hŭi, a soldier-diplomat in the tradition of Ulch'i Mundŏk, to negotiate. Koryŏ agreed to become a tributory of Liao rather than the Song, temporarily replacing the Chinese calendar by theirs, in return for which they were given control of the land up to the banks of the Yalu.

Much of it had been settled by the semi-nomadic Ruzhen people known to the Koreans as the 'Malgal', who had once provided mercenaries for Silla. More recently, many had been enlisted by Wang Kŏn during his last battles with Later Paekche and came to identify themselves with Koryŏ, but they were now being drawn into a tribal federation by their more politically conscious kinsmen on the other side of the border.

Sŏngjong died, childless, in 997 and was succeeded by Mokchong, a son born to the third wife of his cousin and predecessor Kyŏngjong and now a weakly youth of 17. His stepmother, while acting as regent, had an affair with one of her ministers, Kim Ch'i-yang, who was also her brother-in-law, and bore him a son. As he grew up they apparently intended to establish this boy as the crown prince, so Mokchong, childless and now 29, was persuaded to nominate instead Hyŏnjong, whom his father's third wife had in her widowhood born to his uncle Anjong, son of the wife given to T'aejo by Kyŏngsun, the last King of Silla. This led to an attempted coup by Kim Ch'i-yang in 1009, in the face of which Mokchong appealed to the commander on the north-west frontier, Kang Cho. He returned to the capital where he assumed a dictatorial role, even-handedly executed both Kim Ch'i-yang and Mokchong, and put Hyŏnjong on the throne, belatedly bringing the true-bone genes of Silla into the royal line.

Liao, having extracted tribute from the Song, were now ready to squeeze the Koreans, and in 1010, under the pretext of avenging the death of Mokchong, they combined with the Ruzhen to launch a powerful attack under the personal command of their Emperor, Shengzong. They quickly crossed the Yalu and Kang Cho himself was captured when at the second attempt they breached his central fortress at Sŏngch'ŏn and he was executed when, even under torture, he refused to change his allegiance. This opened the way to a siege of Pyongyang, which led to panic in Kaesŏng, and talk of surrender, but Kang Kam-ch'an, an elderly minister in whom the King had great trust, advised him to take refuge in Wang Kŏn's old south-western fortress at Naju and let the Qidan stretch their supply lines while he planned a counter-attack. Although Kaesŏng was occupied and looted, it had the desired effect and after a few months the invaders began to withdraw. The Koreans under General Yang Kyu inflicted heavy casualties and the Qidan temporarily retreated across the Yalu but they did not abandon their demands for the payment of tribute and for Hyŏnjong to present himself before their Emperor, which the Koreans refused to accept.

Instead, they began an intensive strengthening of their defences, despite a short-lived rebellion by the army. The strain on their resources caused by the war led the court to try and reduce the amount of land granted to officers for their upkeep, and this combined with their resentment at taking orders from civilian officials – one of the basic principles of Confucian administration – resulted in a military coup in 1014 in which two senior officers, Kim Hun and Ch'oe Chil, temporarily seized control. They were appeased by the execution of two officials, but there was little real improvement in their conditions which would deteriorate even further once the Qidan threat was removed.

The supreme command remained with Kang Kam-ch'an and over the next few years he would continually improve and deepen the defences, including the approaches to the capital. The Qidan, as well as keeping up the pressure with occasional border skirmishes, were also making larger preparations. They built a fortified bridge across the Yalu, and in the winter of 1018 General Xiao Paiya led an army of 100,000 across it to march on the frontier fortress at Ŭiju. At the next river crossing Kang had dammed the water with a cowhide barrier and laid an ambush before releasing it. The invaders would continue to be harassed and outwitted until, cut off from behind, they had no alternative but to attempt a forced march on the capital which they failed to reach and only a few thousand survived to recross the border. When Kang Kam-ch'an, a small man, now 71 years old, returned in triumph to Kaesŏng, the King went out to meet him with ribbons and flowers of gold for his hair and the country's gratitude was marked by the erection of a pagoda-like stone tower that can still be seen below Kwanak mountain, on the south side of Seoul, where at his birth, it is said, a great star had fallen from heaven.

After this the Korean court made renewed attempts to strengthen their relationship with the Song but the Chinese had no intention of inviting further aggression from Liao, so in 1020 the Koreans, by default, sent tribute to Liao and two years later again adopted its calendar. This was no real guarantee of peace and Kang Kam-ch'an had already initiated the building of an outer wall for Kaesŏng, which was completed by 1029, and he then went on to attempt a permanent solution to threats from the north by building a great wall right across the peninsula. It took 12 years to complete and ran roughly along the line of the fortieth parallel from the mouth of the Yalu to the port of Yŏnp'o on the east coast.

There was now trade and regular diplomatic exchanges with the Qidan. Their central Asian background and their early adaptation of the Uighur alphabet saved them from becoming entirely Sinified but they settled down to peaceful coexistence with both the Song and Koryŏ. The royal family favoured Nestorian Christianity but Buddhism flourished, producing some magnificent art. Many Qidan craftsmen were employed in Kaesong and their influence can be seen in Koryŏ's richly decorated Buddhist paintings.

It was the increasing strength of the Ruzhen that was now threatening Koryŏ's long and hardly defensible northern wall. In 1104, under Sukchong, its height was increased by three feet and three special brigades were created to defend the coastal plain on the eastern side, one of upper-class cavalry, one of peasant infantry, and one of martial monks. Three years later General Yun Kwan led an assault into Ruzhen territory at this point and established a group of nine forts to control the mountain passes north of the wall but lack of support from the court and persistent attacks forced him to abandon them. In 1115 the united Ruzhen, under Akuta, founded the state of Jin and by 1125 they would have overthrown the Qidan and be ready to threaten both Koryŏ and the Song.

Chinese culture flourished again under Emperors of ever increasing refinement who, in contrast to those of the Tang, whom Silla had seen as friends and allies, chose to buy off the nomads and present themselves as spiritual leaders who exercised the Mandate of Heaven in a realm that was above the turmoil of tribal wars and politics. The well-educated Koryŏ élite were receptive to such ideas, and by 1070, after a break of about 80 years, there was a resumption of regular diplomatic and cultural exchanges.

This was a period when Confucianism was being transformed by a succession of philosophers who used a rationalized version of China's most ancient religious beliefs to provide it with a metaphysical frame with which to confront the Buddhists. It would come to be known as 'Neo-Confucianism', though the term, invented centuries later by Jesuit missionaries in Beijing, expresses the exact opposite of what its creators thought they were doing. Just as the Protestants in Europe would imagine that they were restoring primitive Christianity, the Song philosophers thought they were rediscovering the 'Dao', the ancient 'Way' of Confucius and his early successors.

This revival would have ethical, social and ritual aspects of great importance that would find their definitive formulation in the works of Zhu Xi at the close of the twelfth century, but its morning star in eleventh-century Koryŏ was Ch'oe Ch'ung, who has been called 'The Confucius of Korea' and is said to have anticipated some of its main ideas by half a century. Intensely conservative, he did not openly oppose the advocates of Buddhism, but insisted that as it concerned only the individual soul and its fate in other worlds, they should not interfere in political matters.

He was a member of an already influential clan based at Haeju and combined his inherited privileges with academic brilliance and a powerful personality. Born in 984, he became a senior minister at an early age under Mokjong, and after being a strong influence through four reigns he retired in 1055 to found a private academy whose graduates, by a combination of inherited rank and academic success, would find it easy to capture ministerial posts. It set a fashion for the founding of private schools by former government ministers in the regions of their birth, the alumni of which would form powerful networks of influence, so that the National University would lose ground despite the attempts of several Kings to restore its reputation.

China had never had to face any threat from the sea other than pirates, which they had solved by internalizing their waterways, or by land, other than nomads, to be kept out by building walls or by bribery, so that the literati tended to be contemptuous of soldiers, and, to the nation's cost, this attitude would be adopted by most of their Korean disciples. The private schools had no interest in military studies, the status of military families steadily declined and many military posts were downgraded or abolished.

The Buddhist establishment, charged with the protection of the state, had made an immense concentration of effort to keep out the Qidan invaders. Through most of the eleventh century some hundreds of highly skilled monastic craftsmen, organized by a special department of the government, had been busy generating spiritual power by carving the wooden plates to print a complete version of the Buddhist scriptures, the Tripitaka, which ran to several thousand slim volumes.

The royal house, like every other family in the land, if they had any sons beyond those needed to ensure continuity, were expected to give one of them to Buddha. King Munjong's fourth son Hu, joined a monastery at the age of 11 and under his monastic title of Ŭich'ŏn he went to China in 1085 and returned as an exponent of Ch'ŏnt'ae (Tiantai), a school which attempted to marry reason and scripture to the mystical insights of Zen. Like Kwangjong's chief abbot, Kyunyŏ, in the previous century, he hoped to reconcile the older textual schools with their Zen rivals. Again it failed, but Ch'ŏnt'ae would become the dominant school and it stimulated the Zen communities to a renewal which looked back to the teaching of the seventh-century Chinese monk who had been their sixth Great Master, the movement known as 'Chogye'. Ŭich'ŏn brought back hundreds of volumes of scripture and commentary, and as the woodblocks for the Tripitaka had now been completed, he went on to edit a supplement that included commentaries from Liao, Japan and Korea. There were altogether about a hundred thousand wooden plates, each one representing a page of intricate ideograms. They were stored well to the south at Taegu's Puinsa but their reputation as the spiritual power that had protected the country from the Qidan was such that when the Mongols came two hundred years later they would seek it out and destroy the whole monastery.

CHAPTER ELEVEN

A VISITOR FROM CHINA

THE ELEVENTH century saw the rise and rise of the Yi family of Inch'ŏn, an early example of what would later be called *sedo chŏngch'i*, 'power politics', through which a strong in-law family might for several generations dominate the court, made easier in early Koryŏ times by a custom that permitted children to be brought up by the bride's family. As one of Hyŏnjong's three chief ministers, Yi Cha-yŏn had supplied three of his daughters as consorts to Munjong, and after the first had produced a crown prince, they established a kind of family monopoly of royal brides, though after three generations, branches of it would be competing with each other. Chayŏn's two sons and a nephew provided daughters for the next two Kings, Munjong's short-lived elder sons, Sunjong and Sŏnjong, but as Sŏnjong's only son, Hŏnjong, a sickly child, died young, he was, in 1095, succeeded by an uncle, Sukchong.

Yi Cha-yŏn's senior grandson, Yi Cha-ŭi lost his life in an attempt to foil Sukchong, so his cousin Yi Cha-gyŏm was now in a dominant position. He gave his eldest daughter to be the wife of Sukchong's son Yejong, and their son, Injong, having spent much of his life at the Yi home, was at the age of 12 provided with two of Cha-gyŏm's younger daughters as wives, and his relatives and supporters occupied many key posts and continually enlarged their estates. We are given a glimpse of their world in the writings of a twelfth-century visitor from Song China, Xu Jing.

As the Qidan controlled the land route, he came by sea, where, in contrast to the days of Silla, the Chinese were now the masters. The Koreans had nothing to compare with the great ships that they were developing, complete with bulkheads, sternpost rudders and compasses, and their fleets are recorded as arriving at the Koryŏ capital at the rate of about 15 a year over the hundred-year period from 1018, and on two occasions Arab ships are also recorded.

Koryŏ's exports were mainly raw materials such as gold, silver, copper, ginseng and pinenuts but their fans and their writing materials – brushes and ink as well as paper – were also in demand. Imports included books, porcelain, medicine, musical instruments and costly fabrics, of which the celadon, in particular, would stimulate local potters to produce work that would come to be even more highly regarded than that of China. Shipwreck and piracy still took their toll and in addition to the much feared *wako* of Japan, Ruzhen raiders appeared along the east coast so that a small fleet of warships had to be stationed at Wŏnsan and a system of hill-top beacons was set up so that the capital could be warned of any large-scale incursion.

Xu Jing accompanied a diplomatic mission to Kaesŏng in 1123, the formalities of which were now performed with an elegant pomposity. The two biggest ships, the 'spiritual ships', specially built for the occasion, one for the envoy and one for the sacred document, the Imperial Edict, were about 300 feet in length, sufficient in Xu's words, 'to awe the monsters of the deep and terrify the barbarians.' On arrival at the river port for the capital, where a special pavilion had been built for such ceremonial occasions, the Edict, resting in a special palanquin, was met by the royal guard and carried in procession to the palace. To greet it, the King vacated his throne and kowtowed, remaining on his knees to hear it read, but of its actual contents, presumably some kind of paternal blessing, nothing is said.

Xu Jing was a scholar-bureaucrat but, like the Emperor himself, an artist by taste, and he came to Koryŏ to produce an elaborate set of watercolours to illustrate the life and customs of the natives. The pictures have not survived, only the notes he wrote to accompany them, but they give us some valuable glimpses of everyday life. He tells us that within its outer walls the city was five miles across, with a population of about one and a half million. They were crowded together in thatched houses 'like a beehive or an anthill', but he was impressed by the great palaces and temples and by the splendour of the palace guards, and he enjoyed the company of its leading scholars whose learning and courtesy he could not fault. Bookshops, he noticed, were more numerous than in his own country, a remark often echoed by modern visitors.

He tells us that young men were liable for conscription from the age of 16 and the capital was guarded by 30,000 of them in six battalions, of which one manned the walls while the others worked in the fields outside ready to collect their weapons and assemble if an emergency arose. Their main weapon was the bow, about four feet in length, with arrows of willow that he regarded as too light to have much stopping power. He was impressed by their celadon, which though based on Chinese models was beginning to develop its own distinctive forms as well as new techniques in white-slip decoration and the use of copper-oxide for underglaze colour.

He appreciated their generous hospitality but found their clothes old fashioned and mentions a number of ways in which they still behaved like barbarians – the informal style of the upper classes, and even of the royal family, their easy divorces, their mixed bathing in streams, their trust in exorcisms rather than medicine, their carelessness in keeping accounts, their compassion for criminals, most of whom were freed every year in August and very few of whom were ever executed, and their almost entirely vegetarian diet. He gives them credit for not tattooing themselves and not allowing sons to sleep in the same room as their fathers and he is pleased to see that they had made some progress towards teaching the peasants to kneel when they are addressed by those in authority.

A monetary system had been introduced at the suggestion of the monk Ŭich'on after his return from China in 1085 but it had not caught on and Xu Jing found few shops. There was a large market for barter, values being calculated in terms of rice or rolls of cloth, which were also the basis of taxation. The redundant coins were kept in a warehouse and occasionally put on display, while for big deals the upper classes used bottle-shaped ingots of silver. The Chinese had already developed paper money and under the threat of the Ruzhen their annual inflation would soon be running at 100 per cent.

Xu Jing also tells us that their Buddhist culture forbade the direct slaughter of animals, and fishing was disapproved of, though still widely practised. The court was allowed to provide the flesh of pigs or goats for official banquets but they could be killed only by being thrown on to a fire so that, as he remarks, 'even after cooking or in soup a nasty smell remains'. Lotus roots could not be eaten because this was the flower on which the Buddha was enthroned. Another aspect of Buddhism was the provision of soup kitchens where the monks offered free gruel to passers-by.

He mentions that they had had teachers and technicians from China to instruct them in court music and in fact some years before his arrival the Emperor had made them two very generous gifts of musical instruments, of which the second represented the latest Song attempts to regain the perfection of ancient music, known as Yayue (*a'ak* in Korean), 'elegant music'. As yet, he says, they still follow the Tang tradition, but later, for ceremonial occasions at least, they would attempt to maintain the ideals of 'Yayue' and it is now thought that they may well have preserved twelfth-century elements of which the Chinese themselves have lost all trace.

Xu Jing's visit came just one year after the death of King Yejong, and Injong, 14, was under the thumb of Yi Cha-gyŏm, the father of his mother and his two wives. Backed by his son-in-law, General Ch'ŏk Chun-gyŏng, who was the hero of campaigns against the Ruzhen, he had just foiled a bid for power by the supporters of one of Injong's half-brothers. Xu Jing was not favourably impressed by Yi Cha-gyŏm and describes him as living in excessive luxury and continually receiving gifts, so that his storehouses stank of decomposing food, and he adds that he was despised by the people.

The Song had at first welcomed the Ruzhen as allies against Liao, but when, by 1124, Liao had been defeated, the Ruzhen resented Chinese attempts to reoccupy this territory. As Koryŏ failed to support them, the Chinese had to beat a retreat and the Ruzhen chased them back as far as their capital at Kaifeng, where they were then bribed to go home. When the Chinese subsequently broke this agreement and returned to the attack, the Ruzhen flooded back and looted Kaifeng, destroying, among other things, Xu Qing's pictures, which, his son tells us had delighted the Emperor and secured him promotion.

The Song were forced temporarily to retreat even beyond the southern banks of the Yangtze, and the Ruzhen, established in Beijing under the dynastic title of Jin, now called on Koryŏ also to pay tribute, and Yi Cha-gyŏm, with the reluctant support of General Ch'ŏk, agreed. This had been strongly opposed by Chŏng Chi-sang, a minister from a leading Pyongyang family who had the ear of the young King, but the third element in the court, the old Sillan families based on Kyŏngju, led by Kim Pu-sik, backed Yi Cha-gyŏm.

Injong, now 17, was no longer content to be a puppet and he supported a palace coup which succeeded in eliminating some of Yi Cha-gyŏm's chief supporters, but Ch'ŏk Chun-gyŏng had the palace surrounded and then set it on fire, forcing its occupants to flee. All the conspirators were executed or exiled and Injong was kept in confinement by Yi Cha-gyŏm, who appointed himself as commander of the army and was thought to be on the point of proclaiming himself King. He had already made approaches to the Song court and seers had proclaimed that the 'Eighteen Child', a kind of numerical anagram of the ideogram for 'Yi', would rule. At this point the young king was almost forced to abdicate, but the captain of his bodyguard remained loyal, a split developed among Yi's supporters, and he hesitated. General Ch'ŏk, who apparently felt guilty about burning down the palace, changed sides and Yi himself was arrested and exiled to a town on the coast of Chŏlla. Injong, thankfully no doubt, said goodbye to the two aunts he had been forced to marry.

The main division was now between those from the north, led by Chŏng Chi-sang, and those with roots in Silla, led by Kim Pu-sik, both loyal, talented and ambitious men, but of very different temperament. Injong's recent experiences and his friendship with Chŏng Chi-sang, a romantic poet deeply versed in Daoist lore, made him feel more at home in Pyongyang, where he came under the influence of Myoch'ŏng, a prophetic monk who believed that if it was restored as the capital, its geomantic advantages would guarantee the recovery of their lost territories in Manchuria. With this in view, Injong ordered a palace to be built there, but on his return to Kaesŏng, Kim Pu-sik, whom Xu Jing had greatly admired, warned him of the difficulties of moving the capital and the dangers of a reckless attack on the Jin. Then in 1134, as if to confirm the warning, his newly completed Great Flower Palace in Pyongyang was severely damaged by lightning, and he gave up the project. Myoch'ŏng, bitterly disappointed but still confident in the city's destiny, went on to lead a regional revolt, claiming a heavenly mandate to establish a new kingdom. Chŏng Chi-sang, in Kaesŏng, is not thought to have had any complicity in this, but Kim Pu-Sik had him arrested and executed as a traitor and then led the government forces that eventually repressed the rebellion. He would later retire to the Kamno monastery to compile the *History of the Three Kingdoms*, from which most of the information provided in Part One of this book is derived, and to write a poem on the serenity of the autumn hills that ends on a note of penitence:

> Half my life I've spent, to my shame,
> In this small world, coveting fame.

CHAPTER TWELVE

THE REVOLT OF THE SOLDIERS

A HUNDRED years had now passed since the defeat of the Qidan and although for much of that time the forces on the northern frontier had been on the alert, the grievances of the soldiers that had inspired a rebellion in 1014, temporarily alleviated under Munjong, had continued to deepen. For even the simplest military operations civilian control was imposed; their stipend land was still being reduced to provide for the ever-expanding civil service families, and apart from their poverty, under Injong, the military section of the National Academy had been closed, so that they were virtually excluded from the higher education system, and consequently from all the higher posts.

Injong's successor Ŭijong seems to have enjoyed humiliating them and history regards him as the playboy who pushed them too far. He required them to turn out as escorts for his frequent excursions and to stand on guard through cold winter nights, so that on one occasion nine were frozen to death. When they were not being employed in this way, they were used as labour battalions, so that many deserted. For the chief of the three officers who finally initiated the revolt, Chŏng Chung-bu, the last straw had been the burning of his beard, for the amusement of the court, by Kim Pu-sik's son Ton-jung, while another young official struck an elderly officer in the face.

One morning in the summer of 1170, while the long royal procession was returning from an outing, Chŏng Chung-bu gave the order, 'Off with all the heads that wear civilian hats!' and following a premeditated plan heads began to roll. There were coordinated uprisings in the provincial garrisons and a great many officials were ruthlessly slaughtered. There was already in existence a deliberative council of generals called the Chungbang and a lesser one for regimental commanders, and under the direction of the three leaders of

93

the revolution, Chŏng Chung-bu, Yi Ŭi-bang and Yi Ko, these were now developed into instruments of government.

Ŭijong was exiled to an island off the south coast and replaced by his younger brother Myŏngjong, after which, in a manner not unlike the switch from a Democratic to a Republican administration after an American election, all the officials from civilian families were to be replaced by men from military households, with corresponding changes in the allocation of stipend land. Many civil officials who had avoided offending the military were allowed to continue but inevitably the administration was thrown into some confusion.

The three leaders who now controlled the *Chungbang* were vying for power from an early stage, and after Yi Ŭi-bang had eliminated Yi Ko he sought to increase his influence by marrying his daughter to the crown prince, but he was eventually himself eliminated by the followers of Chŏng Chung-bu, who now remained as a virtual dictator. In 1173, Kim Po-dang, the general in command of the north-eastern frontier, led an attempt, based on Kyŏngju, to restore civilian rule on behalf of the exiled King. Ŭijong was rescued from Kŏje Island and set up there, but they were easily defeated and both Kim and the King were executed, followed by a further purge of civil officials thought to have been implicated in the plot.

A year later another counter-revolutionary move was begun from Pyongyang by Cho Wi-ch'ong which gained the support of other commanders in the area and it continued for two years and reached the outskirts of the capital before it was suppressed. Slave rebellions, peasant uprisings and soldiers' mutinies, provoked by local grievances, would continue in other parts of the country. The military leaders made a serious attempt to correct some of the injustices, by giving community rights to manufacturing villages where government slaves were employed as forced labour and removing corrupt officials, but in other places the uprisings were ruthlessly suppressed, so that the rebels would eventually become better organized, with conscious political aims.

The older monasteries, with their large holdings of land and their private armies of military monks were a stabilizing influence, but as royal princes and the sons of powerful families were among their numbers, they were well represented at court and often became centres of counter-revolutionary activity. They were also a place of refuge for condemned civil officials, who made over their land to them to avoid confiscation, and on several occasions small monastic armies would make unsuccessful attempts to overthrow the regime.

This is probably one of the reasons why the military leaders, no less fervent in their beliefs, tended to support the 'Chogye' school, the Zen renewal that had begun in the previous century at the time of Ŭich'ŏn and was now flourishing under the monk Chinul. It condemned the 'worldliness' of the established monasteries and favoured private prayer, or small groups that did not need temples, though as a result of its success it would soon have its own larger communities and become the dominant school of Zen.

Chŏng Chung-bu's success against rebel armies owed something to the prowess of a former slave from Kyŏngju, Yi Ŭi-min. Physically powerful, he had been responsible for the assassination of Ŭijong after the overthrow of Kim Po-dang, and after rapid promotion to the rank of general, he became one of Chŏng's chief henchmen. Chŏng's increasingly dictatorial rule came to an end in 1179 when along with his son-in-law, Song Yu-in, he was assassinated in a coup led by General Kyŏng Tae-sŭng, a talented young man who had become the commander of the royal guards in his twenties. Yi Ŭi-min escaped to Kyŏngju, while Kyŏng Tae-sŭng, now feared by the rest of the generals, kept himself surrounded by his 'Tobang', 100 picked men, but within four years he was dead, at the age of 30, through illness said to have been brought on by the tense isolation in which he attempted to rule.

After his death Myŏngjong called on Yi Ŭi-min to head a reconstituted Chungbang which he would control for the next 16 years during which, despite some return to normality, the country was in effect divided amongst regional magnates whose power depended largely on the size of their private armies. They fought each other at the points where their efforts to acquire more land collided and had to cope with large-scale insurrections from below. In 1193 a peasant rebellion in the Kyŏngju area lead by Kim Sa-mi and one to the north of it led by Hyosim joined forces to control the whole area for about 18 months.

In 1196, after a generation of disorder, a senior member of the Chungbang, General Ch'oe Ch'ung-hŏn, aided by his younger brother Ch'ung-su, gained control and after eliminating all who opposed him and ensuring his own survival by employing a much enlarged Tobang – an élite bodyguard of 3,000 men – he established a dictatorial rule that would eventually restore order throughout the land. With a loyal force stronger than that of any possible rivals, he replaced King Myŏngjong by his younger brother Sinjong, disbanded the monastic armies and removed from the court the royal monks and other relatives who influenced the King, even to the extent of executing his own younger brother when the latter endeavoured to secure his own future by marrying his daughter to the crown prince.

The most serious threat to the new regime would come from an unexpected source within Ch'oe Ch'ung-hŏn's own household. The unsettled conditions and the rise to power of slaves such as Yi Ŭi-min gave hope to others, including Manjŏk, one of Ch'oe's own slaves, but his vision was the wider one of freedom for all of them. The citizens of Kaesŏng used to send their servants out to a large hill to the north of the city to collect firewood, which gave them a chance to gossip and, further, to listen to Manjŏk who said to them:

> Since the recent uprisings many high officials have risen from among the outcasts. Do generals and ministers have to be born to these privileges? When the time is right anyone can do these things. Why should we be the only ones to have to work ourselves to the bone under their whips?

In 1198 a plot to seize control of the capital and burn the slave registers was uncovered and Manjŏk and some hundreds of his followers were flung into the river to drown, this being a form of execution acceptable to Buddhist tradition.

In the following year there were further uprisings on the east coast which spread southwards as far as Kyŏngju and the south coast, and in 1202 a movement to re-establish Silla as an independent state would continue to offer some resistance for the next ten years. In dealing with these disorders the government was hampered by the fact that, divided between rival generals, most of the national army had melted away. Many of its rank and file had simply returned to their own villages while others formed maurauding gangs, until its six divisions existed in little but name.

This enabled Ch'oe Ch'ung-hŏn to reinforce his own power by adding to his Tobang until it became the most powerful military force in the country, at the same time enlarging his estates in the Chinju region to provide the rice to feed them. In this way, rather than marry into the royal family he began to build up an alternative power base in the manner of the earlier *makriji* of Koguryŏ. An attempt on his life in 1209 led to the establishment of a special security office, the Kyojŏng Togam, which grew into a centre of administration attached to the palace that he built in Kaesŏng. It would continue to be used by his successors, so that to be its chief was to run the country on behalf of the King, with whom the traditional forms of respect were fully preserved, and its departmental heads would form the cabinet.

In 1211, while Ch'oe Ch'ung-hŏn was waiting for an audience with King Hŭijong, who had succeeded his father Sinjong in 1204, there was another attempt to assassinate him, the King having locked himself away at the appropriate moment, but Ch'oe overcame his assailant and replaced Hŭijong with his cousin Kangjong. He died two years later to be followed by his son Kojong, Ch'oe's fourth royal puppet since the deposing of Myŏngjong. Ch'oe was now concerned to bring about a reconciliation with the ousted civilian officials, or their families, so that their loyalty could be assured and their talents put to use, but there was strong opposition from some of the members of his council and it would be left to his successor finally to bring this about.

All these internal struggles had taken place during the 90 years of peace that followed the Ruzhen domination of north China, so that the weakening of the national army and a consequent neglect of the country's defences passed almost unnoticed until in 1215 the leaders of Koryŏ were forced to take notice of a new threat, the next, and most fearsome, of the successive nomad federations, the Mongols.

CHAPTER THIRTEEN

THE COMING OF THE MONGOLS

EARLY in the eleventh century when the incursion of Ruzhen tribes was being resisted, a band of them had been captured and brought to the capital. Ch'oe Ch'ung had advised the King that though they had faces like men, they were beasts at heart and would never be corrected by punishment nor improved by captivity – 'They will only fret and pine for their native lairs, so let us return them to the woods and let them go.' By the end of the twelfth century, however, settled in Kaifeng under their dynastic title of 'Jin', the Ruzhen aristocracy had themselves become silk-clad aesthetes, thereby estranging themselves from those who still remained in the tribal homelands as well as being resented by the Qidan minority and the Chinese peasants over whom they ruled. Even so, they seemed safe enough, for beyond their own city walls they had Beijing and the Great Wall and beyond this again they had an outer ring defended by tributary tribesmen whom they subsidized. It is not surprising if they underestimated the threat posed by Genghis Khan and his new-grown federation for they had an army ten times the size of his and had often beaten off Mongol attacks in the past.

The skills and organization involved in the seasonal migration of herds and the rounding up of game had, long before, been translated into cavalry tactics by Koguryŏ, followed by the Qidan and the Ruzhen, but the forces of Genghis Khan were motivated by a unique combination of discipline and comradeship that enabled him to move and coordinate encircling armies with a speed and precision hardly rivalled even by the motorized divisions of modern times. His military skills were matched by an equal expertise in exploiting the resentments of ethnic minorities and the ambitions of their leaders and it was by these means as much as by winning battles that he advanced towards Beijing.

Encouraged by the Mongols, the Qidan in Liao rose against

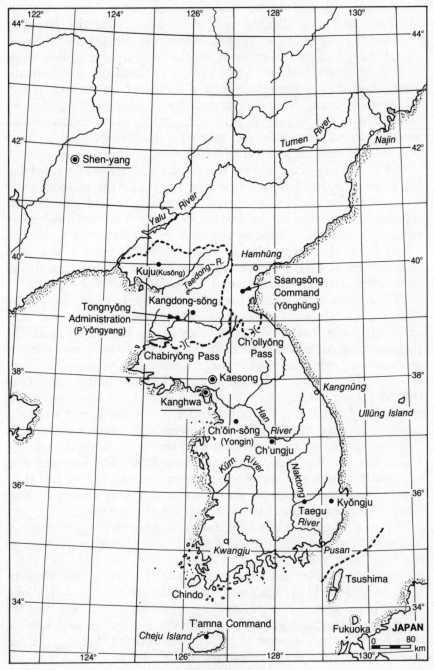

The Mongols

the Ruzhen and asserted their independence, but when, by 1215, the Mongols had taken Beijing and made peace with the Jin, they expected the Qidan also to submit. When they refused, the Mongols joined the Jin in attacking them. In this way a large Qidan army, with their dependants, was driven south as far as the mouth of the Yalu, where they crossed the river and continued southwards, pillaging as they went. A first incursion was successfully repelled by General Kim Ch'wi-ryŏ in 1216 but further waves followed and, avoiding Pyongyang, they ate their way southwards until by 1217 they were presenting a threat to the Korean capital.

Ch'oi Ch'ung-hŏn, now 69, was reluctant to release anyone from his Tobang, and had been attempting to rebuild the national army by conscripting monks, as a result of which he had almost been toppled in a mutiny led by 800 of them. He was also involved in ensuring a smooth succession of power by handing over to his son Ch'oe U, as there were threats from U's half-brother Chun, who though born of a slave-mother had risen to be a notable general, and from other relatives who favoured U's younger brother Hyang.

The Qidan were turned back from the gates of the capital by Kim Ch'wi-ryŏ and driven towards the north-east until they approached the Ruzhen-occupied hills of the Hamhŭng area. The Koreans were content to leave them there as the bitter winter weather was now beginning, but just at that moment the Qidan found themselves confronted by a Mongol force backed by Ruzhen auxiliaries that in a typical long-range move had outflanked them by riding hundreds of miles over the mountains to cross the Tumen from the north-east so that the Qidan survivors were now driven west towards Pyongyang, and by the end of the year they were bottled up in the walled town of Kangdong on the Taedong River. The Koreans were apparently unaware of the Mongol incursion until, having had their supply lines cut by heavy falls of snow, they sent envoys to Kim Ch'wi-ryŏ's headquarters to ask for men and supplies.

Ch'oe Ch'ung-hŏn was reluctant to have any dealings with them, but urged by Kim Ch'wi-ryŏ, Marshal Cho Ch'ung, on a visit to the front, sent them a thousand sacks of rice, and early in 1219 a Korean army under Kim Ch'wi-ryŏ joined them at the siege of Kangdong. The elderly Ch'wi-ryŏ was a famous warrior with a long forked beard that two maids held up while his sword was buckled on. He seems to have got on well with the Mongol general Kachin, who when he had learned of his age had insisted that he take the seat of honour, so that when Marshal Ch'ung, 47 arrived, General Kim had to say that the Marshal was even older in order to get him the best seat at the feast of welcome, at which, in Mongol style, great lumps of meat with a knife stuck in them were passed from hand to hand.

When the Qidan in the besieged town had been starved out, a hundred of their officers were beheaded, and the Korean army were given their fair share of the remainder, including 700 women and young boys. The Mongol leader made a special selection of the younger women and gave nine each to the two Korean generals, along with nine each of the best horses. Cho Ch'ung arranged for the prisoners handed over to the Koreans to be given land in the area on which to settle.

The Mongol general apologized for not having time to call on the King, but with his commanders swore that 'our two nations shall eternally be brothers'. However, the Mongols, as 'elder brothers', would expect an annual tribute, and their demands would go far beyond anything ever required by the Emperors of China, while the gifts they offered in return would be no more than tokens. Their envoys soon arrived at Kaesŏng and when brought before Kojong they walked straight up to him and grabbed his arm to put their one document into his hands, but the purposeful intelligence that lay behind these bluff manners can be judged from the fact that when Kachin had returned across the Yalu he had left 41 officers in the border town of Ŭiju with instructions to learn the Korean language.

By this time Ch'oe Ch'ung-hŏn had handed over to his son Ch'oe U, though after his death a year later there was a struggle in which his younger son Hyang lost his life. Ch'oe U went on to build up the Tobang, still under his personal command, adding a regiment of cavalry, chiefly for ceremonial occasions, and a Night Patrol. This appears originally to have been a kind of army police force, but it would grow into an elite corps, with divisions of Left and Right, and later a third section known as the Army of Spiritual Justice, made up from prisoners who had escaped from the Mongols, and these units, known as the Three Special Forces, would be relentless opponents of the invaders.

With the country now more stable, Ch'oe U began a reconciliation with the families of former civilian ministers, finding places for the more talented, though he took the precaution of providing them with a military guard for their official residences – perhaps really necessary, as the move had been bitterly opposed by some of the military, who had even attempted a further coup. He also restored much of the property appropriated by his father and established a better relationship with King Kojong.

Most notable of the new recruits was Yi Kyu-bo. About 27 years of age when military rule began, he had been banished for his outspoken comments. He was said to be equally learned in the

Confucian classics, Buddhist and Daoist scriptures, and his own country's history and equally adept as poet, harpist and drinker. He became Royal Secretary and began to exchange diplomatic correspondence with the Mongols, one aspect of it being to conceal from them the fact that final authority lay with the junta rather than the palace, and another, in relation to their demands, to emphasize their poverty.

They were minded to resist, but far from ready for war, so for the next five years, while cautiously rebuilding their defences, they would reluctantly respond to the Mongol demands, which were irregular, but frequent and irritating. What they fancied most were furs and falcons, and they could never get enough of these. They also wanted horses, and fodder for them, so that much arable land had to be converted to this end. In 1221, in addition to a request for 500 virgins, which was refused, they demanded 10,000 otter pelts, 3,000 rolls of fine silk and 2,000 rolls of ramie, 100,000 sheets of paper with 1,000 sticks of ink and 200 brushes, and dozens of minor items. Faced with such demands, and the often unruly envoys who brought them, Ch'oe U wanted to turn them back but his advisers were against it – it was a choice between 'slaking the Mongol's greed or making a bloody sacrifice of our people.'

This uneasy peace came to an end in 1225 when a Mongol delegation on its way home with gifts was ambushed and killed on the far side of the Yalu. It was an area still controlled by the Ruzhen but the Mongols blamed the Koreans, who treated the Ruzhen as allies, and broke off diplomatic relations. The troubles that followed the death of Genghis Khan in 1227 kept them occupied until 1230, when under Ogodei they reopened their campaign against the Jin, at the same time giving the Koreans a chance to rehabilitate themselves by opening a second front on their behalf.

The Koreans ignored this request so the Mongols decided to begin by attacking them. In the August of 1231 a powerful force under General Sartai crossed the Yalu and surrounded Ŭiju, where the commander was Cho Suk-chang, the son of Marshal Cho Ch'ung who had first welcomed them 12 years before. He surrendered, to save the population from the threat of annihilation, reminding the Mongols of their promises to his father, as did the commanders of several other Korean strongholds, the result being that they were at first promoted by their own government in order to increase their bargaining power, and subsequently condemned to death as collaborators. This inevitably resulted in some of them actually becoming collaborators and providing invaluable aid to the invaders. Other fortified towns refused to submit, notably Chŏlsan, where after resisting until their provisions ran out, the governor assembled the women and children in a warehouse and set fire to it and then led the men in cutting their own throats.

Two other fortified towns, Kuju and Chaju, had better provisions and held out, so the Mongols left detachments there to contain them and swept on towards Kaesŏng, destroying everything in their path, and even there they left a force to invest it and moved on. Soon, in the face of this devastation, peasants, slaves, monks and even bands of brigands from the hills were organized to fight. At the city of Ch'ungju, which controlled the passes to the south-east, after the officials had fled, an army of slaves held out heroically until they were finally overrun, but in Kaesŏng, Ch'oe U had refused to commit his private army to its defence and the court had already begun to negotiate a surrender. Even after it had been agreed, the defenders at Kuju and Chaju refused to give in and held out for months with incredible courage. When finally Ch'oe U ordered their commanders to be executed for disobedience, the Mongols spoke up for them, saying they were the bravest men they had ever met.

As a condition of their withdrawal the Mongols demanded reparations on a massive scale and they left garrisons in the main cities of the north along with a total of 72 *darughaci*, civil administrators who ranked as personal representatives of the Khan, some of them as commissioners in the capital. The magistrates of several of the west-coast towns in the path of the Mongol advance had saved their populations by evacuating them to offshore islands and this suggested to Ch'oe U the radical idea of putting himself and the King beyond their reach by moving the whole administration to the large island of Kanghwa, which lay conveniently close, at the mouth of the River Han. The proposal was opposed by most of the Kyojong Togam, both the 'doves' who felt it wrong to abandon the people, and the 'hawks', led by General Kim Sae-jung, commander of the Night Patrol, who wanted to stand and fight, but Ch'oe considered that it would be enough to advise the people to seek refuge in the hills or on other islands, while, taught by family experience, he settled the military argument by executing Kim Sae-jung, but his spirit would live on in the Special Forces which never, to the end, surrendered.

About 17 miles in length and ten miles wide, the island has paddies and pleasantly wooded hills. A large part of its population was forced to move to other nearby islands and were replaced by virtually the whole of the bureaucratic and religious establishment of the capital, complete with their servants and the slaves who provided the labour for its industries.

CHAPTER FOURTEEN

THE COURT ON KANGHWA

MOVING the capital to Kanghwa in the early summer of 1232 must have required the shuttling to and fro of a great many ships, large and small, but it was completed with remarkable speed and efficiency, each of the city's five districts being allotted certain days within which its households were to be shifted. Inevitably, it involved the assassination of the Mongol envoys to prevent them from sending a warning, and as soon as this became known a punitive expedition was organized, again led by Sartai. He soon reached Kaesŏng where, apart from a small military unit left to keep order, little remained, and the dispatches he sent to Kanghwa demanding the King's return drew no response. With no equipment for an amphibious assault, he embarked instead on a skilful campaign of psychological warfare.

Aided by the collaborators he had brought with him from the northern borders, he went to Taegu where they sought out the Puinsa monastery and burned the precious store of 80,000 wooden plates for printing the Buddhist scriptures which were believed to have saved the country from the Qidan. From there he went on to besiege the old Silla capital at Kyŏngju, where the great nine-storey pagoda was another of the sacramental objects that, for Buddhist believers, served to protect their country, but failing to take it quickly, and harassed by guerrillas, he decided to withdraw. As he approached Suwŏn on his way back he attacked a mud-walled fort at Yongin where a martial monk, Kim Yun-hu, launched an arrow that killed him. It seemed that the Buddha had been avenged and the Mongols, deprived of their general, retreated to the northern border.

The Korean Special Forces followed it up with an attack that drove the collaborator Hong Pok-wŏn out of Pyongyang and the country would now have a couple of years of respite while the Mongols completed their subjugation of the Jin and the Qidan, but the Court knew that they were using the shipyards on the north-west coast to build boats, and far from abandoning their refuge on Kanghwa they strengthened its defences. Although in places the island is only a few hundred yards from the shore and insults could be traded across the water, the channel is deep, with fierce tidal currents, and on the advice of the Korean collaborator in charge of building the boats the Mongols eventually abandoned the project, for although they had conquered most of the Asian landmass they had no taste for the water. The adviser subsequently escaped and was rewarded by the King.

As the island was in the path of the ships bringing goods and taxation grain to the capital they were assured of regular supplies. Thousands of labourers had reproduced there, on a smaller scale, all the offices, palaces and temples of the capital, each of them given its original name. Lotus pools and polo fields were laid out, the academy reopened, for all its books had been safely ferried across, and the upper classes were able to continue their accustomed way of life. The various ministries were at work in their offices and in the temples hundreds of monks performed the elaborate rites intended to rally the cosmic powers against the enemy, while Daoists and astrologers also bent their minds to recipes for the removal of barbarians.

The country also possessed a tooth of the Gautama, purchased at great cost in the Chinese capital, and kept in a special shrine, but it was now discovered that it had been lost in the move. All the temple staff concerned were put in prison, with the result that on the third day it was anonymously returned, though lacking its jewelled case. On the question of whether they should all be executed or pardoned, Ch'oe U's Supreme Council decided that as it involved the Buddha they should be pardoned.

The Government would stay on the island for 40 years and in 1241 the great scholar and poet Yi Kyu-bo would die there. Visiting professors from the West now seek his grave, proving that he spoke too modestly when in a poem occasioned by his son's desire to write his biography, he asked,

> Who will care, a thousand years from now,
> That a man called Yi once lived in a corner of this land?

The defeat of the Qidan after the carving of wooden plates for the printing of the scriptures, along with the recent fate of the enemy general who had burned them, encouraged a belief that only by repeating the process would the Mongols be driven away, and in 1237 a new government department was set up for this purpose and another great concourse of skilled monks was assembled. The 80,000 plates would be completed by 1251 and would eventually be stored at the mountain monastery of Haeinsa where Ch'oe Ch'i-wǒn had once listened to the midnight rain while his thoughts travelled far, and where they can still be seen.

Despite the move to Kanghwa and the Mongol retaliation there was no formal repudiation of their earlier peace agreement and the Koreans were careful to preserve appearances by offering excuses for everything that they did or did not do: they had moved the capital offshore only because they feared that reprisals would come before they had had time to explain how local rebellions had made it impossible to fulfil all the tribute demands; they had not returned certain captured collaborators because they were not well enough to travel, and so on.

By 1235 the Mongols had completed their conquest of North China and over the next few years they would regularly send raiding parties which made no contact with the court and were simply intended to terrorize the population. The cavalry section of Ch'oe's Special Forces became hardened fighters who in local engagements could challenge the Mongol horsemen on their own terms, and in combination with guerrilla bands and the courage and resourceful-ness of those in the hill forts and walled towns, they would resist them probably for longer, and with more success than any other nation, though at a heavy cost to the common people who, even if they could find shelter in a hilltop fort, had to watch their houses and crops burning below them. In 1236 they penetrated as far as the plains of Chǒlla in the southwest, which provided most of the rice for Kanghwa, and in 1238 they returned to Kyǒngju and finally succeeded in burning the famous nine-storey pagoda at Hwang'-nyongsa.

In the face of this continuing devastation the government sent a peace mission at the end of 1238 to which, early in the following year, the Mongols responded by demanding that the King should present himself at their court, along with the crown prince, who would remain there as a hostage. This was not acceptable to the Koreans, but rather than break off the negotiations they pleaded that the King was unable to leave as he was in mourning after the death of his mother, and sent in his place Wang Sun, a young cousin who pretended to be the crown prince. He was married to a Mongol princess and given royal rank and it would be 14 years before they discovered the deception, by which time he would have proved his worth as the King of Shenyang, an area of Liaoning where many of the settlers were of Korean origin. It would be kept as a seat for Korean crown princes, or Kings who were out of favour.

There was now another truce that, largely through internal struggles among the Mongol leaders, would last until 1247. A hostel was built to accommodate Mongol envoys on the mainland opposite the island, followed by the construction of a palace nearby so that the King could occasionally venture across to receive them. Some of the demands for tribute were fulfilled, but new walls were added to the island's defences, Mongol complaints being answered by saying that they were only to deter Chinese pirates.

On the island, the palaces of the Ch'oe family, who had still never parleyed with the enemy, set in newly planted parkland with their own polo fields, were said to be wondrous to behold. Polo was their favourite sport, and the King was sometimes invited to watch the big games. It would appear that for many of these people what was happening on the mainland, which they had not seen for 20 years, was of little concern. Even there, agriculture was recovering, but the grain was being stored in forts and walled cities, and the walls repaired, in readiness for further trouble, which was heralded in 1247 by renewed demands for the court to return and the King to present himself at the Mongol capital at Karakorum. This was followed by an attack which had not gone far beyond the northern frontier before news of the death of Guyuk Khan led to its abandonment and it would not be until after the accession of Mongke that these demands would be renewed.

Meanwhile, Ch'oe U, failing in health, had two sons from a secondary wife, Manjŏn and Manjong, who in accordance with his enthusiasm for Chinul's reformed Zen, had been brought up as monks on the Island of Chindo. In 1249 he sent for them, and Manjŏn, under his secular name of Ch'oe Hang, was prepared as his successor and took office after his father's death later in the same year. In 1251 the Mongols again demanded that the King should return to the mainland, so, to placate them, it was announced at the beginning of 1252 that he would do so in six months' time. The Mongols sent a secret order to their envoy to find out if this was their real intention, and the Koreans, having been secretly warned of this, proposed actually to take him across the water, but Ch'oe Hang refused to allow it, so once again a royal relative was chosen as a stand-in. The Mongol envoy denounced the trick and ominously departed for home.

In the following year an army led by Prince Yeki began a multi-pronged attack, along with a demand that the King should immediately step ashore. The Koreans replied that he would as soon as the army had withdrawn; so to make it easier for them, Wang Sun, the royal hostage, who had accompanied Yeki, wrote a personal letter to Ch'oe Hang saying that if they would just send across the crown prince, or even his younger brother, the Mongols would withdraw, but this offer also was refused. The people were again told to take refuge in the fortified towns or the islands, and with stronger forces now engaged on both sides the country became a battlefield.

The walled town of Ch'ungju, now under the command of Kim Yun-hu, whose arrow had killed Sartai 20 years before, again offered heroic resistance. He burned the registers of slaves, shared out the supplies and invited everyone to fight as equals. They held out successfully until after 71 days a new truce was agreed. This came about through the King finally coming out as far as the palace that had been built on the opposite shore, where he handed over one of his sons to the care of Wang Sun and the Mongols withdrew in the belief that this marked a virtual surrender, but it was not so, for Ch'oe Hang, whom the Mongols now knew to be the actual ruler, had no intention of giving in.

The result was a terrible onslaught led by Jalairtai, a veteran who had served with Genghis Khan and upheld his conviction that any nation that refused to surrender must be destroyed. Large swathes of the country were laid waste, the villages left in ashes and the fields covered with dead bodies. Each time a town was shaken, its scribes and artisans were sent back to serve the bureaucracy, the women and children of usable age were divided out and the rest were killed. Contemporary records indicate that while about 207,000 were taken as captives it was impossible to estimate the number who were simply slaughtered. The resistance was also fierce and the defenders sometimes had their victories, especially the Special Forces who now had numerous regional units, but inevitably popular support for the struggle declined, and on Kanghwa the intransigence of the military rulers aroused increasing opposition, particularly from the civilian officials.

In the spring of 1255 the Mongols once more withdrew, but in the autumn, the Korean court having given no sign of surrender, they returned, and now for the first time a naval force appeared off the west coast and after pillaging one or two islands it made a sufficient show of force around Kanghwa to give the residents a scare but did not attempt a direct assault. These forces withdrew again early in 1256, due it is said to the persuasive charm of Kim Su-gang, the Korean envoy at the Mongol court. He told them that they could not expect the mouse to come out of his hole while the cat was still sitting in front of it.

Even the islands and fortified settlements were now short of food, and the contrast between the sufferings of the people and the life of those on Kanghwa who seemed to have no thought for anything other than the supply of their own needs was a source of ever-increasing tension. There were several attempts to overthrow Ch'oe Hang and counterplots by military fanatics. He survived them all, but after his death in 1257 his son Ch'oe Ŭi, who had been born of a *kisaeng* while his father was still a monk, proved to be spiteful and petty minded in his dealings with the generals who had kept his father in power. In particular, he made the mistake of rejecting the counsels of Kim Chun, a former slave whose skill as an archer had attracted the attention of his father and led to his eventually becoming his chief minister.

The famine caused by a combination of successive droughts and the depredations of the enemy was now affecting supplies to the overcrowded island, where the soldiers alone numbered almost 50,000, but Ch'oe Ŭi refused all requests to open the doors of his family's vast granaries. The plight of the hungry population encouraged Kim Chun to plan a coup which successfully captured the Ch'oe palace. With the attackers battering at his inner-gate the captain of Ch'oe Ŭi's bodyguard tried to heave him over the rear wall but he was too fat, and falling back had to return to his rooms where he was caught and summarily executed for the crime of 'watching the people starve to death'. The rice from the family stores was distributed and is said to have provided enough to feed the whole population of the island for the next few months.

Kim Chun was willing to cooperate with the civil officials in restoring some authority to the King and allowing them to parley with the Mongols, though he still kept the machinery of government in his own hands and like most of the other generals on its council was reluctant to abandon the struggle. In 1259 a settlement was agreed by which the real crown prince was to go to Beijing where Mongke Khan had his capital. He was engaged in a struggle with the Song for what remained of China while his younger brother Khubilai was attacking them from the western side. It was also agreed that the outer fortifications of the island were to be dismantled under the eyes of Mongol inspectors, which caused some trepidation, and it is said that the price of boats soared.

Before the crown prince arrived in China Mongke had been killed in battle and Khubilai, nominated as his successor, was hurrying to Karakorum, but he met the prince on the way and greeted him warmly. Early in 1260, while he was still accompanying Khubilai, news came that his father Kojong who had ruled for 46 years, 27 of them on Kanghwa, had died, so he returned to become King Wŏnjong and would eventually send his own son to replace him at the Mongol court.

Reconciliation went ahead despite the refusal of the military council to participate in the negotiations or allow the King to leave the island. The Mongol's toleration of these further delays seems to have been due to Khubilai's more civilized attitudes and to his affection for the Korean envoy Kim Su-gang, who negotiated the return of Korean prisoners and permission for the King to remain on the island for three more years while a new palace was built in the now ruined former capital.

The people returned to their farms and crops were sown but the country soon fell behind with the heavy reparations demanded by the Mongols, which included not only great quantities of gold and silver, falcons, horses and furs, but also a human tribute of technicians, attractive young women and castrated boys. This caused much bitterness, but was not universally opposed as it could bring wealth and influence not only to the agents involved but also to the families of the young people, particularly if their progeny attracted the fancy of the great and powerful. The outstanding example would be the small landholder from Haengju, Ki Cha-o, whose daughter became a consort of Emperor Shundi, and as his favourite, helped her brother Ki Ch'ŏl to become the leader of a pro-Yuan faction that for some years would dominate the Korean court, while her son would become the last Yuan Emperor.

CHAPTER FIFTEEN

THE INVASION OF JAPAN

B Y 1264 Khubilai was established as the Great Khan, though in the West wars of succession would still go on, and he returned to Beijing with the firm intention of completing the conquest of Song China. He sought to resume his friendship with Wŏnjong and invited him there in the summer for a stay of several months. In this way he might soon have won from the Koreans the allegiance traditionally given to the rulers of China but he still shared his grandfather's belief that it was their destiny to rule the whole world, while on the Korean side many of the generals, and in particular the Special Forces, were determined never to submit.

With Korea apparently pacified, Khubilai was already looking beyond it to Japan – it is said to have been a Korean interpreter at his court, a mischievous monk called Cho'i, who first turned his thoughts in this direction. It was traditionally a tributary of China and they still traded with the Southern Song. A Mongol mission to Japan, with demands for tribute, left in 1266 escorted by Korean guides and interpreters, but they turned back from Kŏje Island, ostensibly because of bad weather but probably more from reluctance on the part of the Korean officials, for nothing could be worse, from their point of view, than to be swept up in a struggle between these two powers. A second mission in 1268 reached the court at Kyoto where on Korean advice a tactful reply was drafted, but it had to be sent to the Shogunate for approval and they threw it out and sent the envoys back empty-handed. This was not the kind of insult the Mongols could ignore but they were already using Korean shipyards to provide vessels for their campaign against the Song, who would continue to hold out along the line of the Han and Yangzi rivers for another five years, so that they did not immediately pursue the matter.

Wŏnjong had returned from Beijing with the expectation of

moving his capital back to Kaesŏng, but this was delayed by the determined resistance of the Three Special Forces who were discontented with the moderate rule of Kim Chun. In 1269 he was assassinated by Im Yŏn, another forceful soldier who had risen from the ranks through his successes against the Mongols to become a general under Ch'oe Hang. He had supported Kim Chun in deposing Ch'oe Ŭi and become commander of the Palace Guards, which put him in the key position to replace Kim when he and his confederates could no longer tolerate the court's submissive attitude.

Wŏnjong, who had sent his eldest son to Beijing as a hostage, refused to comply with Im Yŏn's demand for a resumption of hostilities so he was removed from the throne and replaced by his younger brother. When news of this reached Beijing the Mongols returned in force with the crown prince and under strong threats from their envoys Wŏnjong was restored and eventually moved his court to Kaesŏng. The Three Special Forces, now led by Pae Chung-son and Kim T'ong-jŏng, refused to leave the island, and having appointed another royal relative, Wang On, as their King continued as an anti-Mongol government in exile. The prospect of a Mongol assault made them less popular on the island but their cause still had strong support in the south so they gathered an armada of about a thousand boats and with their wives and families sailed off to Chindo, largest of the islands off the south-west corner of Chŏlla.

From here they were able to rule an area embracing about thirty of the larger islands, including bases on the mainland and extending as far as Kŏje Island to the east and Cheju Island to the south, obtaining supplies of grain from the fertile plains of Chŏlla at the same time that they prevented it from being shipped north to the capital. The Mongols, always ready for a chance to 'divide and rule', offered them the province as a self-governing region, but eventually lost patience with their delaying tactics and began to prepare for an amphibious assault on Chindo. By this time they had come to appreciate the importance of the Song's naval power and they were building ships at ports all round the Yellow Sea, vessels large enough to carry horses, artillery and supplies for expeditions against either the Song or the Japanese.

In 1271 as their first essay in this type of warfare they assembled an armada to attack the survivors of the Three Special Forces on Chindo, including a contingent from Liao. The Loyalists, who had easily repelled previous attacks, were not prepared for the scale of this one and much of their fleet was away collecting supplies. Wang On and Pae Chung-son were both killed but a considerable remnant under Kim To'ng-jŏng escaped to Cheju.

Meanwhile, another mission had been sent to Japan, but they still refused to parley and stepped up their defensive precautions on the west coast, mainly on the southern island of Kyushu, the most likely area for an attempted landing. Khubilai's preoccupation with this was affecting the fortunes of another island at the opposite end of the world, for he had allowed himself to be cut off from his nephew Abaka in Persia, as a result of which in 1271 Abaka relinquished his support for Prince Edward's crusade in Palestine and the Prince had to sign a truce with the Muslims and begin a leisurely return to England, inheriting the throne on the way.

The Koreans were now compelled to supply an enormous quantity of provisions and labour in the construction of an invasion fleet with a work force estimated at between twenty and thirty thousand. A Mongol official of ambassadorial rank was sent to request a direct meeting with the Japanese Emperor but again the shogunate refused to make any response.

Meanwhile, the Korean patriots on Cheju Island were busy harassing the southern coasts and burning the ships being built there, and in 1273 the Mongols organized an invasion force of 12,000 men to attack them. As Cheju was both larger and more distant than the Japanese island of Tsushima, which they proposed to capture as a staging post on their invasion, it was also useful practice. They had the latest kind of explosive weapons and made simultaneous landings at several beaches, forcing the Koreans back to the island's walled capital where after a short siege they finally submitted, bringing to an end 100 years of military rule and 50 years of brave but costly resistance. The Mongols had lost many horses in Korean winters and recognizing the value of the island's mild climate and extensive pastures they were quick to put it under their direct rule and establish a stud for horses, mules and sheep. Camels, a herd of which had perished in a dried up riverbed in Kaesŏng on their first appearance in the peninsula in the days of T'aejo, were also bred there, but would not outlast the Mongol occupation.

The great armada was scheduled to sail for Japan in June of 1274, but at this point it was delayed by the death of Wŏnjong, so that after the necessary obsequies and the return from Beijing of his successor Ch'ungyŏl, it was cold and dangerously late in the autumn when they left their bases on the south coast, centred on Masan. There were 300 large ships and 600 small ones, manned by some 7,000 Korean sailors, and carrying about 25,000 Manchurian and North Chinese soldiers, with a spearhead of Mongol cavalry and 8,000 Korean troops.

They took Tsushima – though at some cost as the defenders refused to surrender and only two prisoners were taken – and then the smaller island of Iki. On 19 November the first landing-craft came ashore on two beaches in Fukuoka Bay on the coast of Kyushu. Some of the cavalry were landed, backed up by catapults that could throw bombs, and the Japanese were forced to retreat to prepared positions beyond the beaches. Meanwhile, a typhoon began to blow up which threatened the ships in the harbour and prevented more from coming in, so that the Korean pilots had to advise them to re-embark as darkness came on. A great many ships were lost in the storm and soon after the invasion was called off with a reported loss of 13,500 lives. It was not in the nature of the Mongols to give up, but for a while they would concentrate on finishing off the Southern Song.

Before he left Beijing after the death of his father, Ch'ungyŏl had already been married to one of Khubilai's daughters and had followed his cousin as ruler of Shenyang. The first ideogram of his title, *ch'ung* ('loyal'), meant loyal to the Emperor, and this prefix along with a Mongol princess and a residence as crown Prince in China would be imposed on six successive Korean Kings, subordinating them to a fixed son-in-law relationship that would not be seen again until early in the twentieth century when with similar intent the Japanese would arrange a marriage between the last Korean crown Prince and a member of their own royal family.

Ch'ungyŏl's Mongol Queen rode, hunted and flew falcons beside her husband, and from this time onwards Mongol fashions and customs would increasingly influence the court. In 1275 the titles of government officials were changed to fit the Yuan system, which amounted virtually to downgrading them to the level of a province, and in 1278 they were even required to adopt Mongol dress, some aspects of which would survive until modern times, though they soon rejected the half-shaven hairstyle.

In 1280, with the whole of China now within his grasp, Khubilai again turned his attention to Japan and Ch'ungyŏl was invited to Beijing to agree on plans. The Koreans were to provide the ships for 40,000 Korean, Mongol and North Chinese troops and at the island of Iki off the coast of Kyushu they were to be joined by a larger fleet from the south of China with 100,000 men from the defeated Song armies. Meanwhile, an impressive Mobile Headquarters for the Chastisement of Japan was set up in Korea with Ch'ungyŏl as its nominal head, which meant that it had to be serviced by the Koreans.

The Korean-based fleet was ready by the spring of 1281 but there were repeated delays by the Chinese forces and it was well into the summer before all was ready. Khubilai sent his envoys with a final demand to the Japanese Emperor to appear before him in Beijing, to which the shogunate replied by cutting off their heads. In addition to their coastal defences they had built up a naval force and had even considered a pre-emptive attack on the Korean coast. There was now a five-mile defensive wall around the shores of Fukuoka Bay, but the Mongol intelligence knew about this and they came in on either side of it, the Koreans to the north and the Chinese to the south.

Beachheads were secured and had been held for seven weeks without much further advance when the monsoon season began and for two days in August a typhoon swept the coast breaking up much of the fleet and forcing the survivors to retreat with heavy losses. It is said that about a third of the troops in the Korean ships were lost and perhaps half of the 3,500 Chinese ships. This was the Kamikaze, the divine wind, that has given assurance to Japanese defenders of their country ever since.

The Mongols did not entirely abandon their intentions, and the Mobile Headquarters, though folded up for a while, was briefly re-established, under a different title, in 1283 and again in 1299,. but now, like the 'mobile bureaux' in other countries they dominated, it became merely a means of maintaining pressure on the local government.

After the return of the court from Kanghwa there were continuing attempts to restore a system of salary land for officials, but beyond the areas around the capital it proved difficult to enforce and more and more rice land was being absorbed into great estates, reducing much of the farming population to serfdom or even slavery. Powerful families who had acquired their wealth through royal connections or by serving Mongol interests often had holdings in several different areas and used the much improved system of roads and post stations to collect their dues.

As in China, the 'Mongolization' was superficial and far more significant for both countries was the Neo-Confucian ideology brought in by the scholars of the Southern Song, recently returned to the capital. It was known as *Do Xue*, 'Study of the Way', or *Zhu Xue* after its dominating figure Zhu Xi more formally *Cheng Li Xue* (*Songnihak* in Korean). The two ideograms represent 'nature' and 'reason', of which Zhu's doctrines and rituals represented the final synthesis, that ancient harmony of 'The Way' that the contemporary world had lost. An Hyang, also known as An Yu, an official who had accompanied Ch'ungyŏl to Beijing, was greatly enthused by it and on his return in the following year became a tireless activist. It is one of history's little ironies that after the Mongols had finally defeated the Song, their literati could now use the Mongol Bureau in Korea as an instrument for furthering their own ideology. An Hyang, with their backing, royal support, and the services of younger and better-educated men such as Paek I-jŏng and Yi Chin, was able to reorganize the national university, renaming it, after the Chinese original, the 'Sŏngyun'gam' (later the 'Songyun'gwan'), with a temple in which to give a sacramental presence to its doctrines.

It was virtually a new religion, puritanical and patriarchal, strongly opposed to the shamans, relentlessly critical of Buddhism, and persuasive enough to determine the spiritual formation of the literati who would run the country for the next 600 years. They would be committed to absolute obedience to the King, but as the guardians of the divine principles upon which his rule was based they would powerfully influence his decisions and in the case of weak Kings, or during regencies, challenge the influence of the in-law families and gradually transform the whole fabric of society.

The new ideals found an early incarnation in the crown prince, Ch'ungsŏn, just 20 years of age when he came home from Beijing for a visit in 1295. He so impressed the court that his father encouraged him to preside in his place and he planned immediate reforms to help the peasants. His arrival gave them new hope and it is recorded that on one occasion while out on horseback he was surrounded by a great crowd of them and carefully listened to their grievances.

These attempts at reform were bitterly opposed by the powerful families, particularly those associated with the Mongols, and he was recalled to Beijing where preparations were being made for his marriage to a daughter of the Emperor. His parents came for the wedding and did not get home until the following May, after which his mother took ill and died. Ch'ungsŏn hurried home and, influenced, perhaps, by gossip at the court, became convinced that his mother had died because of a shamanistic curse arranged by one of his father's most trusted retainers so had him and another eunuch executed and about 40 others sent into internal exile.

He again replaced his father and continued to oppose Mongol influences in the court, introducing a number of reforms supported by a group of scholars who had accompanied him. When, added to this, he upset his Mongol wife by taking a Korean consort he was forced to return to Beijing to explain himself to her brother. Ironically, the girl he had chosen was the daughter of Cho In-gyu, a man from Pyongyang whose fluency in Mongolian had won him high esteem as a go-between. Cho now found himself, at the age of 71, condemned to seven years in a Chinese prison to appease the Queen's wrath. He survived, and through their royal and Mongol connections his family retained their influence. Ch'ungsŏn resumed his former title of King of Shenyang and his father returned to power.

Ch'ungyŏl had sent numerous students to study at the Yuan capital and when Ch'ungsŏn succeeded him in 1308 he brought some of them back with him, as well as 4,000 books. He resumed his attempts to improve the lot of the peasants and restore the revenues of the court, but with little success. The gradual breakdown of regional administration brought about by the Military and the Mongols had left most of the country in the hands of powerful landlords, many of whom were royal relatives, so that in order to resist them the would-be reformers needed the backing of the Yuan regime, a complex balancing act that for many years would have only small successes.

Perhaps in despair, Ch'ungsŏn abdicated at the age of 45 in favour of his 20-year-old son Ch'ungsuk, and, not wishing to reign over Shenyang either, gave that to a nephew and returned to Beijing to concentrate on working for a Neo-Confucian future. He established the Man'gwŏndang, Hall of Ten Thousand Books, where the leading scholars, calligraphers and artists of the day came to mix with his students, and the Yuan emperor donated some thousands of books collected by the previous dynasty. Unfortunately his family became involved with the losing side in one of the perpetual quarrels that plagued the closing years of the dynasty and he was exiled to Tibet for four years. He took with him on the seven-month journey Yi Chehyŏn, a son of Yi Chin and student of Paek I-jŏng, two of the *songni* pioneers under An Hyang. Chehyŏn would record the snowbound mountains in a vivid poem and go on to become one of the great statesmen of the next generation, a generation that would begin to see the Yuan rulers not as their foes but rather as their saviours from a brutal military regime.

Despite its Confucian critics Buddhism was still a vital force, and as in the last days of Silla the radical Zen communities attracted the political opposition. The new zeal in this tradition inspired by Chinul would gain further impetus from the arrival of Dhyanabhadra, a monk from a North Indian royal family. Known as Chigong, 'Pointed to the Void', his combination of heroic asceticism and metaphysical eloquence had won him favour at the Chinese court. Ch'ung-suk, who had known him there invited him to Korea in 1328. He was given the title of Royal Teacher and spent some years at the Hŭi'am monastery at Yangju, where some of his relics, brought later from China, are still preserved. His two best-known Korean disciples, Hyegŭn and Muhak, would both be influential men, the former as adviser to Kongmin, the last effective King of the old dynasty, and Muhak as friend and adviser to Yi Sŏng-gye who would found the new. One of Hyegŭn's poems, 'In the Mountains' (in Peter H. Lee's translation), may help to convey the flavour:

> With the true emptiness of non-action
> I nap on a stone pillow among rocks.

Do you ask me what is my power?
A single tattered robe through life!

Ch'ungsuk endeavoured to pursue his father's policies, with little success, though with the aid of Ch'ungson's protégé Yi Chehyôn, now his secretary, he was able to dissuade the Emperor from making the country a Mongol province and imposing a poll tax; but he was for two years replaced by his son Ch'unghye to whom he handed over power shortly before he died, still young, in 1339. Ch'unghye's ineptitude and his sexual excesses were severely criticized by the new literati and after four years he was forcibly carried off to Beijing, dying on the way at the age of 29.

Yi Chehyôn now hoped to be able to guide his 7-year-old son Ch'ungmok, nominally under the regency of his Mongol mother, and at this point another of Ch'ungsŏn's protégés, Wang Hu, made a providential appearance. After he had been compelled to send his own only son to the Mongol court at an early age, Ch'ungsŏn had adopted a boy from the Kwŏn family of Andong, giving him the name of 'Wang Hu', and he had received a dukedom from the Emperor. He was thus an influential figure, acceptable to the Yuan as Prime Minister, and, though not himself a great scholar, fully in favour of the reforms. New officials with degrees in *sŏngnihak* were appointed to key posts, and although they came largely from the ruling families and professed loyalty to the Yuan regime they were thoroughly imbued with the new ideals and would continue to build up the educational standards that were needed for the creation of an effective civil service.

CHAPTER SIXTEEN

REFORMERS AND PIRATES

THE MONGOL policy of employing foreigners in the administration of the countries they had overrun, of which Marco Polo was a notable example, had brought a number of Moslems to Korea, a few of whom would settle there. By 1315, however, under the influence of the Song literati from the south the competitive examinations for such appointments had been restored, based now on Zhu Xi's interpretations of the classics. A few places were kept for candidates from the outer regions, including three for Korea. One of the early successes was Yi Kok, a disciple of Yi Che-hyŏn, who after passing in 1333, went on to attain high rank in the Yuan court and 20 years later his son, Yi Saek, would do even better and eventually return to his native land to reform the Sŏnggyungwan and become perhaps the most influential of the Neo-Confucian reformers.

The ineptitude of the Mongol Emperors who followed Khubilai, and their family quarrels, led to widespread revolts by the over-taxed Chinese peasants. Their armies, inspired by a messianic form of Buddhism, came to be known as the Hongjin, or 'Redcaps' (Korean, Honggŏn), because of the red bands they tied round their heads. It meant a weakening of the Mongol grip on Korea, where from about 1350 onwards the main trouble would be pirates from Japan. Civil wars had left them free from control and Korean rice, whether in store, or on its way to the capital, was an attractive target. Mounted bandits would come ashore from fleets of 200 vessels or more, extending their pillage up both sides of the peninsula and even venturing far enough up the estuary of the Han to cause panic in the court at Kaesŏng. The naval forces of the southern provinces were strengthened and a resourceful senior officer, Ch'oe Yŏng, was put in charge of the defences.

In 1348 Ch'ungmok, now twelve, suddenly died and in the hope of continuing their policy of moderate reform, Wang Hu and Yi Che-hyŏn quickly replaced him by Ch'ungjong, the 12-year-old son of one of Ch'unghye's three Korean consorts, but this was contested by the influential dowager Queen Hong, mother of Ch'unghye, and after three years of palace quarrels he was replaced by her younger son from Beijing, Kongmin, then just 22 and married to a Mongol princess. An artist and scholar in the tradition of his grandfather Ch'ungsŏn, he made Yi Che-hyŏn his Prime Minister and was determined to oppose both the Mongols and the powerful families who were collecting more and more of the country's rice land into great plantations known as *nongjang*, with armies of serfs or slaves to provide the intensive labour.

Those who favoured the Mongols had a majority voice in the Todang, the chief council of state, and were accustomed to imposing their will on the court, but after an attempted coup by one of them – Cho Il-sin – was defeated by quick action from General Ch'oe Yŏng, their influence began to decline.

In China, 'Redcap' rebellions were threatening Nanjing and in 1353 Kongmin was faced with a demand for senior officers and 2,000 trained men to lead a conscript force of 20,000 Koreans that the Mongols were raising in Manchuria. He had no choice but to comply and Ch'oe Yŏng was taken from his war against the pirates to lead them, but it was too little too late: by May of the following year the surviving soldiers were home again and Ch'oe reported that the Yuan were losing control.

Encouraged by Yi Che-hyŏn, Kongmin decided to strengthen his authority by getting rid of the powerful Chŏngbang which had originally been set up by the Ch'oe shogunate to bypass the throne in making official appointments, and had since been dominated by Mongol collaborators. When the Yuan Emissary plotted to oust Yi Che-hyŏn and re-establish it, Kongmin, supported by his army leaders, had him arrested, tried, and executed for treason. He then closed the Mongol Bureau, dismissed the pro-Mongol group from the Todang, and approved the assassination of its leader, Ki Ch'ŏl, brother of the Haengju farmer's daughter who was now the dowager Yuan Empress.

They now set about regaining the northern areas that had been kept under direct Mongol rule, beginning in the north-east, where the critical factor was a change of allegiance by Yi Cha-ch'un, a man from a family that had originated in Chŏlla, but had now served in the local Mongol administration for two generations. He commanded the largely Ruzhen military forces deployed in the area and continued to keep their allegiance as military governor of the north-east. After his death in 1361 he was succeeded by his 26-year-old second son, Yi Sŏng-gye, a brilliant soldier destined for ever-increasing fame. He had already played a leading part in recovering the areas to the west and also in repelling a 'Redcap' army from North China, where a failure to gain the support of the local gentry had forced them across the Yalu. For several years they would pillage large areas of the north, occupying Pyongyang in 1359, and in 1361, moving rapidly south in search of nourishment, they reached Kaesŏng, forcing the court to flee to Andong.

On his way home after this incident Kongmin stayed at Hŭngwangsa, near Yŏju, the largest of T'aejo's several great monastic foundations, and here there was an attempt to assassinate him, part of an unsuccessful coup by the pro-Mongol faction who hoped to replace him by Prince Tŏkhŭng, an uncle who had remained with the Mongol court. After this failure one of the chief conspirators, Ch'oe Yu, fled to Manchuria where the Mongols provided him with 10,000 men but they were chased back across the Yalu by Ch'oe Yŏng and Yi Sŏng-gye.

Mun Ik-chŏm, an official who had earlier gone to the Yuan court to confer with Tŏkhŭng, redeemed his political misjudgement by returning home with the first seeds of cotton to reach the peninsula, for although the plant had come to Southern China centuries before, its cultivation and use had been a closely guarded monopoly. Over the next generation or so the comfort and convenience of cotton garments in place of hemp would produce an enormous improvement in the lives of the common people.

Zhu Yuanzhang, a leader of the Chinese 'Redcaps' who had come to an agreement with the landlords in order to unite the country against the Mongols, took Beijing in 1368, proclaiming himself first Emperor of the Ming. Kongmin at once sent an envoy, hoping to be accepted as an ally, but the uncertainties surrounding Korea's intricate involvement with the Mongols would make the new dynasty cautious in its dealings with them. The King sent an army across the lower reaches of the Yalu under Yi Sŏng-gye in the hope of linking up with them in the Liao peninsula but the Chinese were making slow progress and he had to return without making contact.

Unlike his predecessors, Kongmin seems to have been deeply attached to his Mongol wife; after her death in 1364 he built a chapel to enshrine her portrait and spent much time there in meditation. Although he had awarded Chigong's disciple Hyegŭn with the rank of Royal Teacher, from this time onwards he would increasingly come under the influence of Sin Ton, a more radical monk of unknown origins with whom he felt some kind of mystical bond, forged, they believed in a previous incarnation and suspected, by their Confucian critics, of being homosexual. Buddhists believed that people could be of different sex in successive incarnations and that the karma of a passionate affair would live on through several of them, so that homosexual love was readily explained, and regarded, like heterosexual passion, as something better avoided, but deserving of compassion.

Whatever the basis of their partnership, it would have profound and disturbing results, for the two men committed themselves to breaking the power of the great landowners and re-establishing the rights of those they exploited, along with the efficient collection of taxes on which successful bureaucracy depended. If it could be done at all, it would be only by a man such as Sin Ton, free from all family connections. In 1365 he was given the title of 'Kuksa', National Teacher, the highest order of merit for a monk. As a rank it stood next to that of the King himself, with the implication, as with arch-bishops in the West, that his powers would be limited to the realms of the spirit, but he was now put in charge of a new Bureau with dictatorial powers for redistributing land and restoring the rights of those who had been reduced to slavery.

These radical policies did not have the approval of Yi Che-hyŏn, now an old man who had served six Kings, and although they were supported by many of the younger literati, and the people, most of the country's older statesmen and military heroes opposed them. They soon came to detest this upstart monk who had bewitched the King and not surprisingly, he responded with paranoiac hostility. Highly respected ministers such as Yi Kong-su, who had been res-ponsible for organizing the country's defences against the Mongols and the Redcaps, and military heroes such as Ch'oe Yŏng were exiled to offshore islands, but able men of humbler origin like Yi Sŏng-gye, even if they had reservations about the monk, were more in sympathy with the reforms.

Ch'oe Yŏng, loyal to the last, stoically accepted his fate, but others were less restrained and with so much at stake the struggle became increasingly ruthless. As the monk would eventually lose the battle and the conservatives survive to write its history, it is difficult to provide a balanced account, but the accusations against him are suspiciously vague, matters of 'evil doing' and breaches of celibacy, and a petition presented to the King by two officials had to rely heavily on the traditional belief that the weather reflects the judge-ments of Heaven:

Since your majesty has entrusted power to this Sin Ton even the seasons have become confounded: thunderstorms come in the winter dry season, yellow fogs spread over the land for days, spots appear on the face of the sun, red clouds ride the midnight sky, meteors fall with deadly aim, trees are broken with the weight of ice and snow, and wild beasts appear in the streets by day. How can it be said that this man's appointment is in accord with the will of Heaven?

The King threw this document into a brazier and had the authors tried under torture, making martyrs of them. The plots, counterplots and assassinations became more desperate. As chief minister, Yi In-im, a talented scholar from one of the great families, had organized the assassination of Ki Ch'ŏl, driven the Redcaps out of Kaesŏng, and assisted in Sin Ton's social reforms, but recent events had gradu-ally pushed him towards the conservative side and in 1369 both he and the powerful dowager Queen turned against the monk. He was now said to be plotting against the King himself and at the end of 1370 he was exiled to Suwŏn where a few months later he was accused of various crimes and sexual offences and condemned to a traitor's cruel death. His head was taken to the capital and displayed on the East Gate while other parts of his body were sent to provincial capitals, and the conservative loyalists, mostly from military families hostile to the Mongols, were restored to power.

Ch'oe Yŏng was recalled, and in 1374 given the challenging task of storming the last Mongol stronghold, the island of Cheju. After the main part had been recovered the remnant made a last stand on Hodo, a small island with a grassy top and sheer cliffs that stands just outside the southern harbour of Sŏgwip'o. The area is noted for strong winds and it was here that the General dealt the final blow by using man-carrying kites for an airborne assault.

Later in the same year the pro-Mongol landowners, aided by eunuch accomplices at the court, succeeded in assassinating Kongmin as part of an attempted coup that was quickly quelled. Three success-ive consorts provided for Kongmin after his widowing had failed to produce a son so that the only candidate as heir was a boy born to Panya, a girl from Sin Ton's household, with whom the King had had an affair. He had been taken away from his mother, given the title of Prince Kangnyŏng, and adopted by Queen Hong. Now 10 years of age, he was put on the throne as King U and formally married to a daughter of Ch'oe Yŏng, while the Queen, advised by Yi In-im, acted as regent.

Ming suspicions of Korea's involvement with the Mongols were revived by the assassination of Kongmin, and when on top of this a Ming envoy sent to Kaesŏng to obtain cavalry horses was murdered by the pro-Mongol faction on his way home, they refused to recog-nize the legitimacy of Kongmin's successor, demanded a large tribute and asserted their claim to the northern borderlands that had been occupied by their Mongol predecessors. This produced a split in the court between the younger literati who were in sympathy with the ethos of the new rulers of China and wanted at all costs to maintain an alliance with them and the older generation, represented by Yi In-im, who favoured a 'two-legged policy', one limb walking with the Mongols and the other keeping pace with the Ming. When forced to choose between them, he believed that it was more important to defend their northern territories, even if it meant a temporary alliance with the Mongol remnant in Manchuria.

From 1375 onwards raids by Japanese marauders intensified to such a degree that in the south-west many coastal areas were abandoned and the transport of rice by sea to the capital had to be discontinued. Diplomatic relations with Japan, long in abeyance after the Mongol attacks, were handicapped by a north-south divide between rival shoguns backing rival Emperors, but when Chŏng Mong-ju led a new mission in 1377 the Ashikaga Shogun, Yoshimitsu, had won back the south and was prepared to do a deal: if the Koreans would let him have a copy of the Buddhist Tripitaka (about 7,000 volumes) he would suppress the pirates. Chŏng came back with several hundred freed Korean captives but neither side would find it easy to deliver. Chŏng would lose his life in the political struggle that ended the dynasty and long before the scriptures were finally delivered, in 1423, the Koreans would have found their own solution to the problem of the pirates.

It was provided by Ch'oe Musŏn, a man of humble origins who, after wresting from a Chinese acquaintance the secret of gunpowder, went on to win government backing for an arsenal where, by 1377, he had developed bombs, rockets and even a primitive form of cannon. From 1379, with the rank of general, he began to demonstrate their value and when in the summer of 1381 what was possibly the largest ever pirate fleet was spotted moving north along the west coast, the Korean forces were put on the alert.

The Japanese were making for Chinp'o at the mouth of the Kŭm River where, 700 years before, Tang and Silla forces had destroyed another of their fleets. Several thousand of them came ashore from their 500 vessels which they tied together with ropes and left with a few hundred men to guard, while the main body marched inland, heavily armed, with cavalry and with pack horses to carry the rice. Large quantities of grain and many captives had already been brought back from the nearer settlements when the Chŏlla provincial commander arrived with his fleet, which included two other generals, one of whom was Ch'oe Musŏn himself. They used their fire bombs to set the whole armada alight. The Japanese guarding the ships quickly killed their Korean captives but suffered heavy loses through fire or drowning. About 300 escaped to catch up with the main force which had now moved inland as far as Namwǒn, where they were confronted by an army commanded by Yi Sǒng-gye, and it is said that it was five or six days before the reddened water of a nearby stream became drinkable again.

From this time on the raiding parties were more cautious, while the Koreans were preparing to carry the war to their bases, and in 1389 a fleet of about 100 warships led by Pak Wi, the military commander of Kyǒngsang Province, attacked their stronghold on the island of Tsushima to burn about 300 ships, set houses alight and rescue 100 Korean captives. It did not immediately put an end to the raids – eight years later there would be an invasion at Ongjin, north of the Han estuary, and subsequent famines in the south of Japan would, for a time, increase their incidence, but the Koreans had now gained the edge in naval technology.

CHAPTER SEVENTEEN

THE END OF A DYNASTY

THOSE who opposed Yi In-im in his attempts to seek aid from the Mongols found their natural leader in Yi Sŏng-gye. He was now a national hero and he had already taken wives from several of the leading families. He had behind him a kind of independent brigade of about 2,000 well-disciplined men and he had won the support of a large group of gifted young officials and ministers who had grown up since Kongmin came to power and held their posts on the basis of their academic ability, so that even though some of them were from the old families they were all in favour of reform and for closer relationships with the Ming. Important among them were Chŏng To-jŏn, who in 1375 had resigned from the Privy Council rather than agree to reconciliation with the Mongols, and Cho Chun, who would become the chief architect of far-reaching reforms and was already at work on plans for re-registering and redistributing the nation's land.

Perhaps the most distinguished of them ws Chŏng Mong-ju, who had led the mission to Japan in 1377. Kongmin had appointed him to follow Yi Saek at the National Academy, where he had been active in promoting local colleges for the less privileged in each of the five districts of the capital and in the country areas. He was banished for a time by Yi In-im because of his anti-Mongol views but later, in 1384 and again in 1386, was sent as envoy to the Ming, where he was well received by the Emperor.

The Ming had now won control of the Liao peninsula but the Mongols would continue to harass them for another century or more and they still suspected the Koreans of aiding them. When in 1387 the Ming Emperor refused to receive another Korean envoy, Ch'oe Yŏng was persuaded to join Yi Sŏng-gye in ousting Yi In-Im and putting Ch'oe Yŏng himself in his place as chief minister. It was hoped that this would mollify the Chinese, but the Emperor, hard pressed to maintain his northern armies, began to reiterate heavy demands for tribute that he had previously remitted in an audience with Chŏng Mong-ju and to encroach further on the northern provinces. This made even some of the pro-Ming Koreans think again and Ch'oe Yŏng decided that an army must be sent to drive them back. Two forces were mobilized, one from Kaesŏng to be led by Yi Sŏng-gye and the other by Cho Min-su, the military commander of the north-eastern area, while Ch'oe Yŏng moved to Pyongyang to take overall command.

Yi Sŏng-gye's path towards the mouth of the Yalu was the one he had followed 18 years before in his unsuccessful attempt to assist the Ming and now, against his will, he was being sent to make an ill-prepared attack on them. They were delayed by the heavy summer rains and by the time that he had established a base on the island of Wihwa at the mouth of the Yalu supplies were short and he had lost a great many men through illness or desertion. After twice requesting permission to withdraw, without success, he came to an agreement with his fellow general and led the armies back to seize first, Pyongyang, and then Kaesŏng, in an almost bloodless coup.

Ch'oe Yŏng accepted exile but his daughter was still Queen and a new Privy Council, with the two generals, Yi Sŏng-gye and Cho Min-su, as its chief ministers, decided that King U must divorce her. The King, now a confident young man of 24, had backed Ch'oe Yŏng in sending the army to the north and refused to consider a divorce, trusting that he would have enough loyal support to force Yi Sŏng-gye to back down, but it was not so: the couple were exiled to Kanghwa Island, and inevitably his father-in-law, Ch'oe Yŏng, came under suspicion.

There was now a disagreement between Cho Min-su, who wanted to replace King U by his own small son Ch'ang, and the radicals, who wanted to make a clean break by choosing a distant member of the royal family with no powerful connections. Yi Saek, who represented the moderates, argued powerfully for Ch'ang and won the day, but when his supporters went on to oppose the radical redistribution of land planned by Chŏng To-jŏn and Cho Chun, Cho, with the backing of Yi, used the powers vested in him as Censor to purge them, and the reform went ahead.

It was based on the traditional principle that all land was the King's land, but with a new emphasis on the collection of taxes from those who held it. Private holdings were to be modest, and sufficient areas of rice-land around the capital were to be set aside for the stipends of government officials. With radical zeal they began by burning all the existing registers of ownership, and even the monasteries were either expropriated or had their holdings greatly reduced. They may have been ruthless and intolerant but, as in the days of Sin Ton, a strong social conscience was at work and it would give the new regime a solid economic base.

Towards the end of 1389 King U was visited in exile by two sympathizers, Ch'oe Yŏng's nephew Kim Cho and Chŏng Duk-hu. They found him full of anger and resentment: 'Why do I have to sit here helplessly waiting to die? All that is needed is one brave man to deal with Yi Sŏng-gye.' He told them to go and see the Minister of Rites, Kwak Ch'ung-bo, who had always been a good friend. They did, and he reported them to the Privy Council. Chŏng killed himself while Kim Cho, under torture, implicated a great many others who were executed or exiled and it sealed the fate of the brave Ch'oe Yŏng, now 73. It is said that still no grass grows on his grave at Pyŏkche as evidence of his innocence, and his spirit is still venerated at shrines in seaside villages that he saved from the Japanese pirates.

A story was now put around that King U was really the son of the wicked monk Sin Ton, and it was scandalous that his grandson Ch'ang should still be King. He was replaced by the man that the radicals had originally wanted, Kongyang, a feeble-minded descendant of Sinjong, who had reigned at the end of the twelfth century. He had no powerful in-law families to support his authority and is said to have passed his first night in the palace weeping over what he felt to be a cruel fate.

Yi Sŏng-gye was now King in all but name, and the determined revolutionaries, backed by his impetuous 22-year-old son Pang-wŏn, would soon push him on to take the last step. He was a soldier with little taste for the life of the court but he was certainly one of those powerful personalities who are commonly described as 'born to rule'. As the most talented of his statesmen wrote (in J. S. Gale's translation):

> His presence is the mighty warrior, firm
> He stands, an eagle on a mountain top;
> In wisdom and resource none can compare,
> The dragon of Namyang is he.
> In judgement on the civil bench,
> Or counsel from the warriors tent, he rules:
> He halts the waves that roll in from the sea,
> And holds the sun back from its heavenly course.

Yet it was the very man who wrote this, Chŏng Mong-ju, who would persist in loyalty to the old dynasty and lead the last desperate opposition to the new. By the beginning of 1391 the War Office had been reconstituted as The Office of the Three Armies, with Yi Sŏng-gye as the supreme commander, and the two Neo-Confucian ideologues, Chŏng To-jŏn and Cho Chun, as his deputies. All those who had opposed the burning of the old land registers or supported the descendants of Kongmin had already been removed from office, and exiled from the capital but when the final issue of a new dynasty arose, a minority of the radicals, led by Chŏng Mong-ju, were determined to oppose it. His views were publicly expressed only in terms of passionate loyalty to the king, but probably reflected more complex fears of what might happen when the Neo-Confucian philosophers of the Privy Council began to rule in the name of the now elderly Yi Sŏng-gye. There may also have been an element of personal rivalry between To-jŏn and Mongju, for both were polymaths who combined their powers of intellect with physical courage and both would eventually meet violent deaths in conflict with Yi Sŏng-gye's irresistable fifth son, Pang-wŏn.

The chances of turning the General from what now seemed to be his destined path were slim, but Chŏng Mong-ju re-established contact with the moderates and in the spring of 1392 Heaven seemed to offer an opportunity. Yi Sŏng-gye set off from Hwangju to meet the crown prince, who was returning from Beijing, and on the way went hunting, fell from his horse, and was seriously injured. The moderates hastily began to organize a coup but Pang-wŏn got wind of it and managed to rush his father back to the capital before nightfall, where he was put to bed. Chŏng Mong-ju, uncertain about the seriousness of his injuries, paid a courtesy call to enquire. He was given a calm and courteous reception, and afterwards was privately entertained by Pang-wŏn, who failed in a last attempt to win him over. As he rode across the Sŏngjuk bridge on his way home he was struck down with an iron bar wielded by a horseman galloping in the opposite direction. A dark patch on the stone, said to be his blood, can still be seen and as an inspiration to dissidents his shade would haunt the new dynasty for centuries to come.

By the time that Yi Sŏng-gye was fit again the Privy Council had formally declared that, like U and Ch'ang, Kongyang also, was not a legitimate successor to Kongmin. One of Kongmin's three consorts, the dowager Queen An, still survived, so she was called on to name his successor and prudently chose Yi Sŏng-gye. The new King would soon move his capital to a town on the north bank of the River Han but men of principle who remained loyal to the old regime would refuse to set foot in it. One of them, Wŏn Ch'ŏn-sŏk, returned to his home at Wŏnju to set down a true record of these days, after which he revisited the ruins of the palace and wrote:

The wheel of fortune has turned and
    Manwŏl terrace lies under autumn grass
A five-century dynasty sounds only in a shepherd's pipe
    And standing here in the dusk I cannot restrain my tears.

Before he died he sealed up the books containing his history and forbade his sons to open them. Eventually his great-grandsons did, and not wanting to lose their heads, they burnt them. The implication is that many dark deeds were done, and it is believed that it asserted that U was a legitimate son of Kongmin. The *Haedong Yaŏn*, a sixteenth-century unofficial history, alleges that a whole group of royal relatives were drowned by holing the boat in which they were being taken into exile on an offshore island.

King Kongyang was exiled to Wŏnju and subsequently taken even further away to die under suspicious circumstances. Even the bodies of his ancestors were moved, though with a show of Confucian piety they were reverently reburied and a few elderly relatives were settled beside them to tend the graves. When, after another five centuries, the Canadian scholar James Gale visited Wang Kŏn's grave in 1891 it still survived:

> I found a little colony of latter-day Wangs nestled about its feet. One pretty lad with a newly fashioned topknot stood by the side to watch. I asked him his name and he smiled and said 'Wang'. The thirteenth generation removed, and yet as comely as a piece of *Koraiyaki* [Koryŏ celadon]. I would have liked to have carried him home, preserved him, and kept him as a memento of the kingdom of the Wangs.

There can be little doubt that the Wang dynasty's finest legacy is its celadon, examples of which can now be found in most of the worlds' great museums, whilst its creators, like the medieval artists of Europe, remain anonymous.

PART III
CHOSŎN

CHAPTER EIGHTEEN

THE CONFUCIAN KINGDOM

Tℍᴇ ᴘᴇᴏᴘʟᴇ of Koryŏ had inherited from Silla a Buddhist cosmology that, embracing the animistic myths and rituals of the shamans and the Daoists, was rich and mysterious, with many-layered heavens and hells and an infinite variety of demons and fairies, sages and saints, a world in which some of the distinctions between daylight and dream, male and female, or human and animal were still fluid. Progressively refined by the compassionate ethics and metaphysical sophistication of the Mahayana, it had, at its best, served to persuade Kings and nobles that the greatest power belonged to those who were free from worldly wealth or ambition and that noble deeds, or evil ones, would resound through distant stars and many incarnations. The salvation not only of the poor and the afflicted, not only of humanity, but of every living thing was the buddhas' high task, and the buddha-nature lay, waiting to be aroused, in every one of them, but the credibility of such a vision required an apostolic succession of single-minded ascetic heroes, it depended on the integrity of the monastic communities, and it was vulnerable to the scepticism aroused by contact with other cultures and the more rational metaphysics of the Neo-Confucians.

The very success of the monasteries had contributed to their undoing, producing monks 'who abandon their poverty, dress in silk and ride fine horses', very much what would be said of the monks of another faith in Chaucer's England. The enlargement of their estates had given the monasteries a corresponding appetite for workers and with their policy of buying slaves and taking in ex-prisoners, orphans, or any other unwanted children, some of the communities came to be numbered in thousands. Military monks could be rented by wealthy patrons in need of a mob and instead of giving away rice in times of famine they lent it at interest and acquired more land as they foreclosed on the debts.

Confucianism, while seemingly less anthropomorphic than the faith of the biblical prophets, was very similar in the way that it saw barbarian invasions or natural disasters as Heaven's judgement on social injustice. They were sceptical of Buddhist claims to spiritual power and rated the scholar above the monk, but they were humble in their approach to Heaven. Neo-Confucian spirituality is typically reflected in the writings of Yi Sŭng-in, who is ranked along with Chŏng Mong-ju and Yi Saek as one of the three great scholars of the time. He mentions as his favourite texts, 'Deny yourself and live a life of love' and 'Let not the thoughtful scholar forget that he is a child of sorrow.' Like the Protestants of Europe they had their own kind of asceticism and the scholar was expected to be frugal and austere.

There was also a continuing acceptance of Daoism, for its knowledge of the stars, geology, magnetism or chemistry was seen as a matter of science rather than religious belief. When the monk Muhak chose the site for Yi Sŏng-gye's new capital on the north bank of the River Han he used its geomantic principles, and predictions of one's fate by its astrologers and encounters with its vaporous dragons, immortal sages or holy maidens in one's dreams, though they had their rationalist critics, would be generally accepted aspects of upper-class culture.

The unity of the Buddhist state would now be split between the peasantry, for whom the shamans, mostly female, would provide noisy, colourful and highly emotional rituals to promote health, fertility or the appeasement of resentful ghosts, and a male Confucian élite tied to the exacting rituals of ancestor worship which, for parents, demanded three years of sackcloth, abstinence and daily attendance at the grave, and took precedence, except for rare cases of national emergency, over their duties to the state. There were also annual remembrances for earlier generations, and the higher one's rank the further back they went. It did not provide much comfort in the face of sickness, poverty or unrequited love, and in the case of childlessness could lead to an almost pathological concern for the ancestral souls that would be abandoned, so that among all classes devotion to the older religions would survive, particularly among the women, for whom so much depended on the production of an heir. Even the state system would find it necessary to restore traditional rituals for the appeasement of the spirits of those who had died without descendants, or with grievances, as they might assemble to contaminate the atmosphere of a whole area, and there were similar public rituals for times of drought or pestilence.

Yi Sŏng-gye, now to be known by the title that he shares with Wang Kŏn, of T'aejo, 'Great Founder', was very fond of the Zen monk Muhak and the sons and grandsons who succeeded him, while remaining critical of the great monasteries of the Koryŏ establishment, would continue to favour this school and allow their younger sons to enter its communities. The older monasteries would no longer be subsidized by the court or exempted from taxation, and many of them were closed and their property handed over to the army so that from this time onwards, despite occasional revivals, their wealth, learning, and public support would gradually decline.

Apart from a few who rose or fell in the immediate turmoil of the dynastic change, the *kwijok*, the great aristocratic families, would survive, but the new schools and institutions would also produce a more broadly based class of gentry, generally known as the *yangban*. The term had been in use from the early days of Koryŏ, meaning literally the 'opposite files' or the 'opposing orders', and referred to the manner in which, on ceremonial occasions, the higher civil and military officers stood and faced each other, the civil file on one side of the throne and the military on the other. It would now come to be applied to anyone who had passed the official examinations, and any family whose head had once attained this distinction would as a matter of courtesy inherit it for as long as they had the resources to keep up a gentlemanly appearance and preserve a copy of the *chokbo*, the family tree. Although the term *yangban* is essentially a collective noun, in such cases Korean grammar makes no distinctions of number, so that individual members were also described as *yangban*, and in recent times, if the term is used at all, it means about as much as 'squire' does in modern Britain.

There were no automatically inherited titles. Even Kings had to be first approved as crown princes, and the appointment formally confirmed by the Chinese Emperor, and although the eldest son, by the Queen, would normally inherit the title, it depended on good behaviour and a general consensus. Apart from this there were only official titles that depended on examinations and merit, though as a courtesy families were often known by the title of the highest ranking official they had yet produced, even if he had lived several generations before.

Yangban families were, in principle, dedicated to study, in order to serve the state. In early times, at least, they paid no taxes, and would always be exempt from labour service or conscription. They regarded it as humiliating to engage in any kind of manual work, even any form of art other than calligraphy or pale-tinted watercolours. There would be cases of sons who persisted in a disreputable career such as that of an actor or a musician being privately executed to save the family from disgrace, though there would be one great opera singer in the eighteenth century, Kwŏn Sam-dŭk, whose swansong proved so moving that the elders spontaneously pardoned him. A member of the *yangban* could, if necessary, farm his own land without losing respect, but if he lost the land, it was his wife who had to earn their keep, out of sight, by gardening, sewing or weaving, and if required they would work themselves to the bone to keep their husbands in the necessary appearance of idleness.

Below the *yangban* was a less numerous class of artisans, technicians or clerks known as *chungin* or 'middle people' who kept a family tree and had certain hereditary rights, and then the *yangin*, the freeborn 'common people', and at the bottom the *ch'ŏn* or 'base', slaves and those in certain occupations traditionally classed as unclean, such as butchers, leather workers or entertainers, who were virtual outcastes.

The number of official posts would tend to grow over the generations, but the *yangban* population would grow even faster, so that whole areas of the capital, or whole villages, came to be occupied by *yangban* clans. Those with genuine literary ability could expect to obtain a post of some sort, but even a once powerful family that failed for several generations to produce a successful scholar might sink into obscurity, always hoping for the birth of a talented son. It inevitably led to a closing of the ranks so that they became a caste, and this was strengthened by making a strict distinction between the one primary wife, from a *yangban* family, who could not easily be divorced, and secondary wives who whether they were commoners – *yangch'ŏp* – or of the lowest caste – *ch'ŏnch'ŏp*, had no legal status and their children could not inherit their father's property, participate in the burial rites, or apply for official posts.

Traditionally, the sons and daughters of landowners had received equal shares in the family inheritance but, ideally, for a stable social order, according to Zhu Xi, only the eldest son should inherit the ancestral home and its entailed land, and nothing at all should go to daughters who had left to marry and live elsewhere. Similarly, the position of widows, traditionally left in possession of their husband's estates and regarded as the head of the family, would be steadily eroded. Now, if they did not soon follow their husbands to the other world they were expected at least to be chaste. Even in the last years of Koryŏ, upper-class widows had been put under pressure not to remarry, and in the new dynasty they were at first forbidden to remarry more than once and by 1485 would be forbidden to remarry at all, regardless of how young they might be, and they could be very young. After a plague, a war, or a *sahwa*, a purge of officials, there might be a teenage widow living with a widowed mother-in-law in her thirties and a grandmother in her fifties, all equally forbidden to remarry.

These rules would be difficult to enforce as they seemed to be contrary to both traditional custom and ordinary human feelings and it would be a couple of hundred years or more before they became accepted as the norm. Even then, there would still be cases of widows being 'kidnapped' with the connivance of the family, but as a penalty all their sons – even those from the first marriage – would be excluded from office. In time the shame attached to remarriage would spread even to the lowest ranks of society, for these rules were divinely ordained Laws of Nature so that even animals and birds obeyed them, especially ducks, which became popular symbols of marital fidelity.

In theory, at least, peasants ranked above merchants, few of whom could hope to be more than pedlars, as most consumer goods were produced by slaves in government factories, or sent to the capital as a form of tax on local industries, or on specialized crops, and grain was stored in municipal barns. The peasants produced their own shoes, clothes and other necessities – it gave them something to do in the snowbound months of winter. In the main centres there were groups of merchants who imported luxuries from China and Japan, their customers being not only the great landowners but many lesser officials who managed to grow rich by mismanaging government factories and warehouses or by tax farming. For these few wealthy traders, advancement would depend on marrying into a financially embarrassed *yangban* family and adopting their way of life, so that even less than in China or Japan would there be any opportunity for the growth of a prosperous urban middle class.

There were peasants who owned their own land and paid a tenth of their crop, along with other dues, but the majority were tenants who had to give half their crop to the landlord as well as paying certain taxes. They were not allowed to leave their birthplace without permission, and under the 'Tag Law' not only the peasants but the whole population had their movements monitored by the bureaucracy. Every male, from the age of 15, had to wear round his neck a *hop'ae*, a rectangular tag that gave his name, age and district, differences in status being indicated by the material from which it was made – ivory for officials of the highest rank, horn for lesser officials, and five different styles of wooden tags for the lower ranks of the *yangban*, *chungin*, commoners and slaves.

The concept of the Chinese Emperor as the divinely sanctioned leader of the civilized world had not been seriously threatened by their recent contacts with Europe or the Middle East as, apart from Moslem expertise in medicine and mathematics, none of these colourful barbarians had much to offer in the cultural sphere and their ignorance of ideograms classified them, by definition, as 'illiterate'. The Emperor's authority, more 'spiritual' than political, as a kind of Confucian pope would be strongly supported by successive generations of the literati for it provided a divine authority for the ideals they wished to establish.

It was particularly important to Yi Sŏng-gye because he had supported the Ming against the Mongols and if only they would now confirm his royal status he would have the legitimacy denied by those who still professed loyalty to the House of Wang. The Emperor acknowledged him as the de facto ruler and accepted the ancient name of 'Chosŏn' as a suitable dynastic title, but as they were under the false impression that he was the son of the pro-Mongol premier Yi In-im, whom Ch'oe Yŏng had deposed, they were reluctant to grant him the imperial seal and it would not be sent until they were ready to move their capital back to Beijing in 1403, by which time he would already have been forced into retirement.

Thirty-nine leading figures who had supported the coup in 1388 and now formed the Privy Council were enrolled in a special order of Meritorious Subjects and awarded large estates, with slaves, in the area around the capital. Their numbers would later be increased as a reward for support in struggles over the succession so that they threatened to become an oligarchy rather than the truly meritocratic ministerial government favoured by Confucian theory. The various discontents that arose from this would eventually result in a series of three-cornered power struggles between the King, the 'Meritorious Élite' and talented officials from gentry families, who, useful to the King, could be given important posts and even rise to membership of the Privy Council, the Ŭijŏngbu, of whom the 'Three Dukes', the *yŏng'ŭijŏng*, or prime minister, and his deputies of the left and right, in that order, were the King's closest advisers.

When Ta'ejo came to power in 1392 he was 57 and had eight sons and five daughters, of whom the first six boys and four of the girls were the children of his Queen, who had just died, while the two younger boys and the other girl were born to Lady Kang, taken late in life, to whom he was deeply attached. She was now Queen and in a strong position to secure the succession for one of her own two sons despite the fact that his fifth son, Pang-wŏn, then 25 had been instrumental in bringing his father to the throne, had visited the Emperor's court in the company of Yi Saek, and had powerful friends among his father's supporters.

When, in 1393, T'aejo appointed Pang-sŏk, the younger of these two boys, as crown prince, a rift developed between the majority of the Council, under Chŏng To-jŏn, who supported him, and those who sympathized with the older brothers, of whom Pang-wŏn was the leader. When Queen Kang herself died in 1396 T'aejo had a temple, Hŭngch'ŏnsa, built just to the south of the palace to pray for her soul and was even more determined that her son Pang-sŏk should be his successor, with Chŏng To-jŏn as his guide. The older sons had their military retainers and there were now street battles between them and the followers of Queen Kang's boys. Pang-wŏn believed that Chŏng To-jŏn was planning to have him and his older brothers assassinated and in 1398, at a moment when his father was indisposed, he made a pre-emptive strike. The two young princes were killed, along with Nam Ŭn, a comrade of his father, and Chŏng To-jŏn was beaten to death.

Pang-wŏn, having as it were stated his case, was not prepared to force his father out, but the balance of power was on his side. The angry old man took Queen Kang's only surviving child, Princess Kyŏngsun, herself a youthful widow, to Hŭngch'ŏnsa, where weeping, he cut off her hair to dedicate her as a nun and retreated north to the family home at Hamhŭng where he would thereafter conduct himself rather in the manner of King Lear.

He was given the title of 'Great High King' and his eldest surviving son, Pang-gwa, to be known as Chŏngjong, presided in Seoul with the title of 'High King', while Pang-wŏn bided his time. The outbreaks of violence in the new capital seemed to indicate that the site was not propitious and Chŏngjong moved the court back to Kaesŏng, but here another brother, Pang-gan, attempted a coup, after which, with the support of his one remaining elder brother, Pang-ŭi, the original crown prince, Pang-wŏn, was ready to take power, and in 1400 he again attempted a reconciliation with his father. After one envoy who thought he had been successful had been rewarded with an arrow in his back as he departed, a meeting was finally arranged at which Pang-wŏn, after ducking behind a tree to avoid an arrow, was contemptuously thrown the seal of state.

He was established as King in 1401 and can now be known by his eventual title of T'aejong. He moved the capital back to Seoul, which had already been provided with a city wall by a labour force of 120,000 called up by a national levy, and a magnificent palace. Unlike his father who had been content to leave the decisions to the Privy Council, T'aejong changed its title and reduced its influence, using the Prime Minister and his two deputies, of Left and Right, as his counsellors with a secretariat to deal directly with the ministers in charge of the six departments of state. He abolished the private armies, and supervised the embellishment of the city, including fire-walls and a sewage system, and set up a press for the large-scale printing of books.

The fact that in 1402 the fleet of coastal vessels that brought taxation rice to the capital was increased by 250 suggests that the system was now working and spreading its tentacles to the furthest corners of the eight provinces. Settling down to 14 years of peaceful rule, he can perhaps be regarded as having justified the rough assertion of his inheritance by the energy and practical wisdom with which he set up a Neo-Confucian state that would develop into a kind of constitutional monarchy with a sophisticated system of checks and balances.

Under the Ming, trade was again limited to the traditional form of tributary offerings, and as Manchuria was now under Chinese control the envoys followed the land route across the Yalu. Korean cavalry horses, improved and multiplied under Mongol influence, were what the Chinese wanted most and three or four embassies a year made the long dusty journey taking several hundred at a time. Later, when sea trade was resumed, the Chinese took gold and silver, furs, silk, paper and ginseng and sent more sophisticated items such as court costumes, musical instruments, jewellery and books. The Emperors, though professing to restore the civilization of the Tang, were closer to the Yuan in their brutal autocracy and tended to rule through a court conspiracy of eunuchs rather than the Confucian literati.

The envoys sent to Korea were usually eunuchs whose viceregal status required the King to go out and kowtow before them at a specially constructed gate. At first they continued to take the human tribute that had been provided for the Mongols: castrated boys and a bevy of girls aged 13 to 15 for the Emperor's harem, for which a kind of beauty contest was held. They had to be 'well born', but tended to come from lower-ranking families who needed the money or were powerless to resist. It is recorded that in 1408 200 were assembled at the Kyŏngbok palace for the first round, from which the eunuch chose 44 for the second, and finally five. They were given Chinese court titles, as were also their male relatives, and their brothers went as escorts. It is said that the wailing of their families filled the streets, but there seems to have been an element of hypocrisy about this as they received considerable benefits; however, it plainly offended human rights and would be suspended in 1433, and in 1436 fifty-three women would be repatriated.

The rather similar system by which gentry families were required to offer their daughters for selection as ladies-in-waiting would persist until the end of the dynasty, and encouraged the custom of arranging child-marriages among the *yangban*. These girls, as distinct from Queens, who came from powerful families and could not be divorced, were expected to remain as virgins unless the King, or with his permission, the crown prince, fancied them. If they did, the women were in peril from the vengeance of a jealous Queen or a former favourite. If a son was born, after the Queen had failed, they would be launched on a perilous career in which their child might eventually, if it could survive foster mothers, shamans' curses and poison plots, inherit the throne and earn them the status of a secondary Queen.

CHAPTER NINETEEN

THE CONFUCIAN KING

THE NEO-CONFUCIANS placed great emphasis on political science and the study of history, but when they looked back to ancient times it was still with the solid conviction that it had been a golden age of philosopher Kings. Salvation lay in eduction, but primarily in the education of the King. It was not so much a question of what the people should do as what the monarch should cause them to do, not least by example, but also by establishing just laws and rigorously punishing those who broke them.

For State Councillors, to be politically incorrect meant execution or at best a period of internal exile, the death being self-administered by drinking a poisoned cup at the King's request. It could be required not only for outright treason, but for offences such as giving the incorrect advice on political questions, which opponents could construe as threatening the fate of the realm, or mistakes in official rituals, which by upsetting the balance of yin and yang could be blamed for plagues or famines, so that controversies that might otherwise appear as almost comic could provide the pretext for exile or death.

From the earliest age the future ruler was under the guidance of a special government department, the Sejasigangwŏn or Crown Prince's Tutorial Office, and all through his life he would be required to hear lectures, study reports from the censors of the Saganwŏn, and memorials from individual scholars. The test would come with T'aejong's children, the first of the new ruling house to be subjected to this exemplary form of education, as Chŏng To-jŏn's attempt to provide it for the previous generation had been prematurely cut short.

The eldest, Yangnyŏng, was confirmed as crown prince but proved unruly and was eventually sent away as mentally unbalanced – it is thought that, knowing his father did not fancy him as heir, he decided that his safest course was to become a harmless buffoon. The second, Hyo'nyŏng, was attracted by Zen and became a monk, but the third, Sejong, was a veritable incarnation of the Confucian ideal. A keen student from his early childhood, he grew into a youth of such grace, intelligence and good judgement that by 1419, when he was 26, his father decided to abdicate in his favour – it also allowed Ta'ejong to return to military activities on the northern borders or the southern coasts, for which he had more enthusiasm. Yangnyŏng, as he complained to his drinking companions, now had one of his younger brothers appointed to rule over him in this life and the other one in the next!

Sejong applied himself to his country's needs with great energy and imagination, though usually in the name of restoring the ancient ways. He refounded and greatly extended the Chiphyŏnjŏn, or Institute of Sages, a bureau concerned with various intellectual activities that since its original foundation in the twelfth century had been closed and reopened in different forms by Ch'ungyŏl, Kongmin and others. Here he collected a brilliant group of scholars, mostly young, who became his friends, virtually replaced the State Council, and produced reforms, discoveries and improvements in every aspect of life – agriculture, astronomy, medicine, music and printing.

Their finest achievement, after years of research, was *han'gŭl*, a phonetic alphabet in which the shape of the letters indicates the position of the tongue when producing the sounds. It can be learned in a few hours, and enables a reader to be understood even if he himself does not understand. It was produced by a special bureau headed by Sejong's former tutor, Chŏng In-ji, and two younger officials, Sin Sukju and Sŏng Sam-mun, both of whom made trips to Liaoning to consult an exiled Chinese phonologist, Huang Zan. It was not intended to replace the ideograms, for that would have been to turn their backs on civilization, but rather to enable the peasants to understand government proclamations or simple manuals of instruction. It would make possible the slow growth of a vernacular literature, particularly in the verse forms of Sijo and Kasa, provide a literary outlet for women, and eventually come into universal use.

The first notable work to be published in the new script was 'Songs of Flying Dragons', a lengthy epic poem in praise of Yi Sŏng-gye and his ancestors, intertwined with parallels from Chinese history and exhortations to his descendants to imitate him as a paragon of learning, justice and humility, and it could be sung to the accompaniment of popular tunes. The large-scale printing and publishing of books that had been initiated by Chŏng To-jŏn was further expanded and a wide range of Chinese classics and Korean histories and commentaries, in Chinese, became available. A medical encyclopedia was produced, dealing with Chinese medicine in 365 parts and indigenous medicine in 85, and the local cultivation of herbs was encouraged to avoid dependence on imports from China. New books put out in the phonetic script included a practical text-book for farmers based not only, as in the past, on Chinese sources, but on the actual experience of successful farmers from various parts of the country.

There was a continual development of embankments, dykes and reservoirs, along with tread-wheels to lift water from one level to another. This labour-intensive wet-field rice technology, including the use of seedbeds and the transplanting of the seedlings in orderly rows, and the use of mature human excrement, had long since been developed in the 'Jiangnan' area of central China. First described by fourteenth-century visitors to the Southern Song, it had to be slowly adapted to the rougher terrain and the dryer and cooler weather of the peninsula. The new emphasis on research also resulted in the production of rain gauges and anemometers – probably the world's first – along with improved water clocks, almanacs, astrolabes and star maps, and led to the keeping of precise meteorological records in each of the eight provinces.

After his abdication in 1418 T'aejong turned to the problem of raids from Japan which were again posing a threat. He sent a fleet of 227 ships, led by the veteran coastal defender Yi Chŏng-mu, to subjugate Tsushima. The people thought it was the beginning of another Mongol invasion and caused consternation on the mainland by reporting that a Chinese armada was approaching. The So family, who ruled the island, agreed to become tributaries of Korea, in return for which they were granted a licence to trade at Pusan and two other ports, where they established settlements, and to send an annual trade mission to Seoul, the expenses of which would be paid for by the hosts.

After a while there was alarm at the growth of these settlements and the quantities of foodstuff being taken away and a limit was imposed of 50 ships a year – still generous compared with the Ming who allowed them two every ten, and would stop even that in protest at the pirates. The Japanese brought gold, silver, bronze and iron and took back rice, beans, cotton, hemp and Buddhist literature – the complete Tripitaka that had been sent to Yoshimitsu's successor in 1423 was so greatly prized that 20 more sets were ordered, and as each one contained 6,805 slim volumes, it was big business. Trade was also established with the Ryukyus, the string of islands that stretches south towards the Philippines, bringing in southern spices and other exotic items from as far as Indonesia.

In the north-east, where T'aejo, from his base in Hamhŭng, had kept control of the land up to the Tumen, with both forts and trading posts, the Ruzhen had since forced them to retreat, but under Hwangbo In and Kim Chong-sŏ more settlers were moved in, six new fortified towns were built, and by 1443 they had regained all the land up to the river. To the west, the frontier along the Yalu was less hospitable to settlers and more difficult to control, but under Ch'oe Yun-dŏk and later Yi Ch'ŏn, four large forts were established along its upper reaches. Hwangbo, Kim, Ch'oe and Yi were all military officials and all went on to become senior ministers – and three of them, eventually, Prime Ministers – but with the country now at peace the traditional Confucian contempt for soldiers would soon reassert itself and by the turn of the century they would again be completely under the thumb of civil administrators.

CHAPTER TWENTY

EXECUTIONS AND UTOPIAS

IN MIDDLE age Sejong was troubled by poor health and in 1445, at 48, after presiding for 26 years over what would come to be regarded as a golden age, he arranged for Munjong, then 31, the eldest of his eight sons, to take over. He was worthy and studious, but physically weak and chronically ill, while the next son Suyang seemed to possess the same kind of ruthless energy that had already driven T'aejo and T'aejong along bloodstained paths. Sejong was not unaware of the dangers here but he upheld the rights of the firstborn and had a special affection for the grandson Tanjong, born to Munjong in 1441, for his father, nearly thirty, had already discarded two earlier wives as apparently infertile, and the third, Queen Kwŏn, after first producing a daughter, Kyŏnghye, had died the day after giving birth to him. The King had exacted from the two most favoured of his younger scholars, Sin Suk-chu, then 28, and Sŏng Sam-mun, 27, a promise that whatever the fate of Munjong, they would serve the boy with the same loyalty that they had given to him.

The young scholars gathered round the King at the Chiphyŏnjŏn had been contemptuous of Buddhism, and monks had been banned from the city, but he had retained his friendship with the Zen monk Sinmi, who had translated Buddhist texts into *hangŭl* and now, affected perhaps by illness and the early death of his wife, he had a chapel built in the palace grounds and made his reluctant councillors accompany him when he attended ceremonies there. There were strikes and sit-ins at the Sŏnggyun'gwan or, more correctly, 'sit-outs', as the custom was for protesters to sit down outside the palace gates, but nevertheless there was a temporary relaxation of T'aejong's anti-Buddhist laws.

Sejong died in 1450, and Munjong two years later, so that the 11-year-old Tanjong was now King, and with no mother to act as regent,

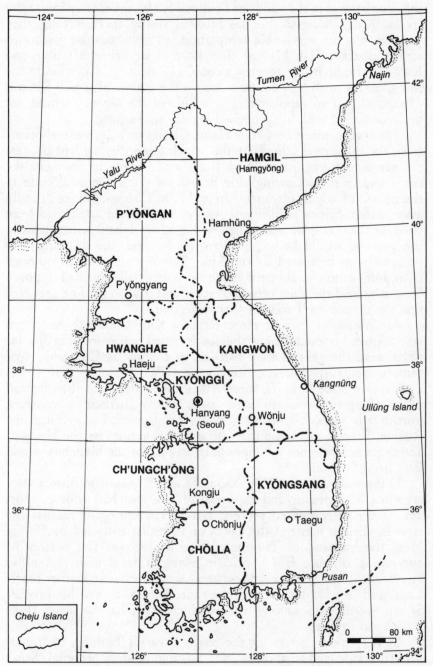

The Eight Provinces in the Fifteenth Century

the country was in the hands of a council led by the elderly Hwangbo
In and Kim Chŏng-sŏ. For his forceful young uncle, Suyang, then
31, this was an irresistible temptation; in collaboration with two
senior officials, Han Myŏng Hoe, later to be Prime Minister, and
Kwŏn Nam, he began to plan a coup. He went on a mission to the
Ming, taking with him Sin Suk-chu, in the course of which Sin was
persuaded that to support him in a bid for the regency would not
be inconsistent with his promised loyalty to Tanjong.

They were joined by Ch'oe Hang, Chŏng In-ji and several others
from the influential Chiphyŏnjŏn, which under Sejong had become
the nerve centre of the country. It allowed Suyang to dominate the
court and in the following year he carried out a sucessful coup in
the course of which Hwangbo In and Kim Chong-sŏ were brutally
assassinated. Sejong's third son Anp'yŏng, a gifted artist, had been
close to them and he was exiled to Kanghwa Island where later in
the year he would be required to die by *sasa*, the drinking of a
poisoned cup bestowed by the King. Tanjong remained as nominal
ruler, but his uncle, after the death or exile of all who had opposed
him, now held the chief offices of state, and it soon became apparent
that the throne itself was his final objective.

As Hwangbo In and more directly Kim Chong-sŏ had been
responsible for establishing the six fortified settlements in the far
north east, the general they had left in charge, Yi Ching-ok, now
came under suspicion and Suyang sent Pak Ho-mun with secret
orders to replace him. Yi, forewarned, killed Pak, and then instead
of marching on Seoul, took his men, mostly Ruzhen mercenaries,
northwards across the Tumen, where he attempted to refound the
Ruzhen Empire of the Jin that had been broken up by the Mongols
200 years before – not an impossible dream, for the Manchus would
later bring it about.

In the walled town of Oguksŏng he and his *kisaeng* consort were
crowned as Emperor and Empress and he also had wide support
among the discontented settlers, but in attempting to recross the
river he died in battle at the hands of a loyalist army led by Chŏng
Jong, the husband of Tanjong's sister Kyŏnghye. The custom of
appointing officials from Seoul in place of local men and other
grievances of the settlers in these areas would provoke further rebellions, and one led by a local magistrate Kim Si-ae and his brother
Si-hap would also involve the Ruzhen and take the army three
months to suppress.

In 1455, two years after the coup, a tearful Tanjong, in fear of
his life, was forced to abdicate, and Suyang, as king, becomes 'Sejo'.
Ch'oe Hang, Chŏng In-ji, Sin Suk-chu and dozens of others who
had supported him became Merit Subjects and were richly rewarded

with land and slaves. Three other great scholars of Sejong's day, Sŏng Sam-mun, Ha Wi-ji, and Pak P'eng-nyŏn, already senior ministers, had been struggling with their consciences, and when Tanjong was deposed they joined with a group of lower officials and a general, Yu Ung-bu, in planning a counter-coup. The reign of fear imposed by Sejo gave it little chance of success, and the leaders were interrogated under torture and condemned to death – the four already mentioned and two others, Yi Kae and Yu Sŏng-wŏn, who killed himself. Another of Sejo's brothers, Kŭmsŏng, and Chŏng Jong, who had put down Yi Ching-ok's rebellion, the last two powerful figures in whom Tanjong could trust, were also accused and sent into exile.

The renowned poet, writer and artist Kang Hŭi-an was tried with them, but released after a passionate plea from the already condemned Sŏng Sam-mun. Kang's sketch of a meditating Zen monk, preserved in the Tŏksu Palace in Seoul, has a vigour and economy that has in recent times won him worldwide fame. Another cry from the heart of Sŏng Sam-mun called on Sin Suk-chu to remember the promise they had made at the time of Tanjong's birth and it is said that Sin went out red-faced, but did not change his mind. On the day of his execution Sŏng wrote:

> The beating drum presses for my life;
> I turn and see that the sun is about to set.
> No inn is provided by the nether world;
> At whose house will I sleep tonight?
>
> (translated by Kim Jong-gil)

They are known as 'The Six Dead Subjects' and remembered in association with them are 'The Six Live Subjects', six others who because they were younger or not actively involved were spared arrest but chose to retire and live out the rest of their lives in silent protest. They included Kim Si-sŭp, about 20 at the time, who abandoned a promising career to shave his head and live as a Buddhist monk. Significantly, he went to a monastery in the hills of 'Yŏngnam', an area of North Kyŏngsang, where a small college and library had been founded by Kil Chae, a greatly revered professor at the Sŏnggyun'gwan who at the fall of Koryŏ had retreated there rather than serve under Yi Sŏng-gye. Settled here, Kim Si-sŭp would write *New Tales of the Golden Turtle*, the earliest known Korean work of fiction, a series of romantic stories in Chinese interspersed with poems, probably inspired by older tales of fantasy and in its turn said to have influenced those of Ueda Akinari in eighteenth-century Japan.

This institution, then under the leadership of Kim Chŏng-jik, the son of Kil Chae's chief disciple, is an example of the *sŏjae*, small colleges founded by dissenting scholars that would keep alive the cause of the Six Dead Subjects and offer biting criticisms of the morals and the policies of the Hungupa', 'The Old Men of Merit'. Their members would be known collectively as the Sallim, or 'Mountain Scholars', a new class of literati who like their Neo-Confucian forebears in Song China would show a genuine concern for the welfare of the peasant communities among whom they lived, and find increasing support at the Court and even among the more conscientious of the Merit Subjects themselves.

Prince Kŭmsŏng, exiled to Yŏngnam, became involved with local leaders in another ill-fated plot for a march on Seoul to restore Tanjong and Sejo was now persuaded that both he and Tanjong would have to die. It is recorded that when Sejo had gone to tell Tanjong of his banishment he himself had broken down and wept, and now administering the cup would be no easy task. The officer sent down with it to the isolated fortress at Yŏngwŏl, faced by the trusting young prince, broke down and finally he had to be simply murdered by an underling who strangled him with a wire. On the same night, in Seoul, the King's own elder son, Towŏn, fell dead, said to have been cursed by the ghost of Tanjong's mother. Nineteen years of age, he left two small sons of his own. Tanjong's brother-in-law, Chŏng Jong, the last survivor, was moved from one place of exile to another until in 1461, in association with the monk Sŏngt'an, he led a final rebellion and was condemned to *nŭngji*, the punishment reserved for the worst of traitors, execution followed by dismemberment and the dispersal of the fragments for public exhibition.

Sejo now became almost paranoiac in his attempts to enforce security. He enlarged the army, divided communities into groups of houses responsible for mutual good behaviour, and instituted the *amhaeng-ŏsa*, high-ranking officials who travelled incognito to keep an eye on provincial administrators. In later times these mysterious figures would, at least in fiction, acquire a more romantic aura, appearing at the last minute to save an innocent victim from execution or a heroine from rape at the hands of a wicked magistrate.

Sejo closed the Chiphyŏnjŏn and abolished or ignored virtually the whole of the bureaucratic system of checks and balances. His decrees no longer had to be discussed with his counsellors or be subject to the approval of the censors; he dealt directly with the heads of the six departments of state and dispensed with the court recorders who were supposed to take down every word that he said to them. Following a theme already developed by Yang Sŏng-ji, a scholar associated with Chŏng In-ji in revising the History of Koryŏ, he put forward the divinity of the country's founder, Tangun, as evidence of his own Mandate of Heaven, thus asserting his independence of the Chinese Emperor. Even so, he cannot be regarded as an irresponsible tyrant – more a conservative authoritarian who saw himself as the head of an ideal state in which the happiness of its citizens could be ensured only by the strict application of its laws.

To this end, from the time of T'aejo, work had been proceeding on a National Code to cover every contingency and every aspect of life in the hope that combined with universal education and the prompt punishment of wrong-doers it would restore society to its primeval harmony. It was completed under Sejo's personal supervision and he added to it a radical reform by which stipend land would have to be relinquished when the holder ended his period of office. We do not know to what extent this was actually enforced, and it seems to have lapsed before the end of his reign, but in his successor's time it would be replaced by a salary system, paid in rice, by the tenants of government paddies.

These Utopian concerns could not silence the echoing cries of pain or wash away the blood that Sejo had spilt. The monk Sinmi had been his confidant since his boyhood and in later life he turned to Buddhism with great passion and penitence. Already in 1457 he had set up an office, under the monk Sumi, to publish translations of texts, and he made pilgrimages to the older monasteries and provided grants for their restoration. On a visit to the temple on Mount Odae set up by Chajang in the seventh century he had a vision of Avalokitesava and returned to Seoul to demolish 200 houses in the city centre and raise up a temple, Won'gaksa, with 80,000 exquisite blue-green tiles on the roof. Only the pagoda survives in what is now a park, laid out in the nineteenth century by Sir John Macleavy Brown, a British customs official who was controlling the country's finances, along with the great bell, or *chong*, which gave its name to Chongro, the main thoroughfare that runs east from there. Sejo's penitence also brought a reconciliation with Kim Si-sŭp whom he commissioned to translate more Buddhist scriptures into the vernacular.

On his death in 1468 he was succeeded by his second son Yejong, then in his twenties, but he died a year later. The family of Sejo's widow, the Yuns of P'ap'yŏng, were the *sedojip*, the most powerful clan of the time, and despite an attempt to put one of Yejong's half-brothers on the throne, Queen Yun succeeded in obtaining it for her own 13-year-old grandson Sŏngjong, the elder son of Sejo's dead firstborn Towŏn, who was posthumously awarded the royal title of 'Tŏkchong'. For the next seven years Sŏngjong was carefully educated in the ideals of Neo-Confucianism and the royal lecturers included the Yŏngnam leader, Kim Chong-jik. He proved an apt pupil and, coming of age, he supressed the Buddhists, restored the authority of the Ŭijŏngbu and the censors and attempted to appoint officials on the basis of their merit, including a number of talented 'Mountain Scholars'; it seemed as though the Confucian State had now attained a degree of maturity.

CHAPTER TWENTY-ONE

HERETICS AND PHILOSOPHERS

T'AEJO'S generous grants of tax-free land to his 'Merit Subjects' had been followed by similar grants to those who assisted T'aejong and Sejo in their usurpations and another 70 had been added to their number for helping Sŏngjong's grandmother to bring him to the throne. Their virtual monopoly of the higher offices of state came under the critical gaze of Kim Chong-jik and the Mountain Scholars whom Sŏngjong had appointed to the Censorates and his sympathy for their views preserved a balance of power. After his death, however, at the age of 40 in 1494, he was succeeded by his 19-year-old elder son Yŏnsan'gun, who seems to have had more taste for wine, women and song than for scholarly lectures or puritanical censors, and a great outcry that they made over the use of Buddhist burial rites after the death of the dowager Queen further increased his dislike of them.

When, after four years, the annals of Sŏngjong's reign were being reviewed, it was discovered that Kim Il-son, one of Kim Chong-jik's disciples who had been responsible for drafting them, had recorded not only the misdeeds of his Merit Subject minister Yi Kŭk-ton but also details of Sejo's usurpation and a lament for Tanjong by Kim Chong-jik, disguised as a tale from ancient China. This was presented by the King as a blatant act of treason and a witchhunt was begun under Yu Cha-gwang, an oppressive survivor from the days of Sejo. This was the Muosahwa, the first of many 'sahwa', or purges, which are distinguished by the name of the year in which they occurred – in this case 1498 – and its victims would subsequently be revered as martyrs. Not only were Kim Il-son and several others of his party executed, and many more exiled, but the body of Kim Chong-jik himself was dug up, after six years in the grave, so that his head could be cut off.

Yŏnsan'gun knew nothing of his real mother, Queen Yun as when he was still an infant she had been forced to poison herself after scratching the King's face in a fit of jealousy, a tragedy brought about, against the King's own wishes, by the hostility of her mother-in-law. In 1504 her relatives told the King of her fate and incited him to another purge in which all those who had been in any way connected with her death, many of them distinguished scholars, were executed. He continued to order indiscriminate executions and to confiscate the property of the victims to pay for his profligate habits, which included keeping 300 *kisaeng* as palace entertainers; and he treated the Buddhists and the scholars with equal contempt.

Eventually, even some of those who had benefited from his unruly regime were alarmed by his apparent mental instability, perhaps connected with the early loss of his mother. Within two years there was another coup, the hundred or so leaders of which were duly added to the roll of Merit Subjects, and he was exiled to the small island of Kyodong, off the west coast of Kanghwa, the site of the provincial naval headquarters, where, through poison or neglect, he soon died. He was awarded no posthumous royal title and remains for ever 'Prince Yŏnsan'.

He was replaced by a younger half-brother, Chungjong, who had been brought up to share his father's Neo-Confucian ideals. He restored the Censorates, done away with by Yŏnsan, and brought in again some of the 'Mountain Scholars', whose chief spokesman was now Cho Kwang-jo, a forceful young man of 25. Appointed as a censor, his trenchant criticisms of the imperfections of his seniors aroused their hostility but won him the ear of the King. The examination system was to be reformed, enabling him to recruit able young outsiders who shared his views, and by 1518 he had the King's backing for a whole programme of radical reforms, based on the ideas of the Song reformers as presented by Zhu Xi. Particular emphasis was put on the Xiangyue or Community Covenant (Korean, Hyangyak) which required the provincial gentry to call regular meetings for mutual edification and self-criticism, probably seen as a substitute for the former role of the Buddhist temples, and this, accompanied by the distribution of basic Confucian writings printed in *han'gŭl*, must have brought some refinement to village life. Individual landholdings were to be limited, and the examinations to be open to men of ability recommended by the provincial authorities, ideas which even if they were not immediately to prevail would remain on the political agenda until the end of the dynasty and beyond.

With a firm conviction that the nation would prosper only if its ruler and his policies were wholly righteous, Cho Kwang-jo was urging the King ever further along the path to perfection. The older religions were banned as superstitious, even the annual Daoistic offering to the Spirits of Earth and Heaven at an altar in the centre of the capital, and on one occasion, at the last minute, to the incredulity of the general in charge, the King was persuaded to veto a planned surprise attack on Ruzhen intruders on the grounds that a surprise attack was a form of deception. Then, in 1519, when there was apparently no more land available to provide stipends for some of Cho's newly appointed officials, he began to question, on Confucian principles, the grants made to the 106 'Merit Subjects' who had supported Chungjong's own claim to the throne.

The leaders of the coup had certainly been generously rewarded, notably Pak Wŏn-jong, who is said to have taken over the care of Yŏnsan'gun's 300 kisaeng and lived with them in a scandalous state of luxury. Under moral pressure from Cho, the King began to confiscate most of their land, but this was a tactical error. These were the people closest to the King and his family, and to them Cho's moral fanaticism was no more than a cloak for unbounded ambition. They claimed that his eventual aim was to revive the old doubts about the dynasty's legitimacy and overthrow the King, perhaps even to seize the crown for himself. They soon succeeded in arousing such doubts and fears in his mind that he was persuaded to put Cho on trial. In June of that year, 1519, there was a month of earthquakes in which many houses were destroyed, evidently a sign of divine displeasure, but open to more than one interpretation. Finally, in the Kimyosahwa, Cho and his chief supporters were executed and many others banished or dismissed.

These violent plots and purges, which seemed to mock the precepts of Confucian propriety under which they were conducted, represented the surfacing of complex struggles within the palaces and the estates of royal relatives and powerful clans, probably exacerbated by the way in which the extremely idealistic ethics of the system tended to encourage self-righteousness and hypocrisy. The Kings themselves were usually men in whom Confucian values had been deeply implanted and their chief ministers were men of conscience and intellect, but paranoical whims and emotions, personal loyalties and, above all, family ties, often proved stronger.

The King was expected to consult the 'Three Dukes' of the Ŭijŏngbu, but he could also side with their official critics in the Censorates, or pay more attention to his former tutors, or his wife, or one of his lesser consorts in whose separate apartments he might choose to spend his nights, for although he could not divorce his primary Queen, who invariably came from a powerful family, he could have secondary ones, while dowager Queens, with the respect due to age, were also a powerful influence. All the ladies of the court had their own female attendants and it is said that when Yŏnsan'gun was dragged away the screams of the palace women were heard beyond the city limits. Through them he might meet shamans who brought him warnings from his ancestors, or astrologers wise in the science of the stars. He could also have favourites who were outsiders such as military heroes, eunuchs, or *kisaeng*, or the illegitimate sons of royal relatives, or Buddhist mystics, purveyors of vast cosmic visions that seemed to dwarf the rational order of the Confucian scheme. Illness, natural disasters, omens, rumours, love potions and poisoned dishes all played their part in determining the nation's destiny.

When Cho Kwang-jo's enemies had begun to accuse him of unlawful ambitions the mood of the court was heightened by the discovery in the palace grounds of fallen leaves perforated with the message 'Cho would be King', produced it is said, by using insects to eat out strokes traced with honey. When Chungjong's second queen produced a son, Injong, there was great rejoicing, but it was not shared by a lower-ranking consort who had already produced one, and one day a dead rat was found hanging on a tree behind Injong's room, accompanied by a curse, as a result of which the woman and a great many of her relatives were executed, though it seems, in the light of later events, that even this was hardly enough to remove the curse.

While some of the literati were, like Cho Kwang-jo, primarily concerned with the social aspects of Neo-Confucianism and the 'Community Covenant', others were entranced by its philosophical aspects. Chief among them were two men whose texts would enter the mainstream of Far Eastern thought and be widely studied in China and Japan, Yi Hwang, better known by his pen name of 'T'oegye' (1501–1570) and Yi I, or 'Yulkok' (1536–1584). In the Confucian tradition two of the basic ingredients of the universe are *li*, 'rational principle', and *qi*, 'material force'. They are long-established terms that carry with them complex echoes of arguments about 'reason', 'will', 'nature', 'spirit', 'matter' and the like, but in combinations quite different from those of the comparable dualisms of Western thought. The original meaning of *qi*, for example, is 'breath', which in the Judaeo-Christian tradition has always been associated with 'spirit', but here represents 'material force', as opposed to 'principle'.

Thus, the centuries of argument as to whether the primacy lay with *li* or *qi*, or with both together, have no exact equivalent in Western philosophy, but in practice tended to divide 'idealists' and 'empiricists' in a rather similar manner and could easily become the banners for party quarrels. It would be another 200 years or so before there would be any serious attempt to analyse the concepts themselves or to see them in historical perspective, nor would there be much attempt to question certain basic assumptions that both sides took for granted, such as that the cosmos was based on strict moral foundations, that it had degenerated from an original perfection, that natural disasters were divine judgements and that dreams and omens foretold the future, though Yi I, in particular, did question some of them poetically, in a manner reminiscent of the Book of Job.

Apart from their intellectual achievements, both men give the impression of being wise and magnanimous, in the tradition of great sages. Yi Hwang belonged to the 'Yŏngnam' school of Kim Chong-jik and advocated the primacy of *li* and the great importance of self-perfection and the 'inner life'. His hero was Yi Cha-hyŏn, a gifted twelfth-century scholar who had abandoned promises of high office to live as a hermit in the mountains. Yi Hwang wrote of him, 'Some say that he did it for a name, but I say 'No', for a name awaited him among the splendours of the world: he did it because his soul was great and he had joys the world does not dream of.' In accordance with these principles he retired early, but many of his disciples attained high rank, including Yu Sŏng-nyong, who would become Prime Minister, and director of the war effort at the time of the Japanese invasion at the close of the century.

This period saw the previously mentioned *sŏjae* develop into officially approved colleges, *sŏwŏn*, which would be given a royal charter and granted books, slaves, and rice land by the state. The first one, Sosu Sŏwŏn, was founded in 1543 by the Yŏngnam scholar Chu Se-bung while he was magistrate at P'unggi, at that time a county town in the T'aebek mountain area of Kyŏnsang Province, and it gained its royal charter through the influence of Yi Hwang.

Yi Hwang's younger rival, Yi I, was born among the mountains of the northern province of Kangwŏn, where at the age of seven he wrote a short treatise on *The Significance of Ancient Writings*. His mother Sin Saimdang, was an accomplished poet and artist, one of the first women in Korea to attain public recognition for her talents, and his grief at her death when he was only 15 led him to enter the famous monastery of Chŏng'yangsa in the Diamond Mountains, founded nearly a thousand years before by King Mu of Paekche and restored by Wŏnhyo of Silla. After a few years, failing to find the expected inner enlightenment, he returned to Confucian studies where he eventually came to argue, against Yi Hwang, for the primacy of 'material energy' and external experience. He preferred the life of a philosopher, but would be summoned by the King to undertake a series of important academic and ministerial responsibilities.

In his fifties, as Chungjong's health declined, the brothers of his second Queen, the mother of Injong, and of his third, the mother of a younger son called Myŏngjong, became bitter rivals, even though both Queens were from the same powerful clan, the P'ap'yŏng Yun. The faction backing Injong, led by Yun Im, was known as the Greater Yun and as Injong was the elder brother they won the first round and he was installed as King in 1544 at the age of 29. A supporter of the Mountain Scholars he restored Cho Kwang-jo's examination system and brought back some of those exiled in 1519, but within eight months he was dead, thought to be the victim of Nanjŏng, the wife of Yun Wŏn-hyŏng, brother of the third Queen and leader of the rival faction the Lesser Yun. Nanjŏng, said to have gained her position by poisoning her husband's first wife, was popularly believed to be a fox in human form because of her extraordinary combination of beauty and ruthless ambition.

Attaching herself to Myŏngjong's mother, who now became regent as the boy himself was only 12, she and her husband initiated the Ulsasahwa of 1545, a vengeful purge of the Greater Yun and all those who had supported Injong. It had no more than the flimsiest veil of ideological justification and for the next 20 years she and her husband, as the virtual rulers of the country, established a network of corruption and ever-expanding personal wealth, largely at the expense of the peasants. It is not surprising, perhaps, that the dynasty's first popular uprising occurred during this period, led by Im Kkŏk-chŏng, the first of a series of folk-heroes who from time to time would demand justice from corrupt officials. Towns and villages in the province of Hwanghae and parts of Kyŏnggi were held and lost, and sometimes destroyed, over a period of three years before the rebellion was finally suppressed in 1562.

The Queen Mother herself was a devoted Buddhist and under her protection the faith, which had been suppressed again by Sŏngjong and reached its nadir when Yŏnsan'gun had used the conveniently empty Wŏngaksa as the Palace stables, was temporarily revived under the abbot Pou, and the examination system for monks restored. After her death in 1565, however, it would again be suppressed. Her death also saw the fall of Nanjŏng, and threatened with impeachment she and her husband poisoned themselves. Two years later Myŏngjong died, childless, and was succeeded by his nephew Sŏnjo.

The most affectionately remembered woman of this age, perhaps of any Korean age, is the poet Hwang Jini, a beautiful and talented entertainer who made good use of the relative freedom of a *kisaeng* through a short but fruitful life. She enjoyed the companionship of some of the country's most gifted men and wrote several of its most popular poems, both in the vernacular and in Chinese. The best known of her six surviving *sijo* goes:

> I wish I could cut out the waist of this long mid-winter night
> And curl it softly, softly under the warm spring quilt:
> And slowly, slowly spread it on the night my love comes back.
>
> (Translated by Chung Chong-wha)

Sŏnjo was 15 when he succeeded to the throne and his aunt, the childless 35-year-old dowager Queen, acted as regent. But when spots appeared on the sun she accepted this as a sign of heavenly displeasure at a woman attempting to rule and made way for the young man, after which came a year of bad weather and poor crops and the great sage Yi Hwang, now 68, sent him a stern warning to repent as even if he was not conscious of it there must be some evil hidden in his heart.

Under Sŏnjo the Mountain Scholars, forced to return to the hills under his predecessor but continuing to win public support, were again able to compete for posts, and the strength of their convictions combined with their well-organized system of education and mutual support made them increasingly influential. The resistance of the conservatives divided the administration into rival factions that would harden into party organizations and make it difficult to obtain even the most minor post without the support of one side or the other. From about 1575 they became known as 'The Easterners' and 'The Westerners', names that orginated in a quarrel between an official, Kim Hyo-wŏn, who was a disciple of Yi Hwang, from 'Yŏngnam', and lived on the eastern side of Seoul and a brother of the Queen, Sim Ŭi-gyŏm, who lived on the western side. Kim Hyo-wŏn, regarded as a leader by the Mountain Scholars, had obtained a key position in the Ministry of Personnel, against the opposition of Sim Ŭi-gyŏm, who accused him of sycophancy, and he, in turn, opposed the nomination of Sim's younger brother on the grounds of nepotism. Both of them were relegated to provincial posts as a penalty for the disruption they caused, but these party divisions, once established, would persist from generation to generation.

The year 1589 saw the culmination of an extraordinary bid for power by Chŏng Yŏ-rip, an ambitious Westerner of great learning and persuasiveness. Having lost his post as a result of party conflict, he tried unsuccessfully to win favour with the Easterners. He then built up an underground network based on the Chŏlla provincial capital of Chŏnju, and while appealing to the literati he also used the monk Ŭiyŏn to attract a popular following, issuing prophecies concerning the appearing of a future King in Chŏnju, and the fall of the House of Yi and rise of the House of Chŏng. This movement, known as 'The Great Eastern Kye', began collecting money and secretly training men for combat on a scale that led to rumours reaching the court. He had to flee, his chief supporters were caught and executed, and he killed himself. Because of his friendships with members of the Eastern Party, some of their leaders were also indited, including the Prime Minister, No Su-sin. For the Easterners it marked the beginning of their decline and it also contributed to an ongoing mutual distrust between Seoul and the inhabitants of Chŏlla that would make it very difficult for them to obtain official posts.

The *kye* has long been a popular feature of Korean society – an informal cooperative that collects from its members regular contributions for some particular object, such as a village bier or a fire-cart, or as a means by which individuals can buy expensive items without falling into the hands of money lenders. In the latter case the members take it in turn to receive the monthly total. In the case of the Great Eastern Kye the aim was a bid for the country itself.

The Neo-Confucian doctrines of the Mountain Scholars were by this time generally accepted, but Easterners and Westerners would now, with ever-increasing bitterness, disagree on every possible occasion and mount great disputes over trivial questions of ritual or procedure. *Sŏwŏn* now began to spring up all over the country, maintaining their links with the alumni who went on to high office in Seoul. In this way, political affiliations came to be based on a combination of family ties and teacher-disciple relations, both involving strong emotions.

Sŏnjo had artistic and literary gifts and made a determined effort to appoint officials on merit and to provide good government, but he was not a decisive leader and he would have the misfortune to live through a period when a brutal invasion coincided with one of the bitterest periods of party strife. In his early days he was fortunate in having Yi I as one of his chief advisers. In 1583, when a Ruzhen incursion overran a whole string of north-eastern forts, Yi was called from his academic responsibilities to take charge of the Ministry of Defence. He found that the long-established system of paying a cloth-roll tax as an alternative to military service had resulted in an army of which the lower ranks existed largely on paper. With an eye to both the resurgence of the Ruzhen, who would eventually threaten both the Ming and the peninsula, and the unification of Japan under Nobunaga, whose requests for recognition and further trade had been casually rejected by both the Koreans and the Chinese, he proposed the raising of an army of 100,000 as the minimum to ensure the country's future safety.

Yi Hwang's chief disciple, Yu Sŏng-nyong, still young, but

already a star of the Censorate, eloquently opposed it, quoting Cho Kwang-jo's witty dictum that to maintain an army in peacetime was like purchasing a misfortune. Yu won the argument, something that he would perhaps regret eight years later when, having become one of the Sŏnjo's three chief ministers, he would be faced with persistent rumours of an impending Japanese invasion. Long before this, Yi I would have died, unexpectedly, at the age of 48, but towards the end of the war one of his chief disciples, Yi Hang-bok, would become Minister of Defence.

CHAPTER TWENTY-TWO

HIDEYOSHI'S INVASION

THE INVASION came in 1592 and is known as the Imjin Waeran 'The Ninety-two Disturbance from the Land of Dwarfs'. *Waeran* was a traditional term for Japanese raids, of which the last serious one, involving about 60 boats, had been in 1555. An earlier *waeran* of a different kind had occurred in 1510 when attempts to discipline the Japanese in the Three Ports where they were allowed to trade had provoked an attack on Pusan from Tsushima in which the district commander, Yi U-chŭng, had been killed, and this had caused enough alarm to bring about the setting-up of the Pibyŏnsa or Defence Council, whose secretary was to call a meeting of generals and senior ministers whenever the country's borders were violated.

Since then Nobunaga's victories and the introduction of firearms by the Portuguese had provided his successor Hideyoshi with a band of well-tried military leaders, a limitless supply of disciplined warriors, and powerful new weapons; he began to dream of conquering China, and perhaps India as well. The Portuguese had also brought in Francis Xavier and the Jesuits, and when in 1563 Omura Sumitada, the first fully committed Catholic daimyo, had put the cross on his standards, defeated his foes and opened Nagasaki to the Portuguese, this appealing combination of spiritual enlightenment, financial gain and military success had enabled Catholicism to spread with surprising rapidity and almost tempted Hideyoshi himself to put the cross on the standards he was planning to carry through Korea to Beijing and beyond.

In 1586 he suddenly turned against Christianity, influenced it would seem by suspicion of the Church's role in the Spanish conquest of the Philippines and the determined hostility of his Buddhist supporters who felt threatened by its intolerance. Even so, several of his favourites were Catholics, notably Konishi Yukinaga, whom he had made responsible for the assembly of an invasion fleet, and Kuroda

Nagamasa, a cavalry general, and these two, along with an older Buddhist rival, Kato Kiyomasa, were chosen to form the vanguard of his continental expedition. All three had won estates on the southernmost island of Kyushu, from which the invasion would be launched. Few of the daimyos relished the prospect and Konishi, in particular, had recently married his daughter to So Yoshitomo, whose father So Yoshimori ruled the island of Tsushima and depended for his wealth on good relations with Korea.

So had already offered the Koreans muskets, without persuading them to buy any, when in 1587 Hideyoshi required him to deliver a summary order for the Korean King to come and present himself before him. Anxious not to offend, he passed it on, after a long delay, as a request for an envoy to be sent, which the Koreans declined. In 1589, with Hideyoshi now threatening an immediate invasion, So sent Genso, a well-educated monk from the mainland who looked after his public relations, supported by his son Yoshitomo, to try to persuade the Koreans to make a favourable response, and they finally sent a delegation early in 1590.

It was led by Hwang Yun-gil, who was a Westerner, accompanied by Kim Sŏng-il and Hŏ Sŏng who were from the then dominant Easterners. Annoyed that the King himself had not appeared, Hideyoshi kept them waiting at Kyoto for some time before he deigned to see them and when he did he told them frankly of his ambitions and gave them a threatening letter to take back. Hwang Yun-gil warned the King that invasion was imminent, adding that 'Hideyoshi has fire in his eyes and is no ordinary man', but the anti-military posture of the Easterners had led them to play down the threat of war and Kim Sŏng-il said, 'Hideyoshi has eyes like a rat and whether you consider his manner or his actions he is insignificant.' Hŏ Sŏng, the secretary, despite being an Easterner, felt compelled to agree with Hwang as to the danger, but the King was finally persuaded that there was no real need to prepare for war.

The member of the Ŭijŏngbu most trusted by Sŏnjo was the Easterner Yu Sŏng-nyong who, as we have seen, had earlier opposed the raising of an army, but he now realized that despite the obstinate opposition of his own party they must warn the Chinese and look to their own defences. He saw to it that the walls of the main fortified cities in the south were repaired, and in what would prove to be a vital decision he recommended a relatively obscure army officer called Yi Sun-sin to fill a naval command post on the western corner of the peninsula, one of two that covered the coast of Chŏlla Province. Yi came from the family of a poor scholar and by the age of 47, as an able but quarrelsome army officer, he had had various ups and downs, but his family had once lived next door to the Yu's and it is through this childhood friendship that he obtained the post.

Appointed early in 1591 he soon sent the King an urgent warning based on his own intelligence reports of the Japanese preparations, along with his plans for building more ships. This should have been backed by the Westerners in the Pibyŏnsa, as it strengthened their case for war preparations, but it was not, because Yi Sun-sin had been nominated by an Easterner, and because their chief military representative, General Sin Ip, opposed the building of ships as he fancied enticing the dwarfs ashore and riding them down with his cavalry, a tactic that he had used to great effect against the tribesmen on the northern border. Sŏnjo was therefore persuaded to veto Yi Sun-sin's proposals, but Yi responded with a second and even more passionate plea for naval defences which so moved the King that without any further consultation he approved the plans.

On his first arrival at his headquarters at the port of Yŏsu Yi had been dismayed at the state of the ships and the shortage of sailors. The boats, developed at the time of Ch'oe Mu-sŏn in the fourteenth century, and apparently little changed since, were well adapted to their purpose, the discouragement of coastal pillage. They were shallow-bottomed galleys carrying archers and cannon that could fire bundles of incendiary arrows as well as shot. They had sails for cruising and a crew of oarsmen for rapid movement in combat. A wooden carapace over the deck protected the crew from arrows and discouraged boarding, which was the pirates' usual form of attack. These vessels, of which at the various harbours under his command he had a total of about 25, where known as 'turtle boats'. He was quick to see that a larger ship on this principle might be the answer to an invasion fleet and with the aid of a gifted technician, Na Tae-yong, he had the first one completed just before the war began.

No reliable details of its size and armament have been preserved but contemporary accounts suggest that it was probably about a hundred feet long, with two cannon facing forward and several more along the sides. The protective shell had iron spikes which were then camouflaged with straw matting to make them a savage man-trap. A great dragon's head at the prow emitted smoke, and there were doors in the sides from which archers could take aim at close range. There were ten oars on either side, presumably with two men per oar, and two teams of oarsmen, and it is said that working in shifts they could cover a 120 miles in a day. It was manœuvred by signals to the oarsmen from the captain's drummer.

Early one morning in the spring of 1592 what appeared to be a large trading fleet came flooding into the harbour at Pusan. It was led by

So Yoshitomo, a familiar figure there, bringing with him about 5,000 men, followed by his father-in-law Konishi with many more. Chŏng Pal, the commander of the garrison town, returned from a hunting trip just in time to shut the gates and from its walls the occupants gazed in wonder at the great assembly of warriors in black and red chain-mail with all the bright flags and trappings of medieval Japan. After Konishi's formal request for the opening of a path to China had been refused they withdrew to set up camp and the Koreans felt safe enough, but these were men well practised at filling moats and scaling walls. At first light the next morning they came tumbling into the sleeping garrison and its occupants were virtually wiped out. A larger force attackd the fortified naval headquarters nearby and the next day the more strongly defended military base at Tongnae also fell.

The commander of Kyŏngsang Province's Left (eastern) Naval Station had been able to do no more than burn his ships to prevent them from falling into enemy hands, while the Right Commander, Wang Kyun, escaped with a few of his and sent a call for help to Yi Sun-sin, the Left Commander of Chŏlla Province. Meanwhile, the senior daimyo from Kyushu, Kato Kiyomasa, had followed in at the Pusan bridgehead with a further 23,000 men and the next day the second Catholic army of about 11,000 under Kuroda Nagamasa landed nearby to take Kimhae. There were three routes to Seoul, the central one, to be taken by Konishi, one that diverged to the east via Kyŏngju, to be taken by Kato, and one to the west to be followed by Kuroda. Konishi had a day start but his rival Kato by marching through the night would catch up by the time their two routes temporarily converged at Ch'ungju.

As the first beacon-fire warnings were followed by confused reports of the Japanese advance the King appointed Yu Sŏng-nyong as Toch'ech'alsa, a special wartime rank that combined the offices of prime minister and supreme commander. He chose Yi Il, who had won a high reputation on the northern frontier, to defend the central approaches to Seoul and Yi set off at once for Sangju but the Japanese got there first and he only just escaped being captured. As news of the continuing advance reached Seoul, Yu Sŏng-nyong sent for the other most noted general, Sin Ip, who rode out at the head of his cavalry confident that by now the Japanese must have outrun their supplies. He vowed that if he did not destroy them he would not come back alive.

At Ch'ungju, the walled city on the other side of the mountains from Sangju, he was joined by Yi Il. The local commander had intended to hold the enemy at the critical mountain pass but Sin Ip wanted them out on the plain beside the River Han where his horses could ride them down. They proved to be better armed and more numerous than he had imagined. Failing to break their lines he fulfilled his vow, with his staff, by galloping over a cliff into the river. Japanese records indicate that after this battle they cut off the heads of 3,000 Koreans. The counting of severed heads was regarded by both sides as the only trustworthy way of assessing battle honours, though for ease of transport, only the most important heads were kept, and for the rest salted ears were sufficient. Thirty-eight thousand Korean ears, after being offered to the Emperor, were stored in jars at Kyoto where the Ear Tomb became a sight for visitors; only after an appeal by a prominent Korean monk in the 1980s would they be returned for burial in their homeland.

As soon as the news of Sin Ip's defeat reached Seoul the King decided to move north across the Imjin to Kaesŏng and amid angry cries from the people he set out that night under the flare of torches, in pouring rain with the leading palanquins bearing the tablets of the royal ancestors and what was still left of the court processing through the mud behind him. The defences at the river Han were mismanaged in a cowardly way by Kim Myŏng-wŏn, a civil official who for this task had been given the highest military rank, while in the city behind him the deserted homes of the wealthy were being looted and the offices that housed the registers of slaves set on fire. The armies of Konishi and Kato followed each other into the city unopposed, and Kuroda arrived a few days later having driven off an attack from the rear by a large Korean army that had been assembled at Taegu.

At this stage the Japanese forces behaved in an orderly manner, ready to pay for what they needed, their leaders expecting to be rewarded with the fiefs of the areas they occupied. They were impressed by the size and wealth of the country, the abundance of food in its walled towns, and the refrigeration systems stocked with blocks of ice cut in the winter. This was a period when Japan was beginning to absorb Neo-Confucianism and though it may not have affected the Catholic leaders there were others whose hearts it had evidently captured. General Sayaga, the youthful commander of Kato's vanguard, was so moved at finding a culture that seemed to be a living example of the 'Way' that, along with his 3,000 warriors, he changed sides, fought valiantly for civilization, and after the war, would settle there under the name of Kim Ch'ung-sŏn, write some books and establish a clan that still remembers him annually in a memorial chapel.

At the Chŏlla Left Naval Headquarters it was two days before Yi Sun-sin heard of the invasion, and shortly afterwards that he received Wŏn Kyun's call for help. He was not supposed to move beyond the borders of his own province without royal consent and in any case he was reluctant to do so before he had had time to call up his own men and assemble his ships from the various parts of the coast where they were stationed. It was just after the fall of Seoul before he was ready to move eastwards towards a rendezvous with Wŏn Kyun, whose eight surviving ships added to his made a total of about ninety, half of them volunteers in fishing boats.

By this time the Japanese had established shore bases at several points to the west of Pusan and were busy looting the settlements on the small peninsulas and islands. Except for the brief period when they had been under threat from the Mongols 300 years before, they had never felt any need for a navy, but Hideyoshi's attempt to buy Portuguese warships having failed, Konishi, in addition to hundreds of transports, had built warships based on Chinese models. Very few of them had as yet arrived, but the failure of the Koreans to oppose their landings had made them feel secure and Yi Sun-sin was able to move around Kŏje and the other smaller islands for several days surprising and burning dozens of their transports before returning to Yŏsu.

As soon as the court at Kaesŏng heard that Seoul had fallen they decided to move on to Pyongyang. Kim Myŏng-wŏn was again left to stop the enemy at the Imjin River, but this time he had the help of another force under the commander of Hamgyŏng Province, Sin Hal. After the Japanese had reached the river and then withdrawn, Sin, against Kim's advice, had his men ferried across to pursue them. A younger but higher-ranking general from Pyongyang, Han Ung-in, then arrived with an army of veterans and insisted on following Sin across the river. When a Japanese ambush forced them all to flee back to it Kim decided not to risk the success of his retreat by sending the boats back across the river.

After taking Kaesŏng the three Japanese generals agreed to divide their routes again, Kato turning eastwards towards the province of Hamgyŏng while Konishi went on towards Pyongyang with Kuroda, who was to establish a base halfway there. The King was now tempted to move east towards Hamhŭng but the wide Taedong River at Pyongyang seemed a reassuring barrier and Yu Sŏng-nyong persuaded him to stay. Indeed, when Konishi reached the river he realized that crossing it would be no easy task. His previous attempts to negotiate with the Koreans had failed but here, for the first time, he had direct contact with the court and he requested a meeting with Yi Tŏk-hyŏng, the minister who had been responsible for earlier diplomatic exchanges with Japan and had now just returned from China with the promise of full support from the Ming.

This time the court agreed and on board a ship anchored in the middle of the river Yi Tŏk-hyŏng met Konishi's representatives, So

Yoshitomo and the monk Genso. They repeated that their only desire was to pass peacefully on an embassy to the Ming, and warned him that as a force of 100,000 men was coming up the west coast by sea, this was their last chance: Yi was able to reply with confidence that a million Chinese warriors were on the way. They returned to their respective camps and while Konishi sat on the southern bank waiting for supplies, the King, about to flee eastwards to Hamhŭng, was finally persuaded by his second minister, Yun Tu-su, to go north to Ŭiju on the Chinese border.

After a few days a large force from the army left to defend Pyongyang crossed the river by night at a secret ford a few miles upstream in the hope of overrunning the Japanese camp but they failed to get there before first light. The few that survived to recross the river found that the rest of the army had already departed, and after a short delay to ensure that it was not a trap Konishi walked into the city unopposed and found its warehouses still filled with stores of grain.

With the conquest of the peninsula now virtually complete, Kato saw his march into the remote north-east as little more than a way of passing the time until Hideyoshi himself arrived to lead his army into China. He would later be opposed by volunteers led by the scholar-patriot Chŏng Mun-bu, but initially he was able to buy food from the disaffected local population and to capture Prince Imhae, Sŏnjo's eldest son, then 18, and his brother Sunwha, who had been sent to Hamhŭng, and but for Yun Tu-su, he would have had the King as well. It was summer, amidst spectacular scenery, and moving on towards the Tumen he succeeded in shooting a tiger, which no doubt requires some courage with a one-chance flintlock musket. This, along with his easy victories, would make him a legend in his own country.

CHAPTER TWENTY-THREE

CHINA INTERVENES

WHEN Konishi's representatives had warned Yi Tŏk-hyŏng that 100,000 Japanese troops were on their way this was no doubt the plan. Their navy, accompanied by marines, was intended to move westwards from Pusan along the south coast and then northwards up the western side of the peninsula, occupying harbours as they went, so that by the time the vanguard reached the north a safe supply route would have been established, but Konishi and Kato had moved much faster than expected, while the navy had started late and was proceeding at a leisurely pace, and the land forces intended to occupy the hinterland were meeting so much locally organized opposition that they too had made little progress towards the west. By the end of May the naval forces were approaching the eastern border of Chŏlla province, happily looting the coastal villages as they went, while Yi Sun-sin, husbanding his meagre resources, was preparing to meet them.

He had planned to make a combined attack with the other Chŏlla commander Yi Ŏg-gi, but before the latter had arrived he received a warning of the Japanese approach from Wŏn Kyun, so, without waiting, he sat off with his 20-odd turtle boats. The big ship with the fire-breathing dragon's head led the way, followed by his own flagship and after two days they met up with Wŏn Kyun's three ships. At Sa Ch'ŏn, at the head of a deep inlet just below Chinju, they found a dozen vessels of the Japanese advance guard anchored along the shore while on the hilltop above they were busily setting up a camp with a dazzling display of red and white flags. The ebbing tide made it difficult to go straight in, but by pretending to flee he enticed them to man their boats and then on the turn of the tide sent his big turtle ship amongst them with all its guns blazing. The others followed it and although they came under heavy fire from the hills on either side and Yi Sun-sin, with a bullet through his shoulder, was amongst the wounded, they destroyed all the enemy ships without losing any of their own.

After a day's rest on the water they moved on eastwards to Tangp'o at the head of an even deeper estuary where twenty-one enemy warships were moored. One of them turned out to be the flagship of Kurushima Michiyuki, the commander of the vanguard. It had a superstructure about 30 feet high covered with scarlet awnings under which the youthful commander could be distinguished, wearing a golden helmet, and during the course of the attack a Korean galley rowing in close brought him down with two arrows, boarded his ship and triumphantly carried off his head, after which most of the Japanese fled ashore. Two attractive Korean girls were found in his cabin and one of them gave the interrogators the impression that in the 15 days since she had been captured she had become deeply attached to him.

A couple of days later Yi's 23 ships were joined by Yi Ŏg-gi's west-coast fleet to make a total of 51 and they moved eastwards along the coast for several days destroying the enemy at sea and on the shore until those that survived had to seek shelter in their bases. A few weeks later a newly assembled Japanese fleet of 73 ships set out from Kimhae, their movements being reported by local people who watched them from the hills. As they threaded their way past Kŏje Island and came out on to the open sea they were enclosed in a semi-circle of Korean ships, Yi Sun-sin's so-called 'crane's wing formation', and the turtle ships were sent amongst them. The Japanese called them the 'blind ships', the invisibility of the crew within their carapace making them more frightening.

The Japanese were themselves adept at psychological warfare, using fearsome masks and manes of hair to make themselves look like demons and giant scarecrows to glare down over the walls of fortified towns but at sea the fire-breathing 'blind ships' turned the tables and Japanese crews often beached their ships and fled into the hills. On this occasion 47 were destroyed and 12 captured, while the remainder retreated into the narrow harbour at Angolp'o where Korean assault parties eventually forced the crews to flee ashore, though not without some losses on their own side. At this point the Japanese seem to have abandoned their hopes of establishing a supply line up the west coast so that all their men and material would have to come in to Pusan, after which, on the long overland trek to the north they were now being seriously harassed by the Ŭibyŏng, the 'Righteous Militia', local forces led by brave amateurs from the ranks of the literati.

Notable among them was Cho Hŏn, a talented official whose plain speaking had often angered the King, causing him to be demoted, dismissed and even banished from various posts. With a few hundred followers, helped by a band of warrior monks, he succeeded in driving the enemy out of Ch'ŏngju but he later joined a larger group led by Ko Kyŏng-myŏng in a disastrous attack on the Japanese base at Kŭmsan, south of Taejŏn, in which all 7,000 of them perished. A martyrs' memorial stands on the spot and in the eighteenth century King Yŏngjo would posthumously award Cho Hŏn the rank of 'Prime Minister'.

There was also the 'Righteous Monks' Militia', many of its members recruited from the mountain monasteries of the north and led by Hyujŏng (Sosan Taesa), the founder of a movement that attempted to reconcile Confucianism, Daoism and the two schools of Buddhism. He would be followed as commander by his disciple Yujŏng who after distinguished service in the war would take the lead in reconciliation with Japan, and the vital contributions of the monks over this period would do much to counter the customary disdain of the Confucians.

The first Chinese troops arrived in July, 5,000 men from Liao under the command of Zu Chengxun, and they encircled Pyongyang, where Konishi was strongly entrenched but with dwindling supplies. His friend Ukita Heide, the supreme commander, now in Seoul, was aware of his plight, but he had to wait for the arrival of Hideyoshi before moving north, and for various personal reasons – the death of his mother and doubts about the loyalty of some of the daimyos – this was repeatedly delayed.

The Japanese navy was now concentrated entirely on defending the Pusan-Masan bridgehead, and the eastern side of the island of Kŏje which guarded its approaches, and by August Yi Sun-sin was ready for an attack on these bases. His shipyards had been busy and he now had a fleet of 166 ships, with 74 'turtle boats'. The Japanese avoided coming out to attack them, forcing the Koreans to brave their powerful shore batteries but, despite some losses, they destroyed about 130 enemy ships.

Early in the new year a Chinese force of 50,000 came across the Yalu on the ice, their commander, Li Rusong, being himself of Korean descent, and they were joined by the monks and other local forces in an assault on Pyongyang. They had no muskets but they had heavy artillery with which to breach the walls. Houses were set on fire and the Japanese had to retreat to a citadel in the centre of the town. Here they were able to enfilade the approaches so well that General Li eventually agreed to a cease-fire that would allow them to retreat towards Seoul.

Before the Chinese could move south they had to have supplies of rice, and by the time that Yu Sŏng-nyong had organized this the

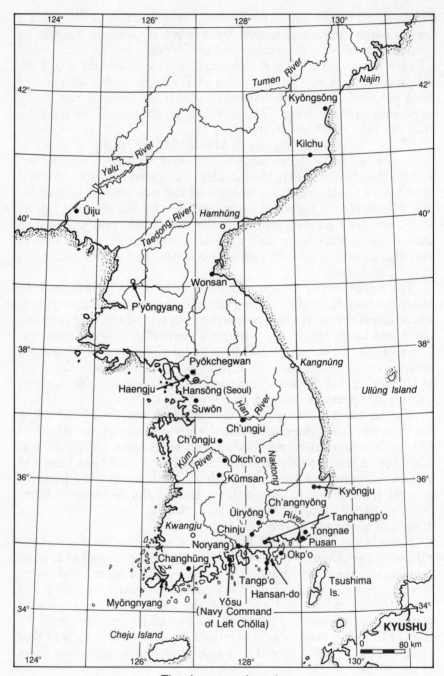

The Japanese Invasion

Japanese were across the Imjin and the ice had broken up so that a floating bridge had to be built. As the Chinese drew near to Seoul they were surprised by a powerful counterattack at Pyŏkche and suffered heavy losses, and this, along with a report that Kato was marching eastwards to cut off their retreat, persuaded them to turn back towards Pyongyang. Before the Japanese could safely pursue them they had to eliminate the nearby fortress of Haengju, which had an almost impregnable position on the north bank of the river and was now occupied by the Chŏlla provincial commander Kwŏn Yul with a force of about 10,000. Their resolute defence cost the Japanese such enormous casualties that with their three generals wounded they finally gathered together the bodies of those who had fallen, burned them, and abandoned the assault.

It proved to be a turning point in the war. With their supply lines broken, and a not unfounded suspicion that Hideyoshi was losing interest in the project, the generals were now ready to negotiate, and agreed to retreat to their bases on the south coast. Kato had to release the two young Korean princes and they returned to their father in a Chinese-occupied capital in which the palaces and virtually all the public buildings had been destroyed, and the streets were filled with the stinking corpses of men and horses. Indeed, as a result of the guerilla warfare and the savage reprisals it had provoked, most of the southern half of the country had been devastated and there was a serious shortage of food.

The Japanese were now concentrated in a series of armed camps along the south coast which they rapidly fortified so that they controlled the whole area from Ulsan in the east to Sunch'ŏn, in Chŏlla, on the west, the only exception being the walled town of Chinju, which had earlier made a heroic stand under General Kim Si-min and a guerilla force led by Kwak Chae-u and continued to defend itself with great courage aided by another Ŭibyŏng leader, Kim Ch'ŏn-il. It made a dangerous bulge in the Japanese line and they were determined to recapture it. It was beseiged by a combined force of 60,000 assembled from the armies of Konishi, Kato and Kuruda, and was finally taken. At a Japanese celebration held in a pavilion on the city wall at the point where it is lapped by the River Nam the victorious general was enticed to the parapet by the *kisaeng* Chu Norngae, whose lover had died in the battle, and taken over the edge in her arms.

Konishi took a Chinese envoy to Hideyoshi's headquarters at Nagoya to negotiate a settlement but as both sides regarded themselves as the victors and neither was really much concerned about the fate of the peninsula the arguments dragged on for years. Meanwhile the ill-fed Japanese soldiers in their scattered forts along the south coast wondered if they would ever see their homeland again; many deserted to till the soil and find Korean wives. Konishi, concerned about their miserable state, asked for a Catholic priest and Father Gregorio de Cespedes, the Spanish head of the Jesuit mission in Osaka, accompanied by a Japanese lay-brother, arrived there via Tshushima in December 1593. They came ashore on a beach not far from Konishi's fortress in the hills south-east of Ch'angwŏn and finished their journey on horseback, the first Westerner known to have visited the country.

He found his congregations homesick, cold and hungry. When he returned a couple of months later he took with him from Tsushima two Korean orphans from the home of So Yoshitomo's wife Mary and had them entered at the Jesuit College. One of them, baptized Vincent, would stay on to be one of 25 of its members burned at the stake at Nagasaki in 1626. Altogether about 2,000 of the captives taken to Japan by the Catholic daimyos would be baptized and many would become martyrs in the subsequent persecutions.

It was not until 1595 that a Chinese envoy set off for Japan, his mandate being to confer tributary status on Hideyoshi if he agreed to remove his forces from Korea. When, with a total entourage of more than 300, he eventually reached Pusan, Konishi thought it prudent to leave them there while he went to see whether Hideyoshi could be persuaded to receive them. He did not dare to go into the details and Hideyoshi was apparently expecting a Korean prince to be sent, as an acknowledgement of its tributary status, and the Japanese King to be offered one of the Emperor's daughters.

While Konishi was away, his rival, Kato, who still loyally supported Hideyoshi's claims, warned the envoy that he would probably lose his head if he crossed the water, as a result of which he fled back to Beijing with his personal retainers. By the time that he had been punished and his successor dispatched another year had passed and it was not until the autumn of 1596 that Konishi finally shepherded the envoy into an enormous palace that had been specially built for the occasion, and then hastily rebuilt after an earthquake in the summer. Konishi and his companions managed to deflect some of Hideyoshi's anger at the Chinese proposals on to the Koreans, who were held responsible for turning them against him, and their envoy, Hwang Sin, was refused an audience. The talks broke off, Konishi was sent back to Korea to take over command of the navy and Kato was promoted in his place. Early in 1597 the war was reopened, and Hideaki, the new commander-in-chief, was given another 100,000 men and ordered to wreak vengeance on the Koreans, sparing neither women nor children, nor even their livestock.

This time the Koreans were better prepared and a Chinese army

would quickly return. Yi Sun-sin's naval workshops had developed
a musket that proved more satisfactory than earlier Korean imitations
and they also experimented with bullet-proof armour, but found it
too clumsy. Conscripts were called up and trained and the naval
forces of the southern provinces had been united under Yi Sun-sin
with new headquarters established on Hansan, a small island on the
western side of Kŏje. Unfortunately, his appointment over the head
of Wŏn Kyun, who was his senior in rank and age, was resented not
only by the man himself, but by the whole Western Party. The two
or three years of peace that had followed the Japanese withdrawal
to the south coast had inevitably led to a revival of the bitter party
struggles and the Westerners, anxious to undermine the King's trust
in Yu Sŏng-nyong, were seeking to destroy his famous protégé.

Their opportunity came when a man from Tsushima, Yoshira,
who acted as Konishi's interpreter, and was probably a double agent,
passed on to the court information about a flotilla that was bringing
Kato back to Korea. Yi Sun-sin was ordered to sail out and intercept
it, but he suspected a trap and decided not to take the risk. Even if
the information was correct, Konishi may well have been using his
hated Japanese rival as the bait to catch his most dangerous Korean
enemy.

Wŏn Kyun had already prepared a dossier that began with Yi
Sun-sin's failure to come to his aid in the first days of the war and
went on to list many alleged breaches of bureaucratic procedure,
independent decisions, unauthorized projects and so on and after
Kato had safely reached Korea they added the accusation that he had
been bribed by the enemy to disobey orders and impeached him on
a charge of high treason. He was arrested, dragged to Seoul, imprisoned and interrogated under torture. He had few friends in the capital
and the triumphant Westerners had already secured the dismissal of
Yu Sŏng-nyong. After several weeks he was found guilty, but with
pleas from two respected state councillors, Chŏng T'ak and Yi Wŏn-
ik, and second thoughts even from some of his enemies, the King
was persuaded to spare his life and merely deprive him of his rank.

Meanwhile, Japanese troops and supplies were pouring in under
the protection of Konishi's much enlarged fleet, and after the Korean
Navy under the command of Wŏn Kyun had been almost completely
destroyed, and Wŏn himself killed, Yi Hang-bok, now Minister of
War, persuaded Sŏnjo to restore Yi Sun-sin. It was the autumn
of 1597 and he found that only 12 ships were left. On his first
engagement, though forced to retreat, he enticed the enemy ships
into a narrow tidal race near Mokp'o in which about 30 of them
were destroyed. A Chinese armada arrived to support him and with
their land forces helping to keep the Japanese within the confines

of their enclave on the south coast they appealed to Hideyoshi to let them go home, but it was not until after his death in the summer of 1598 that they could finally prepare to leave.

With Chinese and Korean ships blockading his headquarters at Sunch'ŏn, Konishi requested a truce to allow his forces to leave, to which the Chinese would have agreed, but Yi Sun-sin was determined to destroy them, so Konishi summoned support from the other Japanese bases along the coast. While the main Japanese fleet was still on its way from Sach'ŏn, Yi Sun-sin intercepted them in a narrow strait at Noryangjin where, on a cold November night, they fought their last battle and at dawn Yi Sun-sin was killed by a stray bullet. He had given orders that his death be kept secret until the battle was over. He was 54. Konishi survived, to be executed a year later at the hands of Ieyasu because, like most of the other Catholic daimyos, he remained loyal to Hideyoshi's young song Hideyori. He was refused a priest but is said to have drawn comfort from a holy image that had been sent to him by Catherine, Queen of Portugal. The executioner had to use his sword three times before his neck was severed. His fief was given to Kato and his adopted Korean daughter Oda Julia was eventually banished to a remote island where she became a legendary divinity.

During the course of the war the Japanese ships that had been taking supplies to the army returned with thousands of captured Koreans, most of them destined to slavery. Neo-Confucian scholars were welcomed, and it would soon become the orthodoxy of the Shogunate, perhaps a subtle Korean revenge, for it would demonstrate that the shoguns themselves were usurpers and lead to an eventual restoration of the powers of the Emperor.

Potters found themselves valued more highly than in their own country, producing vessels that still grace the tea ceremony, and printers provided fonts of moveable type that would enable their captors, by 1645, to publish their own complete edition of the Tripitaka. The returning generals presented Hideyoshi with 3,000 books that would be incorporated into a library founded by Ieyasu. What the Koreans can only look back on as the virtual destruction of half their country and the Chinese see as a major cause of the Ming dynasty's downfall is, for them, 'The War of Celadon and Metal Type'.

The frequent dispatch of envoys to the Ming had brought Korean scholars into touch with the latest developments in Chinese thought and gave them their first contacts with the 'Western Learning' of the Jesuits. The Chinese had, like the West, learned from the Arabs how to predict the movements of the stars and planets, but with their political upheavals and their indifference to mathematics they had lost touch with the theory of it and their predictions were no longer accurate, enabling Matteo Ricci, a gifted pupil of Clavius, to demonstrate the superiority of his 'Christian Science'.

In 1601 he moved to Beijing where he was lodged in the walled foreign quarter with the diplomats and met the Korean envoy, Yi Su-gwang, who was sent there a number of times in the aftermath of the war. Ricci added Korea to his world map and gave Yi a copy in Chinese of his *True Doctrine of the Lord of Heaven*, so that when in 1614 Yi published his *Chibong Yusŏl*, a monumental collection of essays on astronomy, mathematics, geography and so on, he was able to include a summary of it. His essays have a critical objectivity that sounds a new note, particularly in their interpretation of history, seeing it as natural 'cause and effect' rather than as Divine Judgements. It reflected a movement in China that would be known in Korea as 'Silhak', Practical Learning, *sil* being the ideogram that represents empirical 'truth' in contrast to the metaphysical 'truths' of the sages.

CHAPTER TWENTY-FOUR

THE MANCHU INVASION

T HE SEVEN-YEAR occupation of the south coast by the
Japanese army left it haunted by disease and starvation, and
over the country as a whole the exigencies of war had inevitably led
to social changes. Many slave registers and records of land ownership
had been lost, while other slaves had won freedom through service
in the army or by buying themselves out. Shortage of funds had led
the government to sell posts and titles to the highest bidders and this
was a tendency that would continue, along with a steady growth in
commercial activities. The Pibyŏnsa or Defence Council, made up
of senior ministers and generals, had virtually replaced the Ŭijŏngbu
through the war years and, faced with further threats from the North,
would continue as the central organ of government until the end of
the eighteenth century.

The plight of the Korean captives in Japan required some action
and in 1604 the monk Yujŏng led an informal mission which secured
the release of about 3,000 of them. After the reluctant Koreans had
been persuaded to restore diplomatic relations in 1606, more captives
were returned and in 1609 trade with Tsushima was restored, enabling
the So family to block an attempt by Richard Cocks, the head of the
short-lived British trading centre in Japan, to open a station in Korea.

Japan's new-found devotion to Neo-Confucianism, coinciding
with a period of isolation from China, led them to treat Korea with
more of the respect due to an 'elder brother' and its embassies
to Japan became increasingly grand affairs. With soldiers, officials,
musicians and servants they made a party of three hundred or more
and after landing on the western coast of Kyushu they would make
a slow and stately progress towards the Shogun's palace at Tokyo,
then known as Edo, for which roads were remade, temporary bridges
were floated across the rivers and city streets were widened. The
envoys, seated on tiger skins in their palanquins, were preceded by

banners and a band, and followed by specially chosen cavalry who would later give a display of horsemanship.

They brought not only gifts but poets and artists who at nightly feasts in temples or the halls of daimyos would display their talents and judge the efforts of ambitious locals. The artist Kim Myŏng-guk, who accompanied the embassies of 1636 and 1646, was a devotee of Zen and his dashing style, which had already astonished his Korean contemporaries, proved an instant success and became a powerful influence. The expenses were enormous and early in the next century, with his resources dwindling, the Tokugawa Shogun Ienobu would decide to reduce the hospitality to the level provided for Japanese envoys in Korea. The furious leaders of the next embassy in 1711 would threaten to kill themselves, tantamount to a declaration of war, forcing Ienobu to concede a few points, and later, under Yoshimune, most of their former glory would be restored.

In Manchuria the Ruzhen tribes whose ancient empire of the Jin Yi Ching-ok had failed to revive almost 200 years before, were now, under Nurgaci, succeeding. Taking advantage of the Japanese attack in 1592, they had invaded the Liao peninsula, where they won the support of the Chinese landlords and soon established a competent bureaucracy. Calling themselves 'The Later Jin', they looked to Korea for official recognition, causing a split on party lines between the Westerners, loyal to the Emperor, and the Northerners, the dominant faction of the now divided Easterners, who were aware of the Ming's incompetence and reluctant to make enemies of the Jin.

When Sŏnjo's Queen died, childless, in 1600, this controversy became intertwined with the problem of the succession, which would have to go to one of the sons of his several consorts. The eldest, favoured by the Westerners, was Imhaegun, once captured by the Japanese, but he had a reputation for dissolute behaviour and the Northerners succeeded in having his brother Kwanghaegun confirmed as crown prince. This did not settle the matter, as apart from continuing support for Imhaegun from the Westerners, in 1602 Sŏnjo took a new Queen, Inmok, who in 1606 produced a child, Yŏngch'-ang and some of the Northerners would split off to support his claims.

When Sŏnjo died suddenly in 1608, Kwanghaegun was still crown prince and, assuming power, he quickly promoted the two leaders of 'The Greater Northerners', as they were called after the split, Chŏng In-hŭng and Yi I-chŏm. They banished Imhaegun, who had become the centre of a pro-Ming plot to seize the throne, and would have him executed the next year. The other rival, Yŏngch'anggun, would be eliminated by making false accusations against Queen

Inmok so that she and her son could be deprived of their royal rank and sent off to Kanghwa Island.

The Ming soon appealed to the Koreans to join them against the Later Jin, which they did not refuse to do, but in sending off an army of 10,000, Kwanghaegun told its commander, Kang Hong-nip, to weigh up the situation before committing himself. When he found it turning in favour of the Jin he surrendered to them, and although they would keep him as a hostage for the next ten years, it served to preserve the peace.

The King and his advisers could not feel secure while Yŏnch'ang still provided a rallying point for the opposition, and in 1613 the eight-year-old boy was steamed to death by overheating the *ondol* room in which he slept, after which his mother took refuge in a northern monastery. For taking her side the two great statesmen of Sŏnjo's time, Yi Hang-bok and Yi Tŏk-hyŏng, were deprived of their rank, and Hang-bok exiled to the far north where he died in 1618. An anonymous semi-fictional account of Inmok's sufferings, *Kye-ch'uk Ilgi* (Diary of the Year 1613), is thought to have been written by one of her ladies-in-waiting.

Several other early works of fiction appeared in this period, the most important being Hŏ Kyun's *Hong Kiltong*. Hŏ was from a family renowned in literature and politics, his brothers also wrote, and he edited a collection of poems by his sister, Nansŏrhŏn. The hero of the story, Hong Kiltong, based on a legendary figure of earlier times, is a *sŏja*, the child of a *yangban* member by a servant girl, and consequently denied all access to his father. In his righteous indignation he becomes the leader of a popular rebellion, acquires occult powers that enable him to make himself invisible, and finally the government has to offer him the post of Minister of Defence and agree to change the law. Still a popular adventure story, it has a subversive egalitarianism that combined with Hŏ Kyun's active concern for the welfare of such children would cost him his life, as he was accused of complicity when in 1618 a group of them actually attempted a coup.

The public unrest that followed from the murder of Yŏnch'ang culminated in a successful coup by the Westerners in 1623 and Kwanghaegun was removed to Kanghwa and eventually banished to the distant island of Cheju, where a pipe of the recently introduced tobacco plant is said to have been his only comfort. His 28-year-old nephew Injo took his place and the pro-Ming Westerners were again the ruling party.

In the customary awards to the leaders of the coup the man who had provided the military muscle, General Yi Kwal, was disregarded and subsequently posted to the northern frontier, where he suffered the further indignity of coming under the command of a younger man. Convinced that it was his duty to protect the King from such evil men, he began a march on the capital with an army of 12,000, including a company of Japanese who, with their long swords, were particularly feared.

As the towns in his path successively capitulated there was panic in Seoul, a great many people suspected of complicity in the rebellion were hastily executed, and the court left for the old walled city of Kongju, about 80 miles to the south. Yi Kwal succeeded in occupying the capital, where he set up another royal relative as King, but he had been followed all the way down by a loyalist army under Chŏng Ch'ungsin and after a battle fought out on the hills around the capital the rebels were defeated and the King returned. The ease with which Seoul had been taken prompted a revision of its defences: new bases were built to the north of it and the mountain fortress of Namhansan-sŏng a few miles to the south, said to be an ancient stronghold of the Kings of Paekche, was reconstructed to provide a virtually impregnable place of refuge.

It would soon be needed, for the Westerners, determined to support the Ming and defy the barbarians, had given refuge to the retreating Chinese under Mao Wenlong and allowed them to use Kado, an island at the mouth of the Yalu, as the base for a counter-attack. After the death of Yi Kwal many of his followers had fled across the northern border where they now urged the Jin to restore Kwanghaegun as the rightful ruler. Seeing the neutralization of Korea as a necessary prelude to the conquest of China, they made this the pretext for an invasion in 1627. An army of 30,000 crossed the Yalu and by the time they were half-way to Seoul the court had fled to Kanghwa and a parley took place at which the Koreans agreed to abandon their active support of the Ming and accept the Ruzhen as 'elder brothers'.

Soon afterwards, in 1628, three Dutchmen turned up on the south-east coast, part of the crew of the *Ouwerkerck*, a piratical trading schooner from the Dutch East Indies. It had apparently captured a Chinese junk on its way to Xiamen and these three men had been transferred to the junk to take it to Taiwan, but a storm had driven them north, after which the Chinese had apparently recaptured their ship and put them ashore. One of them, possibly the captain, was a big red-bearded man called Jan Janse Weltevree, whose talents included some knowledge of iron founding. He was eventually put in charge of an arsenal where cannon and other experimental weapons were built. Known as Pak Yŏn, he took a Korean wife and would survive to greet the crew of a Dutch ship that would be wrecked on the coast of Cheju Island 25 years later. The other two, serving as gunners on the northern frontier, were killed in action.

By 1636, with the rule of the Ming collapsing in corruption and peasant rebellions, Nurgaci's son Abahai was proclaimed Emperor of a new dynasty, the Qing, and the Koreans were called on to acknowledge its claims, which as with the Mongols 400 years before, they refused to do. The consequences were rather similar, but this time more in the mode of farce than of tragedy, for neither the Sinified 'Manchu', as they now called themselves, nor the even more Sinified Yi dynasty Koreans had the ruthless ferocity of their medieval predecessors.

A Manchu army led by Abahai crossed the border in December to take Pyongyang and the court began a flight to Kanghwa, but an early cold spell had frozen the rivers and the invaders arrived before the King – who had already sent the ancestral tablets and the rest of his family ahead – could follow them. While some of his chief ministers, led by Ch'oe Myŏng-gil, parleyed with the Manchu he was slipped out to the great fortress of Namhansansŏng. The following night, while talks still continued, an attempt was made to smuggle him out to Kanghwa, but there was a deep frost and outside the castle gate his horse slipped on the icy slope and threw him off. He tried to walk down but he could not stay on his feet so his attendants had to seat him on a straw mat and drag him back inside.

He should have been safe enough as the steepness of the wooded hillside made the place almost impossible to storm, and its 9,000-odd defenders had muskets as against the spears and arrows of the enemy. They also had 18,000 sacks of rice, but no adequate way of dealing with the cold, which steadily grew more intense. After kneeling in the open courtyard to beseech Heaven for warmer weather the King gave his fur robe to be cut up and made into earmuffs for his guards. The rough terrain made it difficult for the Manchu to guard the entire perimeter and enabled the Koreans to make brief sallies in the night, so the Manchu put up a brushwood fence and hung it with alarm bells. After a week or two, a force of 300 Koreans, confident in the effectiveness of their muskets, set fire to the brushwood and tried to cut through the enemy lines. The Manchus kept their distance until they reached some level ground and then rode them down with their horses.

A great Korean army from the southern provinces was on its way to relieve them but they were caught in a pass as they approached the castle and dispersed by a relatively small force of cavalry. The invaders then brought up a large cannon capable of breaking up the main gates and on the fortieth day of the siege, despite the opposition of several of his senior officials, the King and the Prime Minister, Kim Yu, decided to give in.

The Qing Emperor staged a public surrender on the south bank of the river at which the King promised his assistance against the Ming and handed over the crown prince and his next two half-brothers as hostages. The youngest, Inp'yŏng, would soon be sent home but the other two would be kept until after Beijing had been taken eight years later. Three senior officials who had opposed the treaty, Hong Ik-han, Yun Chip and O Tal-je, still chose death rather than disloyalty to the Ming. They were supported by an elderly minister, Kim Sang-hŏn, who was taken with the other hostages to Manchuria and would spend three years in jail before returning to be welcomed by the Westerners and made deputy Prime Minister, an early triumph for the notorious clan of the Andong Kim.

Meanwhile, on Kanghwa the Queen and her companions awaited their fate. When the Manchu forces arrived on the other side of the water there was great alarm and Kim Sang-hŏn's elder brother, Kim Sang-yŏng, who had been put in charge of the King's ancestral tablets, shut himself up in the town's gatehouse along with his officials and one of his grandsons, and blew it all up with a keg of gunpowder, while many of the ladies of the court hanged themselves or threw themselves into the water.

At the scene of the treaty, near the village of Sŏngp'ari, the Emperor erected an eleven-foot stele to remind the Koreans that Heaven bestows frost as well as dew and they must remember the severity of its punishments as well as its benevolence to the virtuous. In the 1950s in a fit of patriotic fervour, President Syngman Rhee would order its destruction, but it would be discreetly buried and later restored. Korean prisoners of war were enrolled in special regiments to fight for the Manchus, under their 'banner' system, but many others joined loyalist forces that went north to fight with the Ming, notably General Im Kyŏng-ŏp, who had made a brave attempt to halt the Manchu at Ŭiju and would be the hero of many other losing battles before he was captured, his exploits being the subject of another early novel.

CHAPTER TWENTY-FIVE

WESTERN LEARNING

By 1644 the Qing had captured Beijing, and in the following year the crown prince Sohyŏn and his brother Pongnim, now in their early thirties, were allowed to go home. Sohyŏn, a scholarly young man, had been accompanied by a tutor from the Sejasigang-wŏn, Kim Sin-guk, who had originally favoured peace with the Manchu, while Pongnim had formerly been taught by Song Si-yŏl, a fanatical young supporter of the Ming, and Pongnim's eight years at the Manchu court do not seem to have changed his attitude.

During his brief period in Beijing Sohyŏn came under the influence of Fr Adam Schall von Bell, one of the Jesuit astronomers who had founded a Board of Calendrics in 1629 and would soon be put in charge of the Bureau of Rites. They had revised the calendar on Gregorian lines and Sohyŏn was able to take back to Korea a globe, a calendar, and more books of 'Western Learning'. He was apparently also sympathetic towards Christianity and brought back with him a small group of Chinese lay people, of whom five were eunuchs and three female attendants, making them easy to accommodate within the court.

Injo's Queen, like Sŏnjo's, had no children of her own and Sohyŏn, Pongnim and Inp'yŏng were half-brothers born to different consorts. They now found themselves caught up in an atmosphere of party strife and palace plots, and two months after his return Sohyŏn died, ostensibly of a malarial fever, though Pongnim's mother, Lady Cho, was suspected of poisoning him. The Chinese missionaries were sent home, Pongnim was adopted by the Queen, also a Cho, and after his father's death in 1649 he succeeded to the throne, with the eventual title of Hyojong.

He sent for his former tutor, Song Si-yŏl, who by this time had become the leader of the Westerners and, obsessed with opening a second front to aid the Ming, they concentrated the country's resources on a military build-up. This was meant to be secret, but Kim Cha-jŏm, the embittered leader of a Western splinter group, reported their plans to the Qing, resulting in the death of the earlier pro-Ming loyalist, General Im Kyŏng-ŏp, whom the Qing held as a prisoner, and the execution of Kim by Hyojong.

These preparations for war, including the conscription and training of a large army, went on for some years, evidently stimulating the economy but revealing inadequacies in agriculture and the tax system that would eventually lead to changes. The revision of the old lunar calendar on modern lines was delayed by the fact that to replace the Ming calendar by that of the Qing would imply, traditionally, a total change of loyalty, but in 1653, under the leadership of the gifted Prime Minister Kim Yuk, a new calendar based on the Gregorian system came into use, 70 years after southern Europe and 100 years before England.

The Dutch castaway, Weltevree, now 58 and with a long red beard, was still producing cannon and muskets at the arsenal in Seoul when in 1653 he was sent to Cheju Island to interview the 36 survivors of a Dutch ship, the *Sperwer*, shipwrecked there on its way to Nagasaki. They were accommodated in what had been the residence of the exiled Kwanghaegun while their salvaged cargo, most of it Taiwanese deerskins, was catalogued. Taken to Seoul, they were refused permission to leave the country and treated for a while rather like circus animals. Eventually, under Weltevree's supervision, they were enrolled under the military commander and issued with muskets, *hŏp'ae* and a monthly salary, but an attempt to contact a Qing envoy in Seoul led to their being banished to a remote corner of the south-west where over the next 11 years their numbers would slowly dwindle as they passed through good times and bad under various officials. In 1666 eight of them, led by Hendrik Hamel, the ship's supercargo, would escape to Japan and eventually return to Holland, where Hamel would provide the West with its first detailed account of the country. After two more years of irritable diplomatic exchanges via the Daimyo of Tshushima the remaining seven would be allowed to follow.

This period saw also Korea's first contact with Eastern Europe, as the Manchu requested their aid in repelling Cossack settlers who had reached the northern bank of the Amur and Hyojong gladly agreed as it provided an opportunity to assess the Qing defences. His war plans, which can never have had much chance of success, came to an end with his untimely death at the age of 40, and in the same year, 1659, the last Ming ruler had to take refuge in Burma.

In China, Zhu Xi's interpretation of Confucianism had been under criticism from the school of Wang Yangming, who favoured more subjective and mystical doctrines based on new readings of the ancient texts. He believed that Heaven had placed within us the pattern of moral perfection, needing only careful cultivation. Even before his writings reached them, a few Korean scholars had similar intimations, notably a sixteenth-century minister, Chang Hyŏn-gwang, who resigned at the age of 39 to wander the land with only the *Book of Changes* for company, but such views would never have anything like the influence that they had in seventeenth-century China.

At first forbidden, they would always be strongly opposed by the orthodox, deeply committed to *yehak*, the study and performance of supposedly ancient rituals as laid down in Zhu Xi's 'Guide to Family Rites' and interpreted, in Korea, by Kim Chang-saeng and his disciple, Song Si-yŏl. They took a pessimistic view of human nature and a sacramental view of the rites, insisting that only by meticulous adherence to them could barbarism be restrained and Heaven and Earth kept in harmony. As this was also the period when party strife was at its worst, disagreements about details could result in banishment or even a poisoned cup for any officials whom the King could be persuaded to condemn as 'incorrect'.

The death of Hyojong was followed by a typical controversy of this kind. The Southerners argued that his stepmother, the dowager Queen Cho, should wear mourning for three years, as if he were the elder son, as she had already done for Sohyŏn, while Song Si-yŏl and the Westerners insisted on 12 months, as required for a second son. Hyojong's 19-year-old successor, Hyŏnjong, was eventually persuaded to decide in favour of Song. Yun Hyu, one of the Southerners exiled after this defeat, was a radical of the new school, holding that the scholar must seek the truth itself, rather than any one man's interpretation of it, and claiming that in this he would have been supported not only by Zhu Xi himself, but by Confucius and Mencius as well. Song replied that there had been many evil people in the world, but never one like this, worse even than Wang Yangming.

Even within his own party there was some criticism of Song Si-yŏl's *yehak* doctrines, notably in the writings of Yun Sŏn-gŏ, and after Yun's death in 1669 his son Yun Chŭng brought the disagreement into the open and founded the Soron or 'Young Doctrine' party in contrast to the main body of the Westerners, who followed the Noron or 'Old Doctrine', In 1674 Hyŏnjong's mother died, but Dowager Queen Cho still survived and another controversy arose over how long she should mourn for her stepdaughter-in-law. Again the Westerners opted for the shorter alternative, enabling the Southerners to claim that in emphasizing Sohyŏn's seniority over Hyojong, they were casting doubt on the legitimacy of his succession, an argument that appealed to Hyŏnjong and this time the Westerners were purged and Yun Hyu came home. Even in defeat Song Si-yŏl succeeded in splitting the Southerners as they divided into two factions, Ch'ŏng and Tak, 'Clear' and 'Cloudy', over the issue of whether or not he should die. The T'ak, in favour of mercy, won, and under their leader, Hŏ Chŏk, they occupied the chief offices of state.

Hyŏnjong himself died later in the same year at the age of 33, to be succeeded by his son Sukchong, who was 13, but, as was the custom of the time, already married. Six years later, in 1680, the girl died and at about the same time there was another reversal of political fortunes. Injo's third son, Inp'yŏng, had left three sons, now in their thirties or forties, who apparently had ambitions to put the eldest of them on the throne and Hŏ Kyŏn, a son of the Prime Minister, Hŏ Chŏk, by a secondary wife, was accused by the Westerners of leading the plot. Hŏ Chŏk was compelled to resign, and drink the poisoned cup, along with Song Si-yŏl's old enemy Yun Hyu, and the Noron, again took power.

Kim Su-hang, of the Andong Kim, became Prime Minister and the new Queen that they chose for Sukchong was Inhyŏn, a 14–year old girl from the Yŏhŭng Min, the other most powerful Noron family, but by the end of 1687, with the King now 26 and the Queen 20, no pregnancy had occurred, so he was provided with a consort, Lady Chang, and within the year she had produced a son, whom the King wished to appoint as crown prince. The normal process would have been for the Queen to adopt him, but through some combination of ambition on the part of Lady Chang and of the Southerners, to whose party her family belonged, Inhyŏn was accused of plotting the death of the child and the King was persuaded to depose her. This was strongly opposed by the Noron and in the bitter controversy that followed Inhyŏn was slandered and banished and Song Si-yŏl, now 82, was himself required to drink the poisoned cup, along with Kim Su-hang. Fifteen years later, with the backing of a group of the Soron wing of the Westerners, Inhyŏn was reconciled with the King, the Soron replaced the Southerners, and Lady Chang, accused of various crimes against Inhyŏn, was herself deposed and shortly afterwards took her own life. Inhyŏn's health had also been ruined and the two women, both still in their thirties, died in the same year, 1701.

Inhyŏn became the idealized heroine of two famous novels, one of them, *Inhyŏnwanghu-jŏn*, anonymous, while the other, *Sassinamjŏng-gi*, was written by Kim Man-jung, who had been banished in 1689, with the other Noron officials, for supporting her. It is said to be the first novel to be written in *hangŭl* by a *yangban*. He wisely reset the story in Ming China, giving it a happy ending, with 'Lady Sa' restored, but he died in 1692, eight years before it actually happened. He had been born after the death of his father, the Kim Sang-yong who had died on Kanghwa while blowing up the King's ancestral tablets to save them from desecration by the Manchu, and during his exile he wrote a more famous book, to both comfort and entertain his long-widowed mother, the classic *Ku'unmong*, 'Nine Cloud Dream', a bright poetic tale that provides an elegant blend of Buddhist mysticism and Confucian refinement.

In 1712 Kim Ch'ang-jip, whose father Kim Su-hang had perished in the purge of 1689, was sent as an envoy to Beijing, taking with him one of his five younger brothers, Ch'ang-ŏp, who wrote a vivid diary of their journey through the dry, dust-laden Manchurian winter. He got on well with the cultured Emperor Kangxi, who had ruled for more than 50 years, but was still alert and active, and when the visitor mentioned his diary the Emperor said he would like to see it. This was unfortunate, as in every reference to the Manchu he had used the contemptuous ideogram *ho*, meaning 'northern barbarians', and he had to sit up all night writing an abbreviated version which the Emperor may not have found very rewarding.

Such exchanges with the Qing made the Koreans realize that, despite their feelings of superiority, the new ideas and the lively trade and industry of North China were not to be despised. From this time onwards an increasing body of scholars, particularly from the Southerners, who after the restoration of Queen Inhyŏn never again came to power, would begin to question their traditional scholastic preoccupations in the light of the scientific discoveries and the egalitarian politics that came to be associated with 'Western Learning'.

From the time of T'aejo there had been a continuing concentration of power and wealth in the great land-owning families, either royal relatives or the beneficiaries of 'Merit Land', the two groups being closely interlinked by marriages. Both were equally exempt from taxation, resulting in a steady reduction of government income and heavier burdens on the peasantry, who, in addition to what they had to give to their landlords, had to provide 'tribute' to the government. These had originally been handicrafts from the village people themselves but it had developed into the system known as Pangnap, by which certain individuals were responsible for delivering tribute goods, made by artisans, for a whole area, paid for by extracting their value in rice or cloth from the peasants. In the course of the seventeenth century, under reforms that had begun under the premiership of Kim Yuk, it was gradually replaced by the Taedongbop, a uniform tax of one per cent of the rice crop, and by 1708 this had spread to the whole country.

This income was used to supply the tribute goods through businessmen, known as *kongin*, who employed independent artisans or organized factories, and also sold the goods in the open market. It led to the much greater use of money. Injo had introduced coins made of a mixture of copper and tin, mainly as a way of paying the army or minor officials when the government's stores of rice gave out, but now genuine copper coins were minted on an ever increasing scale, and capital could be accumulated. Merchants began to organize their own transport systems with ships and river boats as well as the traditional strings of ponies. International trade developed with both Japan and China, by sea and through Manchuria, and Seoul being an inhospitable place for merchants, the old Koryŏ capital north of the river at Kaesŏng once more became an important centre for trade with China, as did also the northern border town of Ŭiju. Merchant guilds were established in these cities, and in the countryside they worked through networks of pedlars who were also organized in guilds.

To provide reservoirs and irrigation systems for wet fields and seedbeds required an input of labour that in the past only the great landlords had been able to organize but towards the end of the seventeenth century an Office of Embankment Works was set up and through the following century hundreds of reservoirs would be built. The provision of these services would often be used as an excuse for increasing taxation but there would be a steady increase in productivity and in the number of farmers who owned their own land, many of them going on to become employers of labour. There were also better ways of growing fruit, and specialized crops, chiefly ginseng, cotton and tobacco, were grown for export as well as the home market. Wealthier peasants would be able to buy their way into the ranks of the *yangban* while impoverished members of the *yangban* became farmers. The supply of family trees became a flourishing trade and over the next hundred years or so almost half the population would join the gentry.

CHAPTER TWENTY-SIX

NORTHERN LEARNING

Sukchong died in 1720 at the age of 59 and was succeeded by Kyŏngjong, son of the ill-fated Lady Chang, now 33, childless, said to be impotent, and in poor health. The Noron, now led by the one-time envoy to China, Kim Ch'ang-jip, would have preferred his younger half-brother, Yŏngjo, who had been adopted by Inwŏn, the dowager Queen. They named him as crown prince and advised Kyŏngjong that in view of his declining health he should authorize the prince to rule on his behalf. Their rivals, the Soron, took the King's side and accused them of treason and in yet another *sahwa* Kim and numerous others met their death and about 100 lesser officials were banished. It was a truly fratricidal affair, as the Soron leader, Cho T'ae-gu, who now became Prime Minister, and Cho T'ae-ch'ae, one of the four Noron ministers who had to die, were both from the same generation of the Yangju Cho. Three years later Kyŏngjong died, Yŏngjo succeeded him, and the four chief ministers of the Soron took their turn to drink the poisoned cup.

Yŏngjo, the first strong King for several generations, had seen, twice within four years, gifted men forced to die through party strife and he attempted to put the system on a more rational basis by insisting on his right to appoint the best men of whatever party on the principle of *t'angp'yŏng*, 'even handedness'. It brought the Southerners and the lesser Northerners back into contention and along with the Noron and Soron wings of the Westerners they came to be known as 'The Four Colours', though power would largely remain in the hands of the Noron.

He was a confident and enlightened ruler who reduced the burden on the peasants by halving the cloth tax that financed the army and shared out the rice tax more evenly through the Kyunyŏkpŏp or Equalized Tax Law by which all landholders paid a small percentage of the crop. One of his progressive schemes was to introduce state examinations for the over-sixties so that mature men of talent could try their hand in the bureaucracy. He rationalized many ancient practices and abolished some of the crueller methods of torturing suspects and punishing criminals, though harsh conditions, judicial torture and the practice of leaving the bodies of executed criminals to decay in the fields would continue until the close of the nineteenth century. In the matter of Neo-Confucian rites and morals he remained extremely strict and this may have contributed to the dreadful tragedy that marred his later years.

The Queen was childless and a son born to a consort having died, he then met the love of his life, Lady Sŏnhŭi, who gave him several daughters and in 1735 a son, Changjo, whom, against the wishes of the Queen, Yŏngjo immediately chose as crown prince. The child was separated from his mother at the age of 3 and put in a small palace of his own where the Queen took little interest in him and many of the palace women were hostile. At the age of 8 he was ritually married to a girl of the same age, the daughter of Hong Pong-han, a poor but brilliant scholar of 22 whom the King had already taken note of, and would eventually make his Prime Minister.

The Sejasigangwŏn was expanded to provide him with 13 full-time tutors and he grew up as a strange precocious child. His marriage was consummated at the age of 14 and Yŏngjo, himself under stress and at odds with his ministers, wanted to retire and make him regent, giving him duties that included presiding over the judicial torture of officials, with stern rebukes when he failed. He began to show increasing signs of mental instability which grew from obsessive behaviour to outbreaks of violence, and in his twenties his periods of madness were accompanied by the raping of palace women, the wanton deaths of servants and hostility to his wife and young children. His father came to realize that he had been too harsh but by now it was too late, and his spells of violent behaviour grew worse, his mother and his wife conspiring to hide them from the King.

In 1757 the Queen, Chŏngsŏng, died at 65, and after the two years of mourning Yŏngjo took as her successor Chŏngsun, a 14-year-old girl from the Kyŏngju Kim who soon came to hate the Prince. In 1761, after he had disgraced himself by repeatedly visiting houses of ill-repute, the Prime Minister, Yi Ch'ŏn-bo, loyally accepted responsibility and killed himself, as two lesser ministers had done already after previous lapses.

Worse crimes followed and the King was persuaded that the Prince was plotting against him and he finally decided that he must die. It was accepted that, after consultation, the head of a *yangban* clan could impose the death penalty on any member who had disgraced them, and suffocation was the usual means for these discreet executions. The Prince was summoned to appear before his father, a heavy wooden chest used for storing rice was brought from the kitchens, he was put into it, layers of straw were added to deaden the sound of his cries, and it was left for eight days so that nature might take its course. The King personally prepared his body for burial, comforted in his distress by the Prince's mother. The Princess left the palace with the dutiful intention of killing herself but was persuaded not to by the King, for the sake of her 10-year-old son, Chŏngjo.

The details of the incident, known as the Imo'ok or 'Shutting-up of 62', were removed from the records and only the widow's *Hanjungnok*, a one-sided but deeply moving personal memoir, preserves them. The main party, the Noron, had already split between the Si'p'a, or 'Time-servers', who had sided with the Prince and were backed by the Southerners, while the Pyŏkp'a, 'The Bigots', who had connections with the Queen, backed an alternative candidate as crown prince and had favoured his death. They were now similarly divided as to whether, as Yŏngjo wished, the Prince's son, Chŏngjo, should be the new crown prince. The second Queen, Chŏngsun, remained childless, and at the King's insistence Chŏngjo was confirmed as crown prince. Another member of the Hong family, Hong Kug-yŏng, was appointed as his tutor and went on to play a leading part in securing his succession to the throne in the power struggle that followed the death of Yŏngjo in 1776.

Chŏngjo, now 25, was greatly attached to Hong Kug-yŏng, himself only 28, who now, as Royal Secretary, led a purge against those who had favoured the Prince's death and tried to establish his own family as the *sedojip*, only to perish a year or two later, at the age of 33, in a plot against the dowager Queen. Chŏngjo then did his best to restore his grandfather's principle of *t'angp'yŏng*. He had been ten years old when his father died and, deeply affected by it, he would do much to restore his reputation, and that of his mother, who had been reduced to the level of a commoner. Both had their ranks restored and at the close of the nineteenth century King Kojong, who traced his ancestry to a son of one of the Prince's consorts, would posthumously award him the royal title of 'Changjo', so that he came to be known as 'The Rice-Box King'.

As befitted a child of the eighteenth century, Chŏngjo had a great enthusiasm for science and technology, setting up his own research institute, the Kyujanggak, within the palace grounds where like Sejong he could employ scholars on various projects. Stimulated by frequent exchanges with China, there were further advances in geography and map-making and a new enthusiasm for investigating and recording every aspect of national life. The new attitude towards history reflected in the essays of Yi Su-gwang had been continued by Yi Ik, whose father, an envoy to China, had built up an impressive library of 'Western Learning', and by his disciple An Chŏng-bok. They had learned from the Qing historians the need for 'evidence' and a critical approach to historical sources, and a younger follower, Yi Tong-mu, went to China specifically to study their methods. This historical research also served to arouse a new sense of national identity, reviving memories of the days when Koguryŏ had controlled Manchuria and held out against the military might of the Sui and the Tang. Any thoughts of regaining this territory would be pre-empted by Russia, and then by Japan, and not until the latter half of the twentieth century would they revive.

These new perspectives on history also raised deeper questions of social justice, reinforced by the somewhat idealized picture of Christian civilization presented by the Jesuits. Were not the King and his officials intended to be the servants of the people? Should not the land belong to those who tilled it? Yu Hyŏng-wŏn, another seventeenth-century follower of Yi Su-gwang, had proposed a return to the ancient Chinese 'Well-Field System', so-called because the ideogram for a well is like the grid that children use to play Noughts and Crosses, providing eight paddies for eight families, and a communal one in the centre to grow rice for the government. This theme was further pursued by Yi Ik, who held that scholars should learn to use the plough and farmers be encouraged to study, and that the sole purpose of education was the welfare of the people. These ideas, while they led a few members of the élite to ignore the examinations and even to resign from office, had a stronger appeal to those like the Southerners who rarely gained high office, and it was mainly among these groups that Catholicism began to spread.

Yi Ik himself never became a convert and An Chŏng-bok was a thorough sceptic, but around 1779 a group of their younger disciples, mostly relatives, from the same area of Kwangju County on the south-east side of Seoul, formed a Society for the Study of Western Doctrine, and after they had been joined by Yi Pyŏk, who through reading Ricci had independently come to believe, they met regularly at Ch'ŏnjinam, a disused Buddhist hermitage. In 1784 one of them, Yi Sŭng-hun, accompanied his father on a mission to Beijing, where he was baptized as 'Peter' and given a quantity of prayer books, scripture readings and devotional material. He baptized Yi Pyŏk, who became an eloquent advocate of the new movement, and it now spread rapidly, leading them to appoint their own priests and bishops. The original group included three gifted brothers, of whom the youngest, Chŏng Yag-yong, was a universal genius and a valued contributor to the Kyujanggak. He would be the chief architect for a grandiose project to rebuilt the walls of Suwŏn, in memory of Chŏngjo's father, and Chŏng also designed a system of cranes and multiple pulleys to speed up their construction.

In later life Chŏng Yag-yong's main concerns would be better farming methods, better local government, and a better life for the farmers themselves. He pointed out that in earlier times rulers had been chosen by the people, and replaced if they did not serve them well, and only through corruption had it become 'politics from above' rather than 'politics from below'. The cultivation of rice, with its need for reservoirs and systems of irrigation, required communal effort, as did the education of the farmers' children, and he advocated a collective system based on village units. His best-known work, *Mokminsimsŏ*, 'The Nurture of the People', is said to have been the bedside book of the Vietnamese leader Ho Chi-minh and has probably had more influence on the politics of Eastern Asia than the works of Karl Marx.

Catholicism thus came to Korea in conditions very different from those of Japan two centuries before. There, it had been heroic Western monks preaching to feudal princes, while here it was an indigenous group looking for spiritual enlightenment and social justice and welcoming it as 'Liberation Theology'. If this was, to some degree, a misunderstanding, it was a potentially fruitful one made possible by Ricci's insistence on interpreting the gospel in terms of Chinese culture, accepting the Confucian concept of 'Heaven' and approving the practice of piety towards one's ancestors. The irony was that even before the first Korean convert had been baptized the Church had already condemned every aspect of Ricci's 'indigenization', and the Jesuits themselves had been temporarily disbanded. There was thus a crisis for the Catholic group in Korea when they discovered that their election of priests and bishops from among their own number was invalid, and that their traditional burial rites and mourning customs were to be totally forbidden.

The mourning rites and the offerings to the dead which were regarded as the *yangban*'s primary social duty, and observed with great solemnity and emotional commitment, also served to distinguish them from the lower classes, so that the new religion, by both forbidding the rites and welcoming the outcast as 'children of God' seemed both blasphemous and subversive. When in 1785 it was discovered that a group was meeting inside the city walls of Seoul, in the area where the Catholic cathedral now stands, it had to be outlawed, but the Prime Minister, Ch'ae Che-gong, was a Southerner with Christian friends and relatives so that up to the end of Chŏngjo's reign only instances of deliberate and public rejection of the burial customs would be punished.

In contrast to these idealistic adherents of 'Western Learning', a newer, more urban-minded Silhak tendency, known as 'Northern Learning', was taking its inspiration from China's own new-found enthusiasm for commerce, finance and industry. An early pioneer was Yu Su-wŏn, who as a close relative of one of the four Soron leaders overthrown at the time of Yŏngjo's accession in 1724, had spent eight years in prison, during which he had written an influential book advocating wide-ranging reforms that included equality of opportunity and government assistance to start up new businesses, with better transport, more shops, and so on. In the next generation, several travellers to Beijing, notably Pak Chi-wŏn and his disciple, Pak Che-ga, combined lengthy descriptions of developments in China with far-reaching proposals for reform and the use of new technology.

These were typical of the men who gathered around Chŏngjo at the Kyujangkak, which by this time had replaced the Pibyŏnsa as the nerve centre of government, and would remain influential until its absorption into a revived Ŭijŏngbu 100 years later. Countless books appeared and there would be further improvements in irrigation and agriculture, better roads, along with more bridges and wheeled vehicles, and the use of bricks for building.

Although the Jesuit astronomers in Beijing had enlisted the aid of Kepler to complete their Gregorian calendar and perfect their predictions of eclipses, they had not risked their credibility, or Papal wrath, by claiming that the earth moved, and the Koreans appear to have developed their own first theories in this direction. In his account of his trip to Beijing in 1780 Pak Chi-wŏn mentions that the seventeenth-century astrologer Kim Sŏng-mun had claimed that the sun, the moon and the earth were all spheres engaged in mutual circulation and that more recently Hong Tae-yong had astonished the Chinese with a celestial globe that demonstrated his belief in the daily rotation of the earth.

In 1795 a Chinese priest, Fr Zhou Wenmo, was smuggled into the country and Catholic believers were soon to be numbered in their thousands. They were discreet, and the majority were from ranks of society not bound by the ritual laws, but the rapid growth of this subversive foreign cult aroused great alarm and outrage in the ranks of the gentry, the extent of which does not seem to have been fully appreciated by the King. He had always favoured the Si'p'a and their Southern allies because of their support for his father, and in his later years he relied heavily on the Catholic sympathizer, Ch'ae Che-gong, whom he had allowed to become successively Third

Minister, Second Minister and finally Prime Minister, without appointing anyone to the ranks he had vacated, so that he became a virtual autocrat. Ch'ae died in 1799 followed by the death of Chŏngjo himself in the following year.

His son Sunjo was only 11, and Yŏngjo's widow, Chŏngsun, as the senior dowager Queen, became regent. She was associated with the rival party, the Pyŏkp'a, now dominated by the P'ungyang Cho clan, and they saw the Catholic issue as a chance to restore their fortunes. The tolerance they had enjoyed under Chŏngjo had no legal basis and in 1801 the laws were vigorously enforced. Six of the leaders were arrested, and, refusing under torture to recant, were executed. They included Yi Sŭng-hun, the first to be baptized, and Chŏng Yag-yong's elder brother Yak-chong, the leader of the laity. Five women who refused under torture to betray the whereabouts of the Chinese priest died with them, and he also was eventually caught and killed. Another Chŏng brother, Yak-chŏn, was banished to the distant Yellow Sea island of Hŭksan where he would keep himself occupied with a scientific study of its many and varied forms of marine life and publish a learned work that covers 155 species. Yag-yong was also banished for 17 years, during which he produced *Morkminsimsŏ* and numerous other works, including accounts of how the Church had begun among his friends and relatives at Ch'ŏnjinam.

They had been closely linked by family connections, and Hwang Sa-yŏng, who had married one of the Chŏng daughters, had become an interpreter to the Chinese priest. After the priest's death he retreated to a cave and wrote a long letter to the Bishop in Beijing asking him to summon a Christian army from the West to come to their aid. This 13,000-word message, written in tiny ideograms on a tightly rolled piece of silk, was, unfortunately, intercepted by the government. It confirmed their worst fears and in a renewed persecution there would be about 300 martyrs. The letter itself, buried in government files, would be recovered in 1925 and is now preserved in the Vatican.

In the following year, 1802, the dowager Queen, Chŏngsun, died and with the end of her regency the Cho family lost some of its influence. Before his death Ch'ae Che-gong had appointed as tutor to Sunjo, then crown prince, a talented, and evidently ambitious, scholar from the Andong Kim, Kim Cho-sun, who by providing his own daughter as Sunjo's Queen was able to keep the King under his influence for the whole of his reign and to bring more and more of his own relatives into positions of power. He was opposed to the persecution of Catholics, though local arrests and executions would continue.

At about this time there were droughts and famines and growing discontent among the farming population, particularly in the remoter areas that had few friends at court to air their grievances. In 1804 a complaint about conditions in P'yŏngan, in the far north, was affixed by night to the four city gates of Seoul, a serious offence which implied a serious threat. Nothing was done and a few years later there was a well-prepared rebellion there led by a charismatic member of the *yangban*, Hong Kyŏng-nae, who came to be credited with miraculous powers. It was widely supported by the local gentry as well as the public and although he was eventually killed in battle the rebellion took five months to quell and would serve as an inspiration for further uprisings.

Sunjo had a son, Ikchong, who in 1819, at the age of 11 was married to a girl from the Cho family. Sunjo had poor health and in 1827, when he was 37, he handed over the presidency of the State Council to his son, then 18. Ikchong attempted to have officials appointed according to their talents, but he died before his father, and the Andong Kim continued to extend their power, though Ikchong's widow, Dowager Cho, a powerful personality, would haunt the court for another 50 years or so to fight for their rivals, the P'ungyang Cho.

For several decades the magnates of the Andong Kim would use their powers of patronage to sell offices, and the holders, having bought them with borrowed money, had to recoup it, either through their intermediaries or directly themselves, by the exacting of taxes. The main burden fell on the farmers, many of whom built up debts until they lost their land, and the change to a money economy, and compound interest, made the effects more drastic than in earlier times. And apart from these growing internal problems the Great Powers of the world outside were now about to make their presence felt.

CHAPTER TWENTY-SEVEN

WAR WITH THE WEST

NINETEENTH-CENTURY Western maps of Korea show a coastline littered with the names of European princes, politicians and seamen, evidence of expeditions that, largely unknown to its inhabitants, had been charting its waters: the Great Powers were sizing-up their prey. With Russia's pioneers moving towards the shores of the Pacific, some of the capes and bays down the eastern side would be given Russian names, but not before La Perouse in 1787 had left a sprinkling of memorials to France. The large island in the Eastern Sea that in the year 512 Isabu of Silla had peacefully subdued with his wooden lions was given the name of the French astronomer Dagelet, only to have it changed to 'Matshushima' by the Japanese and not until 1950 would it be marked on our maps as 'Ullŭngdo'.

A more detailed survey of the east coast was made in 1797 by Captain Broughton of the British Navy who called the harbour at Wŏnsan 'Broughton Bay' and the water between Pusan and Tsushima 'Broughton Strait'. The west coast was charted in 1816 by two more naval vessels under Commander Basil Hall, who named various islands, capes and bays after himself, his relatives, and the children of the Queen. He had friendly and sometimes quite hilarious contacts with the local people, who were obviously torn between curiosity, Korean traditions of hospitality, and fear of execution if the bureaucrats found out. Hall had some tinted drawings made of them which he showed to Napoleon Bonaparte in the course of a courtesy call at St Helena on his way home and used to illustrate his popular *Account of a Voyage of Discovery to the West Coast of Corea and the Great Loo-Choo Island* which was published in 1818 and served to introduce the country to the English-speaking world.

In 1832 the East India Company's *Lord Amherst* arrived off the west coast in quest of trade. Turned away by apprehensive officials near the mouth of the Han they moved down to the mouth of the Kŭm, once the outlet of Paekche's capital, which Hall had marked as 'Basil's Bay', and the local people sent their request on to Seoul, where it was refused. They had on board a wandering German evangelist, Charles Gutzlaff, who went ashore to distribute leaflets in Chinese and to plant some potatoes. Neither of his gifts was as novel as he may have imagined – he was visited by some Catholics, who did not know quite what to make of him, while potatoes had been introduced from China about ten years before but were not as well liked as the sweet ones, which had arrived much earlier via Japan. As with Hall, the people knew that to encourage the intruders was to put their own lives at risk.

When Sunjo died in 1834 his grandson Hŏnjong was only 10 so that his mother, Dowager Cho, became regent, which meant a return to power of the P'ungyang Cho and their anti-Catholic Pyŏkp'a associates. In China, also, Catholics were now being persecuted and in 1831 the Vatican had separated Korea from the diocese of Beijing, though Chinese priests would continue to minister there for some years. It was allotted to the Paris Missionary Society which was already working in the French dependencies in South-East Asia. The first Vicar-Apostolic, Fr Brugière, died on the way, in Manchuria, and it was not until January 1836 that his comrade, Fr Maubant, crossed the frozen Yalu and was smuggled into Seoul, to be followed by Fr Chastan and in 1838, by Bishop Imbert, the new Vicar Apostolic. Their presence meant mortal danger for themselves and for everyone associated with them. They had to be kept hidden, and when they moved they were disguised as mourners, wearing hemp and a hat like an inverted basket intended to conceal the mourner's face, or carried in the curtained palanquins used by upper-class women.

That they and their followers were prepared to take such risks was in itself a recommendation for their beliefs, which won the allegiance of many of the literati as well as of the poor and the dispossessed. From early times they became associated with the small pottery villages that were scattered through the hills, people regarded as outcasts, who were happy to find themselves 'children of God', and would provide places of refuge in times of persecution. The integrity of these converts can be judged from the case of Chŏng Kuk-bo, who was arrested in the new persecution of 1839 which followed the death of Sunjo. Having recanted under torture, he was released, only to return the next day and insist on being rearrested, after which he died from the beating that he received.

Bishop Imbert and his two companions voluntarily surrendered themselves in the hope that this would appease the government, but they, along with 200 others who had been rounded up in house-to-house searches, were tortured and executed. A few young Koreans had been sent to study at the seminary at Macao and in 1844 the first to be ordained, Kim Tae-gŏn, was smuggled ashore from Shanghai, as also was another Bishop, Ferréol, and another French priest, but two years later Fr Kim would be caught in a further attempt to contact Shanghai and condemned to death.

Another British request for trade was made in 1845 when Edward Belcher, in command of *HMS Samarang*, came ashore on Cheju Island, but he was probably more interested in Komundo, a group of three islands with a fine harbour about halfway between Cheju and the coast, which he put on the map as 'Port Hamilton'. The request for trade was again turned down, though not without some lively protests from Silhak scholars keen to encourage it. The court may have been hostile to subversive doctrines and indifferent to trade, but at least shipwrecked sailors were now treated with more civility. In 1855, for instance, when four Americans from a whaler came ashore on the east coast in a small boat they were fed, reclothed, and returned via Beijing and Shanghai, and they subsequently contrasted their rough treatment in China with the kindness of the Koreans. The official who dealt with them compiled the first Korean-English dictionary, which was entitled *The American System of Writing*.

In 1849 Hŏnjong died, at the age of 20, with no named successor, and few near relatives. The choice lay with his grandmother, of the Andong Kim clan, who had the advantage of both rank and seniority over his Cho-clan mother, and Kim Mun-gŭn, now the head of the clan, was already a powerful man. They chose Ch'ŏlchong, a 19-year-old great-grandson of the 'Rice Box King'. He had been banished to Kanghwa Island with the rest of his family in 1844 after his elder brother had become involved with rebels, and that was where he was ploughing their patch of paddy when Prime Minister Chŏng Wŏn-yong arrived to take him to the palace. His father was posthumously promoted to royal rank, he was married to Kim Mun-gŭn's daughter, and Kim himself was made *Puwŏngun*, a kind of life-dukedom often bestowed on royal fathers-in-law.

While the King, known affectionately as 'The Young Master from Kanghwa', enjoyed the pleasures of the court, the Kim family residence in Seoul became, under an outward form of pious Confucian etiquette, the centre of a web of influence that was, in effect, an employment agency that controlled all government appointments. Gale's *History* offers a contemporary picture:

Before the great gate were wheeled carts and horses no end, servants and followers galore. Some sat gazing dreamily into space, some sound asleep, some were fighting in a death grip. It was a greater confusion than any marketplace ever saw. Within was worse still, the inner court all a hubbub: a theatre could not equal it. Every schemer in the land was there: a stream flowed in from morning till night without interruption. Some sat and waited the day through, some came twice in the same morning. People cast aside the duties of their distant country home and came up to spend years in this outer court of the capital.

The Catholics were largely left in peace and their numbers rose to 20,000 or more but the same period saw also the rise of a rival cult that its founder Ch'oe Che-u, deliberately called Tonghak, 'Eastern Learning', to emphasize his hostility to the West. It was a heady mixture of magical beliefs from Tantric Buddhism, revolutionary brotherhood and hostility to foreigners. While Catholicism continued to spread among those prepared to suffer in patience, the Tonghak would appeal to the more militant and provide the leadership for local protests.

In 1862 there was an uprising in the southern town of Chinju provoked by a series of extortions by the provincial military commander Paek Nak-sin in which the city hall and granaries were surrounded by rebels with bamboo spears and burnt to the ground with the officials inside them. It spread to other towns and to Cheju, and a well-respected official, Cho Tu-sun, was sent as special inspector. He punished or dismissed the officials responsible for the extortions, but he also arrested and executed the leaders of the uprisings, and popular indignation was not appeased.

Originally known as the Chinju'ran, it would spread far enough to become the Samnamran, the 'Samnam' being the three great rice-growing provinces of the south, Kyŏngsang, Chŏlla and Ch'unch'ŏng. It would also be known as the Samchŏng'ran, the 'Samchŏng' being the three government systems by which, at every level, the farmers were fleeced – the land tax, levied on the rice crop, the cloth tax payable by every male as a substitute for military service, and the hwan'gok, the system by which rice was put into government stores at harvest to be distributed in the spring when food was short but now usually done the other way round – lent in the spring at exorbitant rates of interest to be repaid at harvest.

The riots, and the death of Kim Mun-gŭn in the following year, did nothing to shake the power of the clan and the Prime Minister, Kim Chwa-gŭn, along with his brother Kim Hŭng-gŭn and his son Kim Byŏng-gi still had the young King in their hands. Ch'ŏlchong had not yet produced an heir, but was doing his best – from various palace women he had fathered 11 children, but with the exception of one girl, all had died in infancy. Then, suddenly, in 1864, he himself died, at the age of 33. The Kims were caught unawares – they were ready to fill every vacancy in the country except this one, while their rivals, the Cho, were well prepared. Dowager Cho, Ikchong's widow, had adopted the charming 11-year-old second son of Yi Ha-ŭng, another great-grandson of the 'The Rice Box King'. She was now the senior Queen, and entitled by tradition to nominate him as King. The Kims reluctantly agreed, not expecting the boy or his elderly stepmother to interfere with their regime. The boy was hastily fetched from flying his kite outside his large but crumbling family home to become King Kojong, his father being given, as a formality, the princely title of 'Taewŏngun.'

Before making a deal with Dowager Cho, the boy's father had approached the Kims, but they had seen no need for another beggarly pretender to the throne and had dismissed him with contempt. He was known as a gambler and a drinking man, but this was a mask that concealed a strength of character unmatched since the founders of the dynasty. A contemporary Western observer described him as 'about five feet six inches tall, erect and vigorous, with grey, wonderfully bright eyes', who 'looked what he was, a real leader of men'. When Queen Cho told her chief ministers, two of whom were Kims, that she had appointed him as regent, they protested that it was unconstitutional, but she declined to discuss it with them. The Kims were well experienced at ritualized corruption but they had no stomach for a palace revolution, and anyway they could afford to pay the new regent's gambling expenses, if that was what he required, so the next morning they sent Kim Byŏng-gi to pay their respects to him.

Meanwhile, the Cho clan expected that now it was their turn, but no, for the first time since the death of Yŏngjo the country had a leader determined to choose his own ministers, though like Yŏngjo, he also knew that the great clans could not just be ignored, they had to be balanced. After naming the well-respected Cho Tu-sun as Prime Minister he appeased the Andong Kim by appointing Kim Byŏng-hak as second minister with Yi Ŭi-ik as third and another Kim as head of the Board of Revenue. As a resolute, astute and incorruptible leader he might have been, at any earlier period, the country's saviour, but now it was too late. Ignorant of the world outside, he saw China as the centre of civilization, the Westerners as cowardly pirates and the Japanese as half-educated barbarians, which was, whatever its element of justice, a fatal misjudgment.

As far as the social unrest at home was concerned, he would support Cho Tu-sun's simple policy of purging corrupt officials and cutting off the heads of rebellious peasants. He was also hostile to the influential provincial colleges, the *sŏwŏn*, centres of clan influence that undermined the authority of local government, and he had most of them closed down, a move which made him many enemies.

By this time the Tonghak had become a national movement, proclaiming that, like Silla and Koryŏ before it, the present dynasty had come to the end of its allotted 500 years. Its founder, Ch'oe Che-u, was arrested, along with 20 of his disciples, and in 1864 he was executed. After his martyrdom, under the leadership of Ch'oe Si-hyŏng, the movement went underground, and scriptures began to appear, and hymns proclaiming that the New Age was coming to birth. The Taewŏngun had his own agenda for a new age: the great palace that T'aejo had built on rising ground at the centre of Seoul had lain in ruins since the Japanese retreat in 1593, a symbol of the country's decline. He would rebuild it on a grander scale. If the treasury did not have the funds for it, more coins would be minted and the wealthy would be squeezed for 'voluntary' contributions.

Meanwhile, the Western powers were already beginning to make their presence felt. The Japanese agreement with America had passed almost unnoticed, as had the arrival of the Russians in Manchuria, but Western aggressiveness in China, and particularly the Anglo-French march on Beijing in 1860, raised Korean fears to a new level. There were now about a dozen French missionaries in the country, some of them, after ten years or more, thoroughly at home with its language and customs. In 1864, at the behest of merchants looking for timber concessions, Russian officials crossed the Tumen and reached the garrison town of Kyŏnghŭng where they presented a request for trade. This was routinely rejected without arousing much concern, but there was more alarm when, in 1866, a Russian flotilla anchored in the harbour at Wŏnsan with a further demand. Some Catholic laymen, led by Nam Chong-sam, saw it as a chance to gain acceptance for the missionaries by proposing as a countermeasure an alliance with the French, which Berneux, their Bishop, offered to negotiate.

Up to this point the Taewŏngun had not concerned himself with the Catholics, who had long had unobtrusive members in the court, including his own son's nanny, and later, unknown to him, his own wife, but this proposal aroused all the old fear of them as the agents of a foreign power. Another nation-wide persecution of Catholics was begun and would run on for several years, resulting in at least 8,000 deaths. The Bishop and eight other missionaries were arrested and after refusing to deny their faith or willingly to leave the country, were executed. They included Fr Pourthie, who had been working for years on a dictionary and grammar of the language, which was produced as evidence of his guilt and then destroyed.

In the same year, 1866, two unsuccessful attempts at trade were made by a British ship chartered by a German merchant from Shanghai, Ernst Oppert, while in June the crew of an American ship wrecked on the coast were carefully escorted across the Yalu with their belongings to return via China. Then in July the *General Sherman*, a large armed trading vessel from Shanghai, made its way up the Taedong River towards Pyongyang in a more forceful attempt to open trade. It so happened that the governor of the city was Pak Kyu-su, a son of the pioneer of Northern Learning, Pak Chi-wŏn, and a leading advocate of foreign trade. He was now about to see his dream turn into a nightmare. The Taewŏngun's isolationist policy forced him to refuse their request for trade. He warned them not to come any further up the river, but offered to provide them with any provisions they might need.

The ship's captain ignored the warning and took advantage of an exceptional flood tide to sail up to the city walls with the result that when it receded the ship was caught on a shoal. The Taewŏngun sent orders that it was to depart at once or be destroyed. The official who had been acting as intermediary was seized as a hostage by the frightened crew and shots were exchanged. The ship's powerful guns and the crew's modern rifles terrified the townspeople and kept their attackers at bay for several days, a number of people being killed. A venerable 'turtle boat' was dragged out to fire at it, to no effect, so eventually a chain of small boats loaded with burning firewood was floated downstream and the ship was burned to the waterline. Those who escaped to the shore were instantly beaten to death by the angry crowds. Apart from three American officers, most of its company was Chinese, but included, as interpreter, a Welsh evangelist, the Revd R. S. Thomas, who had brought some Chinese Bibles and would be counted as the first Protestant martyr. As there were no survivors it would be a long time before their fate was known to the outside world.

Meanwhile, Fr Felix Ridel, one of three French priests who had been smuggled out of the country, contacted the French minister in China and they invited the Americans to join a punitive naval expedition. The Americans declined, so it was left to Admiral Pierre Roze, the commander of their Asiatic Squadron, which had a base just across the water at Yantai. He made a preliminary reconnaissance of the mouth of the Han, during which he returned the fire of some forts and went on to scare the citizens of Seoul, and later came back with seven ships and a force of 600 marines. The French minister in Beijing, Bellonet, was heard to say that they were about to 'conquer

Korea'. The Taewŏngun had notice of it but found that, as when threatened by Japan 250 years before, there were very few officers capable of mounting a horse and most of their men existed only on paper. He had some larger cannon installed in the forts on Kanghwa Island and strengthened its musketeers with a core of experienced tiger hunters. They also sank some ships across the mouth of the river, as most of their traffic came through the coastal port at Inchŏn.

The French marines were put ashore at the southern tip of Kanghwa where they lost some men in a foolhardy attempt to take the fortified hill top above the monastery of Chŏndŭngsa. The next day they moved on to the main town at the northern end of the island which they looted and burned. A temple bell proved too heavy and had to be dropped on the way, but they got away with some hundreds of books to provide their National Library with Europe's first Korean collection. It included a copy of *Pulcho Chikchi Simch'e Yojŏl*, a treatise on Zen published in 1377, the earliest extant example of printing with moveable type. Another detachment that had attacked the fort at Munsusan on the mainland was also driven off, and the Taewŏngun was able to send an account of his victories to the court in Beijing. It served further to justify the persecution of the Catholics, which continued.

In the same year Kojong, now 14, was married to a niece of the Taewŏngun's wife, who came from the Yŏhŭng Min clan, as had the famous Queen Inhyŏn. Apart from being attractive and intelligent the girl had the advantage, from the Taewŏngun's point of view, of being the daughter of a poor widow who, as his niece, would, he thought, be completely under his control. His position as regent naturally implied that when Kojong reached the age of discretion he would assume power, but he was a quiet good-natured young man and his father might have kept the reins in his own hands indefinitely if he had been less thoughtless and arrogant in his treatment of the Queen. Her position would never be secure until she had given birth to an heir, and unfortunately for her, at the time of their marriage the young King was already in love with Lady I, a young palace attendant with whom he preferred to spend his nights, and by whom he soon had a son. The Taewŏngun, perhaps realizing the advantages of an heir to the throne who had no aristocratic connections, moved with unprecedented haste to have the child confirmed as crown prince, threatening the young Queen with the same cruel fate as her ancestor Inhyŏn, but she knew that story, and would show that she had learned something from it.

By the end of the year 1866 the American minister in Beijing had failed to elicit any details about the fate of the *General Sherman*, so a warship under the command of R. W. Shufeldt was sent to Pyongyang, but it was now January 1867 and fear of being trapped by the ice forced him to leave before a reply had arrived from Seoul. Another ship sent in 1868 could get no more than a confirmation that there had been no survivors. The next attempt to open up the country came in the same year with characters and a plot worthy of a Victorian story for boys. The German villain, Ernst Oppert, appears again, accompanied by a French priest, Fr Féron, who knew enough about the country to realize the importance of the ancestral grave. The plan was, with the aid of some Catholic laymen, to steal the bones of the Taewŏngun's father, whose tomb lay near the shore of the Asan Gulf, and use them as a bargaining counter against a trade agreement and recognition of the Catholic faith. They anchored offshore, rowed up the Sapkyŏ River in a whaleboat, left some men to occupy the district office, and marched on to the hillside tomb armed with four spades. It was a large burial mound with a cist of granite slabs, and as they had to be back on the ship by eight in the evening or be stranded by the tide, they had not made much impression on it by the time they had to leave.

In 1871 five American warships arrived at the same isolated spot, the Asan Gulf, with their minister in Beijing, Frederick F. Low, his aim being to claim compensation for the loss of the *General Sherman* and to persuade the Koreans to open their ports. A group of officials was sent from Seoul to meet them but Low demanded the appearance of a minister with authority to negotiate, which they declined to provide. The American fleet moved north towards the mouth of the Han and sent a vessel to take soundings in the narrow strait between Kanghwa Island and the mainland. The defences of the island had been considerably improved after the earlier attack by the French and they were fired on by the two shore batteries on that side, Ch'ojijin and Kwangsŏngjin, under the command of O Chae-yŏn. A force of 1,200 marines was landed to overrun them. The defenders had little in the way of firearms but fought desperately, with heavy losses, while the Americans, after silencing the cannon, withdrew with 13 wounded and three dead. A further attempt to land at Kapkot, just below the island's main town, met such heavy resistance that it was abandoned and the fleet returned to China. The Taewŏngun had fought his wars with the Western barbarians and he had won.

CHAPTER TWENTY-EIGHT

OPENING THE DOORS

ABANDONED by her father-in-law after the birth of a son to Lady I, the young Queen concentrated on winning the affection of her spoilt but kindly husband and of the still influential Dowager Cho. She succeeded in finding a good post for her 40-year-old cousin, Min Sŭng-ho, whom her father, before his death, had adopted as his son, and they began to recruit other talented members of their clan. Then, having won the King from Lady I, she gave birth to a son of her own. The Taewŏngun called to congratulate her and offered a present of rare mountain ginseng for the health of the baby, which immediately took ill and died. Infant mortality was high but the Queen inevitably suspected her father-in-law and there would grow up between them an implacable hatred.

The Taewŏngun was contemptuous of the new-style Japan and refused to accept the credentials of the envoys they sent in 1870, as they were not presented in the traditional way. When they came again in 1872 it was even more in the modern manner, with two British-built warships, but they were not allowed to proceed to Seoul and after a long wait, returned in fury. There was strong pressure from the samurai for an immediate invasion, but their leaders felt that they were not yet ready to challenge the Chinese and appeased the samurai by attacks on Taiwan and the Riukiu Islands.

However low his opinion of the Western barbarians, the Taewŏngun could not ignore the destructive power of their technology and he set up a new department to test and produce the necessary defences. They included bigger naval guns, a charcoal-fired warship, bulletproof vests and helmets and a crane-winged flying boat. In view of the country's lack of flat dry land and its concern with coastal defence, the aircraft was a far-sighted project. If it had left the water, it would have beaten the Wright brothers by 30 years, but the country lacked the necessary minimum of scientific and industrial resources.

By 1872 Kojong was 20 years of age and, in theory at least, ready to replace the Regent, while the Queen's clan, led by Min Sŭng-ho, had managed to push about 40 of their members into influential positions. The Taewŏngun had made many enemies among the literati by his closure of the *sŏwŏn* and their spokesman, a fiery junior minister called Ch'oe Ik-hyŏn, offered an impeachment summarizing the Taewŏngun's evil deeds – the impoverishment of the people for the sake of the new palace, the selling of honours and offices, the closure of the Confucian academies, and his failure to prevent the continuous intrusion of foreign ships. He followed it with a memorial in which he urged the King, in view of his father's venerable age, to follow the path of filial piety and allow him to pass his declining years in peaceful retirement.

The object of their concern was a vigorous man of 50 at the height of his powers, with enormous popular support in the capital. There was such a storm of protest that Ch'oe Ik-hyŏn's life was in danger and he had to be temporarily 'exiled' to Cheju Island, but under pressure from the Queen the Chief Ministers accepted his proposals and proclaimed that the King would now take charge of the country's affairs. The Taewŏngun retreated in fury to his country estate at Yangju and summoned his cronies for a council of war. The chief object of his hatred was Min Sŭng-ho, under whose influence Yi Yu-wŏn, the former puppet Prime Minister under the Andong Kim, was reappointed, along with another of his enemies, the former governor of Pyongyang, Pak Kyu-su, who favoured dealings with the Westerners and even with the Japanese. One evening early in 1874 a monk delivered a parcel to Min Sŭng-ho's house, which exploded when he opened it, and the Regent's name was the one he uttered as he died. His 9-year-old only son and his nanny were also killed, and the family adopted a 14-year-old cousin, Min Yŏng-ik, to take his place as future head of the clan.

The new government restored the status of the provincial *sŏwŏn* while in response to the reformers they extended to commoners various *yangban* privileges in dress and behaviour. When a further request for trade was rebuffed in 1875 the Japanese decided to do what the Americans had done to them, they sent warships, one of which landed troops and bombarded a fort on Kanghwa, and on the way home they also made an attack on the harbour at Pusan, after which they issued a report that accused the Koreans of firing on peaceful ships. Soon afterwards they sent Kuroda Kiyotaka as a plenipotentiary minister with a larger force of ships, including troop transports, to demand negotiations. On the advice of Pak Kyu-su, the only one of his chief ministers who had much knowledge of the outside world, the King agreed and in February 1876 the Treaty of Kanghwa was signed on Kapkot point where, five years before, the Americans had been repulsed and where, in 1893, a retired British naval officer would establish, too late, a naval academy.

It gave to the Japanese the various rights and extraterritorial privileges that the Western powers had initially exacted from them, but it also laid great emphasis on the country's full autonomy, as they wanted to break its ancient ties with China. This respect for China, which for centuries had been little more than a polite formality, would now become important to the conservatives in both countries as an insurance against the growing power of Japan, while the progressives were concerned rather with modernizing themselves, with Japanese help if necessary, so that they no longer needed to be afraid of them.

A Japanese minister, Hannabusa Yoshitada, was allowed to occupy a legation just outside the city wall and Kim Ki-su was sent as special envoy to Japan. His progress from Kyushu to the capital was more rapid than of old but he upheld tradition by processing out of the railway station in Tokyo in a palanquin hung with red and yellow fur, surrounded by guards with spears, and preceded by a band with gongs and drums. He sat on a tiger skin and he put on spectacles because those who approached the Emperor of China were required to take them off. Rather lacking in the awe and gratitude of former times, his hosts awaited him with gold-braided uniforms and a suitable air of disdain.

The King was particularly interested in improving the army and in 1879 sent a delegation to Tianjin where the provincial governor-general, Li Hongzhang, had been, in the traditional Chinese manner, made responsible for dealing with the barbarians on his own borders. He had thus become China's de facto foreign minister, and forced also to provide his own coastal defences had developed factories to make modern weapons. The Japanese also offered to provide an officer and the equipment to train a modern army unit, and this was readily accepted. As a result, not only would the army be divided into modern units, in which the King took a special interest, and the old army, whose welfare would be neglected to a degree that would provoke local mutinies, but the new 'drill squad', generally known by its Japanese title of *kunrentai*, would grow into a force of 1,000 well-trained men who, without being consciously disloyal, would become a pro-Japanese élite.

Modern ideas were now spreading rapidly through the younger generation of the literati, one of the pioneers being Kim Hong-jip (also known as Kim Koeng-jip) who while on a mission to Japan in

1880 was startled by their industrial development. The councillor at the Chinese legation in Tokyo, Huang Zunxian, gave him a detailed policy document in which he expressed the view that Russia, with its eventual need for an ice-free port on the Pacific coast, was the greatest threat, and advised an alliance with the United States. He also recommended trade with the other Western nations and the rapid adoption of their technology. In the following year another forward-looking official, Kim Yun-sik, led a party to Tianjin where Li Hongzhang also warned him that unless they forestalled the Western powers by making treaties with them they would be forced to do so at gun point, as a result of which, like the Chinese, they would have to accept both opium and Christianity which, in contrast to Marx, he clearly distinguished, but regarded as equally objectionable.

As a result a party of 12 officials was sent to Japan to inspect their new industries. Their title, *sinsa yuramdan*, 'gentleman's sightseeing party', was in itself a sign of change – the *sinsa* was not the old-style *yangban*, but the 'man about town', who would wear *sinsabok*, a business suit, with short hair and money in his pocket. The King, having read and given his approval to Huang Zunxian's proposals, had copies distributed to various leading scholars in the hope of producing a consensus, but in fact it had the opposite effect, provoking memorials and mass petitions against foreign influence, Catholicism and the Western barbarians. The general effect was only to strengthen the hand of the Taewŏngun, who had become the rallying point for all who opposed the Japanese, the reformers being regarded as their cat's-paws, and even his old enemies, the provincial scholars, were now on his side.

He was generally believed to be planning a coup and the Queen kept a close eye on him. He called Lady I's son, the former crown prince, now 12, for an interview and 11 days later the boy was poisoned, in response to which the next day the Queen's private maid died. A well-planned coup was betrayed the day before it was due and all the leaders were summarily executed, though the old man himself, father of the King, and a national hero, could not be touched. The Queen believed that only by spiritual power would he ever be defeated and every night her corner of the palace grounds echoed to the drums and prayers of her several attendant shamans. Meanwhile, she sought to ensure the continuing power of her clan by having the crown prince Sunjong, now 9, married to the 11-year-old daughter of the Minister of Rites, Min T'ae-ho.

The King was now entirely in favour of modernization and an accommodation with the Western powers, though on Chinese lines rather than with the aid of Japan. Kim Yun-sik was sent back to Tianjin to approach the American Naval Attaché, R. W. Shufeldt, who 14 years before had waited among the ice-floes off Pyongyang for news of the *General Sherman*, but had now become a kind of roving ambassador of American trade. In the spring of 1882 he arrived at Inch'ŏn in the USS *Swatara*, where, having set up a tent on the shore and raised the Stars and Stripes to the tune of 'Yankee Doodle', he was pleased to be able 'without any show of force' to persuade 'the hermit kingdom' to open its doors. One of the two signatories on the Korean side was Kim Hong-jip who two years before had brought back from Tokyo Huang Zunxian's suggestion of such a move and was now a senior minister. Treaties were also concluded with Russia and Germany, while Britain and France would follow more slowly, as the British wanted to insist on opium and the French on Christianity. Neither was acceptable, but the French gained the right to perform private religious ceremonies, as a result of which the priests of the Paris Mission would occasionally be expelled but would never again be executed.

There was now a continuous and energetic effort to modernize the country, based very largely on the reforms taking place in China, and involving a whole group of new departments to deal with such things as diplomacy, foreign trade, industrial production and military ordnance. They provided new opportunities for the *chungin*, the small 'middle class' of doctors, interpreters and technicians, who became fertile soil for the ideals of democracy and universal suffrage, as did many Buddhist scholar-monks who were now extending their contacts with their better educated and more highly regarded brethren in Japan. It led to the formation of a group that met at the house of Yu Hong-gi, better known by his pen-name of 'Yu Tae-ch'i', a herbal doctor, and included O Kyŏng-sŏk, an official interpreter employed on missions to China, who had brought back forbidden books on the history, technology and political ideas of the West, and the monk Yi Tong-in, who had studied in Japan, and had been employed to draft the agreement with the United States. They had all been influenced by the writings of Fukuzawa Yukichi, the founder of Keio University and prime mover in the modernization of Japan.

Meanwhile, the Taewŏngun was still waiting for the right moment to launch a coup. It came later in 1882, when a group of soldiers who were almost starving through the government's failure to maintain their rations became involved in a disturbance in Seoul and appealed to him for help. Led by his associates, they attacked the homes of the Min clan officials responsible for their plight and those of the Japanese army instructors. They were joined by other regiments and the next morning they besieged and burnt the Japanese Legation, forcing the Minister and 28 of his staff to flee down the river by boat. Putting out to sea, they had the luck to be picked up by the British survey vessel, *Flying Fish*, and were taken to Nagasaki. The soldiers then stormed the gates of the palace, causing the King to send for the Taewŏngun, while the Queen went into hiding, as the soldiers believed that it was her shaman rites, including the floating of endless bags of government rice down the River Han as offerings to the Dragon King, that had deprived them of nourishment.

The Japanese, convinced that this was their moment of destiny, anchored off Inch'ŏn with a flotilla of warships and issued an ultimatum, but thanks to the quick action of Kim Yun-sik, who had remained in Tianjin to liaise with Li Hongzhang, they were preempted by the arrival of four Chinese transports with 4,500 soldiers, and knowing that the Taewŏngun was the man the Japanese held as responsible, they enticed him to their legation, put him aboard a steamer and whisked him off to China.

The King, greatly relieved, sent for the Queen, who was with a relative at Changhowŏn. Yi Yong-ik, a palace water-carrier, ran all the way with the message, 40 miles in one day, and as a reward was made a palace official. He would become one of the King's most trusted advisers and in the last days of the dynasty, the leader of the pro-Russian party. The Queen brought back with her a local shaman who would come to exercise such influence over the court that she would eventually become Chillyŏnggun, a Princess, and a professor from the Confucian College who accused her of being one of those foxes in female form with which the country was occasionally plagued was sent into exile. In her later years she would join the congregation of Dr James Gale, the scholarly pastor of the central Presbyterian Church, who found her 'gentle and charming'.

CHAPTER TWENTY-NINE

THE YOUNG REFORMERS

D ESPITE their dramatic confrontation neither the Chinese nor the Japanese were ready for war. Under Chinese guidance, Japanese demands for compensation were met and the Treaty of Chemulp'o (Inch'ŏn), which followed, allowed them to keep a company of soldiers to protect their legation. The much larger Chinese force remained, under the control of Yuan Shikai, only 23 years of age when Li Hongzhang sent him to Korea as 'Resident', with the rank of general. This was something new in the relations between China and Korea, a 'Governor General' on the lines of Western colonialism, who would be resented by the King, and opposed, but eventually imitated, by Japan. Despite his 'imperial robes and his high-falutin' paraphernalia' James Gale saw him as 'a young man of pleasant manner, genial expression and agreeable tone', but to the Koreans he would appear as 'forceful and arrogant', as no doubt Li Hongzhang intended him to be, for as he told the American consul in Beijing, 'I am King of Korea whenever the interests of China require me to be' and he believed the peninsula to be in imminent danger of being carved up between the Russians and the Japanese.

They also provided two advisers on foreign affairs, the diplomat Ma Jianchang and a young German from the Chinese Customs, P. G. Mollendorff, who would set up a similar system in Korea. He also established an English Language School, engaging as the first teacher, Thomas Halifax, an English engineer with a Japanese wife. Mollendorff dressed in Korean style, supported the conservatives, and would for the next three years provide some rather irresponsible advice. The Japanese merchants who had been rapidly extending their trade and establishing settlements in the recently opened ports of Pusan, Wŏnsan and Inch'ŏn now had to compete with the Chinese, who were granted special privileges.

The new Japanese minister in Seoul, Takezoe Shinichiro, was

cultivating the friendship of the reformers gathered round Yu Hong-gi and Yi Tong-in. They had been joined by two gifted young officials, Sŏ Kwang-bŏm and Hong Yŏng-sik, and two others who had the ear of the King, Pak Yŏng-hyo, the husband of King Ch'ŏlchong's one surviving child, and Kim Ok-kyun, a talented representative of the Andong Kim. With Kim as their leader they would come to be known as the Independence Party. Dangerously naïve in relation to both Japan's real intentions and their own countrymen's deep aversion to change, they favoured breaking all ties with China and seeking Japanese aid to modernize the country as quickly as possible.

They succeeded in gaining the interest of the Queen's adopted nephew, Min Yŏng-ik, now the leader of the clan, and in 1881 Yi Tong-in was made the head of a new council concerned with modernization and he frequently conferred with the King. Pak Yŏng-hyo and Kim Ok-kyun went to Japan, ostensibly on official business, but more concerned with their revolutionary aims. While there they spent some time with Fukuzawa Yukichi and there can be little doubt that his encouragement of these able and influential young men along the path of revolution, though done under the semblance of concern for Korea, was purely in furtherance of his country's dreams of empire.

In 1883 the first American minister, General Lucius C. Foote, arrived in Seoul and was well received by the King who would come to see America as his chief protector. He was followed in 1884 by a British consul, William G. Aston, sent from Beijing, and committed to supporting Chinese influence. Min Yŏng-ik led the first diplomatic mission to the United States, taking with him some of the young reformers, including Sŏ Kwang-bŏm and Hong Yŏng-sik. They had as their secretary the young American, Percival Lowell, who had settled in Korea after some years in Japan, and on their return some of them were accompanied by George C. Foulk, on his way to join Foote as Naval Attaché. He learned the language and became their friend, but the Americans were careful not to take sides. Min Yŏng-ik, an older man with scholarly tastes, felt alienated by America and became increasingly suspicious of Japan, so that after his return he turned against the reformers and favoured the conservatives.

Meanwhile, another powerful influence was about to appear – the Protestant religion. As with Catholicism, literature in Chinese preceded personal contacts and the first congregations arose without direct missionary supervision. John Ross, a Scottish Presbyterian settled at Yingkou on the Liao delta and fluent in Chinese, visited the Korea Gate at Ŭiju on the border several times in the 1870s and in 1882, in Shenyang, he engaged two Koreans, Sŏ Sang-ryun and Yi

Ung-ch'an, to work on a translation of the Gospel of St Luke. Both of them were converted through this experience, and by 1884, back in his own village of Sorae in the province of Hwanghae, Sŏ had gathered the first group of believers. The Anglican Church was already well established in Japan and in 1880 the Japanese congregation in Tokyo had sent an evangelist to learn the language, but from lack of finance he had to return before he had established a church.

The first American missionary was a doctor, Horace N. Allen, described as 'tall, thin, red-haired and quarrelsome'. Sent to China by the Northern Presbyterians but unable to settle there, he moved on to Seoul in 1884 where Lucius Foote, keen to have a doctor in the community, found him a house and encouraged him to stay. He would soon be joined by a considerable number of Americans from the Northern and Southern divisions of both the Presbyterians and the Methodists. Under the treaties the propagation of foreign religions was forbidden, but relaxations were thought to be imminent, and there was no time to lose as the French missionaries, whom the Americans habitually referred to as 'Jesuits' and regarded as their natural enemies, were already negotiating a site for their Cathedral.

When in 1884 the Chinese became involved in a war with France on their southern borders, Li Hongzhang moved some of his troops from Seoul and there was talk of a Korean force being sent to fight with them in Indo-China. The young reformers had the sympathy of the King in opposing the Chinese and were confident of his support if only they could free him from the grip of his wife and her oppressive family. They had been joined by another brilliant young man just returned from a Japanese Military Academy, Sŏ Chae-p'il, and began to plan their coup. They had the Japanese soldiers attached to the legation and some of the Japanese-trained officers in charge of the palace guards as a small but deadly Trojan horse but perhaps underestimated the larger horse of another colour that was under the command of the 25-year-old future ruler of China, Yuan Shikai.

One of their number, Hong Yŏng-sik, had been put in charge of setting up a postal system and the central office was to be opened on 4 December. It was built in traditional style, just outside the palace gates, and is still preserved as a postal museum. A banquet there in the evening, hosted by Hong, along with Pak Yŏng-hyo and Kim Ok-kyun, was to be the stage for the coup. Fifteen guests were invited, including the American Minister, Foote; the British Consul, Aston; the Chinese Commissioner, Chen Shutang; Mollendorff and Takezoe Shinichiro; along with the intended victims, the city's chief military commandants and the head of the Min clan, Min Yŏng-ik.

At the last moment Takezoe pleaded illness and sent his chargé d'affaires instead, the result apparently of secret instructions just delivered by the *Chitose Maru*, which ran a monthly service to Inch'ŏn.

The plan was to start a fire in the adjoining buildings to create a panic in which Min and the military commanders would be assassinated as they left, while the plotters rushed to the palace to tell the King that the Chinese were attacking them and he must flee at once to the safety of the Japanese Legation. By the time the fire had taken hold all the intended victims had already gone home except for Min Yŏng-ik, who was severely wounded, and thought to be dying, but Mollendorff had him carried to his house, which was nearby, and sent for Dr Allen. The wounds were already suppurating and it would take three months of care to restore him, by which time Allen would be the Court physician and a foothold for Protestantism would be assured.

Kim Ok-kyun and his followers rushed to the palace where the King refused to go to the Japanese Legation but agreed to move to the nearby Kyongŭi palace which was easier to defend. He sent for his military commanders and chief ministers who were killed by the Japanese soldiers, one by one, as they approached. They included Min Yŏng-ik's father, Min T'ae-ho. In the morning the foreign diplomats were informed that a new government had been established, and on the following day a programme of sweeping reforms was announced, along with a demand for the return of the ever-popular Taewŏngun, and an end to Chinese domination. Yuan Shikai still had 1,500 soldiers, and having received a note from the Queen requesting his assistance, he stormed the palace, easily scattering the Japanese, and carried the King off to his Residence, where he would remain for a few days until the city was quiet again.

The Japanese soldiers, along with Kim Ok-kyun, Pak Yŏng-hyo, Sŏ Kwang-bŏm and Sŏ Jai-p'il, retreated to their legation, which was besieged by an angry crowd. They sent an appeal for help to the Japanese consul at Inch'ŏn, and held out through the night. The next day the party of 200 or more, including women and children, fought their way through the snowy streets of the city to reach Map'o, where they crossed the river in small boats and made their way to Inch'ŏn to board the *Chitose Maru*. In the streets of Seoul a Korean bystander picked up a heavy suitcase abandoned by one of them and found it full of colourful paper money which he used to decorate the walls of his living room. He would subsequently accept a very generous offer for his house and the new owner would begin to grow rich slowly.

Just before the *Chitose Maru* was due to sail, Mollendorff arrived with soldiers to arrest the Korean conspirators. Takezoe was ready to hand them over, but the ship's captain refused, on humanitarian grounds. The King could not forgive Kim Ok-kyun for the death of his own two closest advisers and one of his wife's closest relatives and from Japan he would be enticed to Shanghai, assassinated, and his body brought home in triumph. Of the others, Hong Yŏng-sik had been killed in the Chinese assault, Pak Yŏng-hyo would later return to further the cause of reform only to be chased out again by the wrath of the Queen, and after eventually accepting Japanese rule, would die in 1939 with the rank of 'Marquis'. Sŏ Kwang-bŏm would return, forgiven, and be sent as an envoy to America where he died. Sŏ Chae-pil studied medicine in America and, as we shall see, would return to work for his country's independence.

The Japanese government refused to admit any implication in the affair and demanded heavy reparations. Their Foreign Minister, Inoue Kaoru, arrived at Inch'ŏn with a flotilla of warships, his officials marched into Seoul with two battalions of infantry and the Koreans had no choice but to pay up and replace the burnt-out legation. The Japanese proposed a mutual withdrawal of their own and the Chinese forces which was agreed at Tianjin in April 1885, along with a promise that neither side would again send troops to Korea without giving prior warning to the other.

PART IV

THE EMPIRE OF THE SUN

CHAPTER THIRTY

THE SINO-JAPANESE WAR

THE TREATY of Tianjin had stipulated that both sides should withdraw their military instructors as well as their troops, so the Koreans now had to look elsewhere. A treaty with the Russians had just been signed, so their first minister, Karl Waeber, arrived at an opportune moment. He was an able diplomat, and with the support of Mollendorff and the Queen, who liked his wife, he frequented the court and rumours began to circulate of a secret agreement that would, in return for military aid, give the Russians various favours, including the use of a harbour on the south coast. This greatly alarmed the British who, with the acquiescence of China and without asking the Koreans, occupied the Komundo group, which they had already surveyed and named as 'Port Hamilton'.

It also alarmed Li Hongzhang, who had Mollendorff recalled, and as Henry F. Merrill, whom the head of the Chinese customs, Sir Robert Hart, was sending to take his place, would be an instrument of British interests, he persuaded Judge Owen N. Denny, a former American consul-general at Shanghai, to accept a separate post as adviser to the King. He also concluded that the return of the Taewŏn-gun would be preferable to leaving Queen Min in control, a proposal to which the Japanese agreed, and with Judge Denny as a fellow passenger the Old Tiger was taken home to be ceremonially welcomed by Yuan Shikai, who appeared to be about to put him back on the throne.

The Court put a heavy guard on his palace, a number of officials who had been his allies, or whose names had once been linked with the reformers, were executed or banished, and finally the King sent a note to Waeber requesting Russian protection. It was leaked to Yuan Shikai, who closed down the international telegraph line and threatened to depose him. His doctor, Horace Allen, was now his last resort and Allen, with Japanese aid, contacted an American warship off Cheju Island to appeal for help but there was no response from Washington. The King was thus forced to repudiate his note to Waeber, saying that it was a forgery delivered by officials who had stolen his seal, and four junior civil servants were duly charged with this offence and banished to an offshore island.

To avoid trouble with the Japanese, Li Hongzhang restrained Yuan from replacing the King. The Russians were allowed to trade overland through the border town of Kyŏnghŭng and to operate concessions for timber cutting, but they were refused the use of any ports as coaling stations. As a result of this the British were persuaded to withdraw from Komundo in 1887, with an understanding that neither they nor the Russians would make any more territorial demands. All that now remains of the occupation are the stone foundations of some jetties and the graves of ten seamen. In 1983 the graveyard would be landscaped, with a plaque to commemorate a 'hundred years of Anglo-Korean relations'.

Chinese merchants were now providing about half of the country's imports, mostly British cotton goods, but the Japanese were steadily increasing their economic grip and by the end of the decade would be taking 90 per cent of its exports, carried in Japanese ships and paid for through Japanese banks which had branches in the main ports. The export of rice, soya beans and other food stuffs caused serious shortages, but when later some of the provincial governors, faced with famines, banned the sale of grain, the Japanese, under threat of military action, extorted large sums in compensation. They also acquired extensive fishing rights and began to exploit the country's rich stores of gold at such increasing pace that within 50 years it would become the world's greatest supplier.

The churches continued to extend their influence. In 1885 the Anglicans in Yantai sent two Chinese missionaries to Pusan, and in the same year Dr Allen managed to establish a Royal Hospital in Seoul, jointly funded by the government and the Presbyterian Church. The King provided some medical kisaeng from the palace as nurses, as no respectable woman could be allowed to have contact with strange men. A lady doctor, Lillias Horton, arrived and was made welcome at the palace as Allen had not been permitted to do more than examine female tongues through a slit in a screen. In 1886 they began medical teaching and sent a few students of both sexes to medical schools in America.

In 1890 an Anglican bishop, Charles Corfe, arrived in Inch'ŏn, with two doctors, followed by nuns and clergy, and hospitals and churches were set up there and in Seoul. One of the doctors, an American, Ellis Landis, though short-lived, became a noted scholar of the country's culture, as would also James Gale, sent in the same year by the Canadian YMCA. Australia sent its first Presbyterians to settle in Pusan, followed by Canadians of the same ilk who went to the north-eastern port of Wŏnsan. The Roman Catholics continued to grow, a seminary being established in 1891, and work would begin on the Cathedral in the following year. The King appointed Allen as his foreign secretary in 1887 and in the following year he escorted a mission to the United States, where Pak Chŏng-yang was established as their first envoy. Allen returned in 1890 as secretary of the American Legation.

The Tonghak, seeking social justice and the expulsion of foreigners, won increasing support from farmers, craftsmen and labourers and its leaders were anxious to have the name of their executed founder, Ch'oe Che-u, cleared of what they regarded as false charges. To this end mass meetings were held in Chŏlla in 1892 and in the following year they extended to a rally in Seoul where the leaders knelt before the Palace gates for three days and so much anti-foreign fervour was aroused that Westerners and Japanese were afraid to leave their homes.

Later in the year a rally at Poun in Ch'ungch'ŏng Province attracted 20,000. They erected barriers and raised banners to urge an immediate crusade to remove corrupt magistrates and drive all foreigners out of the country but were eventually persuaded to disperse. In February 1894 there was a riot at Kobu in Chŏlla where there had long been discontent with the rule of a particularly oppressive magistrate. Their leader was Chŏn Pong-jun, whose *yangban* father had already been executed for supporting an earlier protest. They succeeded in having the magistrate replaced and the unrest subsided, but then a government inspector arrived with troops and after compiling a list of members of the Tonghak he had some executed, while others were imprisoned or had their homes burned.

The southern Tonghak leaders issued a nation-wide call to arms which was rejected by those in the northern provinces as inconsistent with their religious teachings, but it had a wide response in the south, where village groups attacked the local government offices and appropriated their weapons. In May hundreds of them converged on Kobu, some with captured rifles or swords, but most with little but staves or bamboo spears. They carried yellow flags and many had tantric amulets which they believed would protect them from bullets. The Provincial Governor in Chŏnju, about 20 miles to the north-east, led his soldiers out against them, and appealed for help from Seoul. The rebels, ably led by Chŏn Pong-jun who because of his diminutive stature was known as the 'Greenpea General', succeeded in dispersing their opponents before the soldiers from Seoul had arrived. They swept southwards for days with the army in pursuit, collecting more followers as they went, and after winning a battle near Chŏngju continued south as far as Naju. Now numbered in thousands, they turned back to face and defeat the full force of the government troops at Changsŏn, after which they went on to occupy the walled city of Chŏnju, the provincial capital. By this time committees of Tonghak supporters controlled the local government in many parts of the province, and would continue to do so over the months of unrest that followed.

There were rumours that they had appealed to the Taewŏngun, whose aims were very close to their own, and consequent fears that the Japanese would intervene to protect their own people. The Court, in a state of panic, chose what it believed to be the lesser evil and called on China for military aid. Meanwhile, Chŏn Pong-jun had arranged to parley with the military commander, as a result of which the government agreed to consider their grievances, the city gates were opened and the rebels returned to their homes.

On 8 June 3,000 men from Li Hongzhang's provincial army came ashore on the Asan Gulf and secured Kongju, which would have blocked any rebel movement towards the capital. In accord with the terms of the Treaty of Tianjin, Li had notified Japan and three days later a battalion of Japanese marines arrived at Inch'ŏn and marched into Seoul, to be followed by transports with about 7,000 troops and an escort of seven warships.

The rebellion having ended, the Chinese proposed a mutual withdrawal, but the Japanese insisted, quite correctly no doubt, that the problems that had given rise to it had yet to be dealt with. Virtually in possession of the capital, and fully prepared, with far better weapons than the poorly trained Chinese, they were now determined to drive them out and enforce a whole series of reforms, along with more economic concessions for themselves. Their minister in Seoul, Otori Keisuke, presented their plans to the Court on 20 July and demanded that the aspects relating to Japanese interests be put into effect within ten days. The Koreans insisted on a prior withdrawal of the troops and appealed to the Chinese, who still had a fleet anchored in the Asan Gulf, but before dawn on 23 July Japanese soldiers forced their way into the Palace, took the Royal Family back to their Legation at gunpoint, and restored the Taewŏngun, without providing him with any means by which to exert his authority.

A Japanese force of about 2,000 marched south to prevent the Chinese at Asan from reaching Seoul and on 25 July they had a decisive victory on the banks of the Ansŏng, the river which flows into the Gulf. While more Chinese troops were attempting to land there and further north, at the mouth of the Yalu they were attacked by the Japanese navy and the *Kowshing*, a British transport, was sunk in the Asan gulf with the loss of 1,800 lives. It caused an outcry in the British press, but the Japanese claimed that the captain had ignored their signals.

Meanwhile, in Seoul, without any consultation with the Taewŏngun or the King, a new Advisory Council was formed under Japanese direction. It was led by the veteran reformer Kim Hong-jip, who had brought back the Chinese proposals of 'A Policy for Korea' after his visit to Japan in 1880, along with Kim Yun-sik, but they were outnumbered by pro-Japanese members including several of those who had been involved in the coup of 1884. They drew up a new constitution which ended the traditional relationship with China and separated the Royal Household from a new State Council, to be made up of a Prime Minister and a cabinet of seven.

There followed a whole series of edicts which more or less echoed those under which the modernization of Japan had been enforced. The traditional examination system was abolished, along with all legal distinctions between *yangban* and commoners. The whole structure of local government was revised and the independent provincial army, navy and judicial authorities were put under central control. A Ministry of Finance was set up to control the collection of taxes, banking and currency, and all official salaries were to be paid in money instead of allowances of grain or cloth. Radical social reforms included abolishing slavery, child marriages, the collective punishment of the families of criminals, and confessions under torture, with new rights for outcastes, widows and illegitimate children. They are known as the 'Kabo' reforms from the name of the year, and despite the unhappy circumstances in which they were introduced, and many delays in implementing them, they would eventually be generally accepted as just and necessary.

The Taewŏngun, determined to resist, sent secret dispatches to the Chinese in Pyongyang in the hope that a new offensive there supported by a nation-wide uprising by the Tonghak and a coup by his own supporters in Seoul might yet turn the tables. He was still bitterly opposed to the Queen and her clan and had another of his grandsons ready as pretender to the throne. In the south, at least, the Tonghak were eager to do battle with the Japanese, but first the rice crop had to be harvested and by 16 September the Chinese were retreating again towards the northern border and the war would move into Manchuria. On the next day the navies of China and Japan, both built and trained by the Western powers, met off the mouth of the Yalu in what was probably the first naval battle ever fought with modern weapons. Though roughly equal in size and firepower, the Japanese fleet was in better condition and its commanders more competent, so that a third of the Chinese ships were lost and the remainder retired.

It was October before the Tonghak leaders could assemble two great peasant armies, one in Chŏlla Province under Chŏn Pong-jun and the other in Ch'ungch'ŏng Province under Son Pyŏng-hŭi. They joined forces at Nonsan and with a total of about 20,000 men advanced on Kongju, but they were opposed by their own government troops as well as by the modern weapons of the Japanese. With an unshakable belief in the justice of their cause and the Mandate of Heaven, they continued attacking for about three weeks until after heavy losses they began to disperse and were relentlessly chased and slaughtered. Chŏn Pong-jun was captured and taken to Seoul to be executed but Son Pyŏng-hŭi would survive to become one of the leaders of the later independence movement, as did two other notable men, An Chung-gŭn and Kim Ku.

During his last days in prison Chŏn wrote:

> At the moment of destiny the world was with me,
> With the Mandate gone, the bravest is lost.
> Was it a crime to love the people and ask for justice?
> Who will understand my patriot's heart?

In November, after the fall of Port Arthur (Lushun), Li Hongzhang was forced to sue for peace and under the Treaty of Shimonoseki he relinquished all claims to the suzerainty of Korea and ceded to Japan Formosa, the Pescadores and Liaoning, though under pressure from France and Germany, and a direct threat of military intervention from Russia, they would eventually agree to relinquish their claim on Liaoning.

CHAPTER THIRTY-ONE

THE MURDER OF THE QUEEN

IN THE final stages of their war with China the Japanese had taken the precaution of replacing their aggressive minister in Seoul, Otori Keisuke, by the distinguished former foreign minister, Inoue Kaoru, who used his charm to persuade the foreign diplomats and even the Queen of his country's good intentions. On his initiative, Pak Yŏng-hyo, the only one of the exiled reformers for whom the King had any affection, was allowed to return and received a ceremonious welcome. The Taewŏngun was once again forced out of office and Pak became the joint head of a new cabinet, along with Kim Hong-jip. Japanese advisers were supplied to train the heads of the new ministries, and a number of students were sent to colleges in Japan.

After the well-disciplined first-line Japanese troops had moved on into Manchuria those who replaced them began to ill-treat the population and they were followed by an uncontrolled flood of immigrants whose behaviour varied from the merely ignorant to the blatantly criminal. The extraterritorial privileges of the one-sided treaty of 1876 left the people with no defence against them. In a letter quoted in the influential *Fortnightly Review* the Anglican Bishop, Charles Corfe, called for the nations of Europe not to be 'deluded into believing that Japan is a civilized power, or desirous of becoming one.' Inoue himself expressed disgust at their behaviour while persistently pressing ahead with the reforms.

In January 1895 the King, accompanied by the Taewŏngun and the crown prince, processed to the Ancestral Shrine where he vowed to his forefathers that he would respect the new constitution. It abolished all deference to China and all the privileges of the aristocracy, leaving him as an isolated autocrat, with no mention of an elected parliament or of citizens' rights. Thus, the whole complex bureaucracy of councillors, censors and provincial administration, already weakened by the clan politics of recent decades, was finally swept away. It seemed to leave the King as simply the puppet of Inoue and his army, but they had reckoned without the one powerful piece that still remained on the chessboard – the Queen.

She knew that the Russians were their only possible allies, and aided by the notable American adventurer General Charles Legendre, who had replaced Denny as foreign advisor in 1890, she was able to keep in touch with Karl Waeber. The Prime Minister, Pak Yŏng-hyo, appears to have been a man of integrity, and certainly not a mere puppet of the Japanese, but he saw the Queen as a baleful influence, opposed to all reforms, and tried to push her aside, as a result of which she forced the King to dismiss him and aroused so much public indignation against him that he had to flee back to Japan. Inoue, keen to reassure her, had allowed the original palace guards to return in place of the *kunrentai*, officered by the Japanese, and the King was able to move some of the reformers to posts in the provinces, and replace them by pro-Russian ministers, notably Yi Pŏm-jin, and also the less reliable Yi Wan-yong who would later change sides, while others of them had already themselves become distrustful of the Japanese.

In September 1895 the urbane Inoue was replaced by a man of a very different kind, Miura Goro, a shaven-headed former general, who appears to have had, if not specific orders to get rid of the Queen, a mandate for decisive action, and the obvious instrument for his purpose was that other old soldier, and enemy of the Queen, the Taewŏngun. A considerable number of educated Japanese hit men of the kind known as *soshi* were seen in Seoul and at about 3 a.m. on the morning of 8 October they, along with the *kunrentai*, began to escort the Taewŏngun's palanquin from his summer residence, joined on the way by the Japanese soldiers and police from the Legation and some volunteers from the Japanese community. They were exhorted to 'deal with the fox' by whatever means were necessary.

They took the palace guards by surprise and forced their way through the paths and passageways to reach the Queen's sleeping quarters, about half a mile from the gates. Those who tried to protect her were struck down and she was stabbed and dragged into a courtyard where her body was drenched in kerosene and burnt. The King's bodyguard was slaughtered and the Taewŏngun was brought in to take control. An elderly American, General Dye, who taught at the military academy, and a Russian technician, who both lived within the grounds, alerted their respective legations. Miura and his first secretary, Sugimura, arrived at the palace and in the presence of the Taewŏngun the trembling King was presented with a series of papers to sign, replacing his ministers by pro-Japanese nominees, and also one, which he refused to sign, that accused the Queen, of whose death he was still unaware, of various crimes. It was nevertheless signed by the new ministers and issued in his name.

Waeber and Allen arrived in time to see the *soshi* departing. They were kept waiting for two hours before they finally forced their way into the room where the King was being held. He was obviously too frightened to say anything that contradicted his captors. The Japanese could not be indifferent to world opinion and allowed Allen, Waeber and other diplomats to make regular visits. Some of the King's family had taken refuge with the American missionaries, and as he was in fear of being poisoned they visited him daily with food prepared in their own homes. He conveyed his thoughts in occasional whispers to Allen or on smuggled scraps of paper.

Allen bombarded Washington with telegrams and letters accusing the Japanese of murdering the Queen, but their denials were accepted by the diplomats in Tokyo. Against them, and orders from Washington, Allen refused to accept a policy of neutrality, or to recognize the new pro-Japanese government, and he succeeded in uniting the diplomatic corps in Seoul against Miura, while the Koreans staged nation-wide protests. As a result, Inoue was sent back to Seoul, where he praised Allen, condemned the assassination, and arrested Miura, who was sent back for trial. Not surprisingly, in view of the readiness of the Taewŏngun and the Korean *kunrentai* to be his instruments, the prosecution failed from 'lack of evidence'.

The pro-Japanese ministers remained in control, the *kunrentai* still guarded the Palace, and Allen was reprimanded by the State Department but did not abandon his visits to the King whom, he said, 'depends on me like a child on his father'. The Japanese needed the King's presence to give legitimacy to their rule, so that if only he could escape from them he would provide a rallying point for resistance. The government, under Kim Hong-Jip, continued with their radical reforms, culminating at the end of the year in a 'Short Hair Edict' which required the male population to cut off their topknots, which, if not carried out voluntarily, would be enforced by the police when they passed through the city gates. To their minds it represented a symbolic castration, and there were uprisings all over the country. Market traders refused to enter the capital, threatening it with starvation, and the order was rescinded, and forgotten.

In January 1896 the Russian legation, where Waeber was about to be joined by his eventual successor, Alexander de Speyer, had its guard temporarily reinforced with 120 marines from a Russian ship at Inch'ŏn, giving Waeber the chance to offer the King a refuge. After careful preparation he was smuggled out of the palace early in the morning in a curtained palanquin, and once safely ensconced in the Russian Legation he issued decrees for the arrest and execution of the pro-Japanese leaders. Kim Hong-jip and two of his ministers were killed by angry mobs before they could even be arrested while two others escaped to Japan. A new pro-Russian cabinet was formed and they issued an amnesty to all who had been imprisoned in the recent rebellions. The other European diplomats gave them their support, and the Japanese, not yet ready for war with Russia, agreed that the King should be free to stay at the Legation or return to the Palace as he chose, and that they would not keep more troops in the country than were needed to protect their own facilities and residents. This improbable victory over the politics of terror was made possible only through the extraordinary courage of Horace Allen in opposing both the Japanese and his own government, and in the fortunate chance that his superior, Sill, was out of the country at the critical moment.

CHAPTER THIRTY-TWO

THE RUSSO-JAPANESE WAR

T HE King's horrifying experiences permanently affected what earlier Western visitors had described as a lively and enquiring mind, and he was reluctant to leave the security of the Russian Legation. It was February 1897 before he could be persuaded to move, and then no further than a small disused palace nearby which was redecorated and renamed the 'Tŏksu'. He was then, ironically, persuaded to promote himself to the rank of Emperor, 'Emperor of the Great Han', making him the social equal of the rulers of China and Japan, and an altar was built where, like the Emperor of China, he could have direct dealings with Heaven. The three storey pagoda-like 'Temple of Heaven' that stood beside it can still be seen near the City Hall, hedged in by high-rise hotels.

Despite the continual growth of Japanese economic activities, the Russians now had considerable influence. Japanese technical and military advisers would be replaced by Russians and when Min Yŏng-hwan was in Moscow for the coronation of Nicolas II in May 1897, they made promises of military forces and monetary loans on a generous scale. That they would never really fulfil them was doubtless due to a new agreement with China by which they leased the Liao Peninsula, enabling the Trans-Siberian Railway to be linked with a line across Manchuria to Port Arthur (Lushan), providing them with an ice-free naval base and the Chinese with a friendly fleet to replace the one they had lost. The British had hoped to lease Port Arthur and instead they took over the former Chinese base at Weihai, just across the water from Inch'ŏn, mutual hostility to the Russian move strengthening the bonds between Britain and Japan.

Meanwhile, a flourishing international community was growing up in Seoul, competing for mining and timber concessions or attempting to set up agencies and manufactures, but apart from the missionaries, who took the trouble to learn the language, they had little meaningful contact with the people. With help from Allen, the Americans won franchises for electric lighting, waterworks, trams and a telephone system. The French, as allies of Russia, obtained a contract to build a railway from Seoul to Ŭiju on the Northern border, but the Japanese were already building one from Pusan to Seoul and quickly bought them out. The rights to build one from Inch'ŏn to Seoul, gained by Japan in 1894, were revoked and given to the United States, but the difficulty of mustering enough skilled labour would enable the Japanese to buy it back, half-completed, in 1899.

Russian influence had also threatened John McCleavy Brown, who had run the Korean customs and advised their treasury as a branch of the Chinese customs and had since continued, with Japanese approval, but Brown had local support, strengthened by the arrival of the British fleet off Inch'ŏn, and the Russians were not inclined to pursue the matter. His rigorous collection of revenue enabled the Koreans to pay off a loan of 3 million yen from Japan which Min Yŏng-hwan had tried to pass on to the Russians, and the subsequent income would be enough to pave the streets of Seoul and provide it with sewers and parks.

In the farming communities there was little improvement in the corruption, poverty and exploitation that had fuelled the Tonghak rebellions, to which was added fierce indignation at the murder of the Queen and the continuing presence of Japanese troops. An alliance with the gentry led to a revival of the Ŭibyong, the 'Righteous Army' of guerrillas that had fought the Japanese in the sixteenth century. In 1896 the government had been reluctantly forced to send their newly modernized troops against them, but the Japanese reverses that followed the King's escape to the Russian legation quietened them for a while. When the British traveller Isabella Bird Bishop visited Korean settlers in the Russian areas just north of the border in the 1890s she reported that only there could one find the relative contentment and prosperity they had once enjoyed in their homeland.

What the country needed if it was to catch up with Japan was state schools, public hygiene, communications, newspapers and the arousing of a national consciousness, but most of those who had been working in this direction had through their association with the Japanese been driven out. A new effort came from So Chae-p'il, who after the failure of the young reformers' coup in 1884 had fled to America where he qualified as a doctor, practised there, and lectured at medical school until, after 12 years, now 33, he returned to become a voluntary adviser to the government. In 1897 he founded the first popular newspaper, *The Independent*, printed in Korean script, to which was added an English edition which helped to bring the Western community into dialogue with the Koreans. It was followed by the Independence Club which brought together several earlier groups concerned with reform, and had the support of the King.

Its meetings were open to all and proved so popular that it grew into a kind of citizens' assembly, run on democratic lines, and similar groups were formed in the provinces. One result was the emergence in 1898 of a women's movement, the Ch'ang'yanghoe, which advocated state schools for girls, the first private one having been established by the Methodists in 1886. As these movements and the readership of *The Independent* continued to grow, there was increasing alarm among the more conservative elements, including the King himself. To treat outcastes such as butchers, shamans or entertainers as the equals of the scholarly élite seemed like anarchy, and it was not difficult to persuade the King that the inevitable outcome would be the abolition of the monarchy itself. Many of those in senior positions resigned from the Club, and So Chae-p'il gave up his government post.

Certainly some check on the King's decisions was urgently needed as the consuls of the Western powers could claim direct access to him, offer him cash sums or promise loans for rights and concessions, and walk away with them. In 1896, for example, an American gold mining company obtained, with Allen's assistance, a concession at Unsan in the hills to the north of Pyongyang, and when the Scottish explorer Angus Hamilton called there a few years later he found that it employed 100 Westerners, 130 Chinese, 17 Japanese and 4,000 Koreans. The constant cries of 'No touch!' from the Americans led to it being known locally as the 'Notouchi Mine'. It paid the Court 600 *wŏn* a month and by the time it was taken over by the Japanese during the Second World War it would have delivered gold worth more than $14 million.

In October 1898 the Independence Club organized a mass meeting in the centre of Seoul attended by high officials as well as a great crowd of ordinary citizens, and they produced proposals that foreign loans and concessions should be approved collectively by the cabinet, the national budget be made public, and a proportion of the King's ministers be chosen by some form of election, which in the beginning the Club itself would organize. The King promised to consider these ideas, but in the end the government's response was to arrest the leaders of the Club and to bring in the Pedlars' Guild, which had become an organization of thugs, to break up its meetings. When they proved inadequate, and the police refused to help them, the

Army was brought in to clear the streets and the gatherings came to an end.

Another profound, and less controversial, change came from the introduction of Western music. While Christian hymn tunes spread through the villages, in Seoul the powerful influence was Franz Eckert, who in 1901 came as 'Court Composer and Military Music Master' after 20 years as government director of music in Japan. He had two marriageable daughters, Anne and Amelie, who caused a flutter among the expatriates, one marrying a Belgian advisor to the government and the other the head of the French language school, the ceremonies at the cathedral being accompanied by their father's Imperial Band. He composed a national anthem in 1902 and would remain there until his death in 1916, by which time Western music would have begun to dominate the taste of the educated and to influence the style of traditional music at every level.

Less obvious was the influence of Western literature, for the all-pervasive spread of Western ideas had been largely through Chinese or Japanese sources, and the first translations of non-religious works, mostly historical or biographical, were from Chinese or Japanese versions, presenting heroes of Western nationalism such as Garibaldi, Washington or Joan of Arc. A critical event would be the publication, in 1906, in serial form in a daily newspaper, of the first modern novel, *Tears of Blood*, by Yi In-jik, based on his own family's experiences in the Sino-Japanese War 11 years before.

At the time of the Boxer Rebellion in China in 1900, Russian troops moved into Manchuria and the Japanese, with British support, constantly demanded their withdrawal, claiming that the Korean peninsula had now become a Russian gun pointed straight at the heart of Japan. In 1902 Japan entered a close offensive and defensive alliance with Britain, which acknowledged that it was 'interested to a peculiar degree, politically as well as commercially and industrially, in Korea'. The Russians were willing to recognize Japan's 'preponderant interests' there, but expected a corresponding recognition of theirs in Manchuria, including their already agreed timber concessions along the Yalu, and suggested the 39th parallel as a possible demarcation between their respective zones of influence.

The Russians were building a loop round the southern half of Lake Baikal, where the ice in winter blocked the ferries and made a fatal gap in their supply line, but it was difficult terrain and the Japanese, determined to seize Manchuria's rich deposits of coal and iron, began a desperate bid to get there first. They speeded up their own work on the railway from Pusan to the north and in January 1904 they began a military occupation of Korea, forcing the King to sign a new agreement that authorized them to protect his country's independence by occupying strategic points throughout the land. Their offensive was timed to coincide with the period when Lake Baikal would be frozen, hoping to prevent any rapid movement of Russian troops or supplies, but the Russians would respond by laying temporary tracks across the ice.

In the early hours of 9 February they attacked the unsuspecting Russian battleships in the harbour at Port Arthur and sank a cruiser and a gunboat at Inch'ŏn, which an editorial in the London *Times* described as 'an act of daring which is destined to take a place of honour in naval annals'. The Russian Baltic fleet, setting off to replace them, feared an attack from the British-built torpedo boats which were collected by crews sent from Japan, and in the North Sea they opened fire on a fleet of fishing boats that loomed out of the darkness. They were excluded from the Suez canal and it would be May 1905 before they approached the Korean coast, where the Japanese, lying in wait behind the island of Tsushima, crippled all but three of the 35 ships.

On land, after enormous losses on both sides, the battle for the Manchurian capital, Shenyang, had ended in a stalemate in March, and despite their victories at sea, the Japanese were at the end of their resources. In August, through the mediation of Theodore Roosevelt, a conference was called at Portsmouth, New Hampshire, at which the Russians handed over their lease on Liaoning, the southern half of Sakhalin, and control of the Manchurian Railway south of Shenyang, and agreed to recognize Japan's 'paramount political, military and economic interests' in Korea.

The war brought to Korea, for the first time, newspaper correspondents from the West. The Japanese controlled all the transport and tried to confine them to Tokyo, but the novelist Jack London, representing the Hearst press, smuggled himself on to a ship to Pusan where he hired a fishing boat with a crew of three and set off in freezing weather to sail round the coast to Inch'ŏn. It took a week and he lost some fingers from frostbite, but immediately rode off for Pyongyang, where the Japanese put him in prison for two weeks, by which time the other correspondents had been given a visit to the battle front. He eventually took back with him a devoted Korean boy, 'Manyoungi', later to be settled with Jack's mother, and ten years on would write *The Star Rover*, which features an episode in seventeenth-century Korea, using material from Hendrik Hamel.

More substantial contributions would be made by two British journalists, F. A. McKenzie of the *Daily Mail* and E. T. Bethell, who came from Tokyo as a temporary correspondent for the *Daily Chronicle*. McKenzie was immediately shocked by the way the Japanese treated the Koreans, and having looked into the history of it became even more indignant. His reports were censored by the Japanese and he was forced to leave, but he would return as a special correspondent in 1906 and by his dispatches and subsequent books would become the chief spokesman for Korea in the West.

The *Chronicle* was committed to supporting Britain's pro-Japanese policy and soon dismissed Bethell on the grounds that they could get more satisfactory information from the Japanese Embassy. Bethell, who had worked in Tokyo and could speak Japanese, decided to stay on in Seoul and set up a newspaper that, like the former *Independent* would be published in both Korean and English. Despite his sympathy for Japan, the objectivity of his reporting soon began to create problems and would eventually threaten the smooth flow of Anglo-Japanese relations.

With the demise of the Russians the Koreans were entirely in the hands of the Japanese. Horace Allen, now the American Minister in Seoul and almost the King's last foreign friend, was told by Roosevelt's adviser on the Far East, W. W. Rockhill, that the annexation of Korea was inevitable as 'the one great and final step westward of the Japanese Empire' and would be 'better for the Korean people and also for peace in the Far East', and in March 1905 Allen was turned out to be replaced by a minister who supported this policy. Japanese control of the ports and communications was now so tight that when in October 1905 the King decided to send a personal appeal to Roosevelt it had to be done in secret. He chose as his emissary Homer B. Hulbert, an American, fluent in the language, who had taught at the government school since 1886, edited an English language monthly, the *Korea Review*, and had just completed a two-volume history of the country.

The importance of Korea to Japan's imperial ambitions can be judged from the fact that the man they sent to enforce the occupation was their most senior statesman, Ito Hirobumi, who had been Prime Minister at the time of the murder of the Queen ten years before. On 15 November, while Hulbert was on the last stage of his journey to Washington, Ito entered the royal palace with an escort of troops and a treaty that would place their foreign relations entirely in the hands of Japan, while their internal affairs would be his personal responsibility as 'Resident General'. He would be aided by a dozen 'Commissioners' who could respectively act as 'advisers' to the heads of the three treaty ports and to the governors of Seoul and the eight provinces. The King refused to sign the document, and after five hours of pressure Ito retired. For the next two days the King and his chief ministers, surrounded by soldiers with fixed bayonets were, sometimes collectively, sometimes individually, bullied at gunpoint. The Prime Minister, Han Kyu-sŏl, a former leader of the Independence Club, behaved with extraordinary courage and it was only after he had been dragged out and, as the other members thought, shot that they finally broke down.

On the same day Hulbert reached the State Department with the King's letter and was told that they were too busy to deal with it immediately. A few days later he was informed that the Emperor had made a new agreement which disposed of the matter, so no action would be taken. By the end of the year the Commissioners were in place and in March Ito returned from Japan to take power, and all the foreign diplomats in Seoul were finally withdrawn.

CHAPTER THIRTY-THREE

PARTISANS AND JOURNALISTS

For the early reformers Japan had been the main source of ideas, information and assistance, and they had had no choice but to learn from them. As a consequence many were drawn into organizations such as the Ilchinhoe, or 'Society of Progress', which the Japanese were now using to their own ends. Members of it, if willing, were nominated to jobs in the ministries, the police, the banks and the education system, to all of which Japanese advisers had been appointed, although the public saw them as traitors and even attacked them in the street. In continued uprisings Ŭibyŏng forces won temporary control over small areas but were hopelessly outgunned by the modern weapons of their opponents.

Min Yŏng-hwan, returned from his fruitless appeals to the West, wrote a passionate last testament and killed himself, and several others followed, while in London the closing of the Korean Legation had been accompanied by the suicide of the chargé Yi Han-ŭng. The King sent a youthful former member of the Independence Club, Yi Sŭng-man, to make another appeal to the American president. It had no effect, but Yi would go on to organize continuing protest from Hawaii and eventually return as 'Syngman Rhee', the South Korean leader of the 1950s.

In February 1906 Bethell's newspaper, the *Daily News*, published a letter from the King in which he stated that he had not agreed to the protectorate and appealed to the nations with whom they had treaties to come to their aid. There was no diplomatic response, but the London *Tribune* sent a journalist, Douglas Story, who had a secret interview with the King and smuggled out an open letter from him which after its publication in London was reprinted by Bethell. The Japanese requested the British to suppress his newspapers – because of Britain's extraterritorial rights only they could do this. The Foreign Office was ready to oblige, but found it difficult, as

Bethell's offence was that of supporting the King, who was still the legitimate ruler. They would therefore have to invent some new ordinance under which he could be indicted, which would take their legal experts some time. The Japanese started a rival English-language newspaper of their own, published by J. W. Hodge, who had originally come to Seoul to set up a printing press for the Anglican Church.

The *Daily Mail* sent F. A. McKenzie back to report on the situation. The Japanese forbade him to leave Seoul, but he evaded them and travelling south found a whole division of the Japanese Army engaged in a savage war with the partisans of the 'Righteous Army'. He travelled for day after day through burnt-out villages where the men had been shot and the rest forced to flee. When he finally met up with the partisans he found them tattered and weary with ancient muskets or Chinese shotguns and little ammunition. The remaining units of the Korean Army were disbanded, resulting in further suicides among their officers, though many joined the Partisans, and this influx of new men with better weapons enabled them to mount a march on Seoul with 10,000 men, and they came within eight miles of it before they were driven back by the machine guns and artillery massed against them.

Meanwhile, the International Court established by the Hague Convention was to meet in June 1907, and two representatives, Yi Sang-sŏl and Yi Chun, with Hulbert as interpreter, were smuggled out through Siberia and joined by Yi Wi-jong, a consul in Russia, but their country being a Japanese 'protectorate', they had no legal existence. They did succeed in meeting the press, and gained a little publicity, which so infuriated the Japanese that they removed Kojong from the throne and replaced him by his dim-witted 33-year-old son Sunjong. His coronation was thoroughly up to date – his topknot was cut off and he was put into a Western-style uniform laced with gold to match those of the Japanese, with the Korean politicians in tailcoats and striped trousers, and the court orchestra replaced by one of the bands trained by Eckert.

While the English-language edition of Bethell's paper reported Japanese atrocities, the Korean version, edited by Yang Ki-t'ak, encouraged the people in their resistance. As an employee of Bethell, Yang was included in the extraterritorial protection, so the Japanese demanded that Bethell be charged with sedition by the British Consul. The problem was that such a charge could be brought in a British court only if it were British citizens who were being urged to rebel. The Japanese kept up the pressure and finally in October 1907 Bethell was summoned to the Legation, and with the Consul Henry Cockburn as judge and his assistant as complainant he was accused of publishing articles likely 'to produce or excite a breach of the peace'. He was found guilty and required to enter into a bond of £300 to be of good behaviour for six months. Cockburn was not unsympathetic towards Bethell but he was under orders from London to have him silenced.

The King's American adviser, Charles Legendre, had died in 1899 and been replaced by William Franklin Sands, formerly Allen's assist-ant at the Legation. When American indifference to Korea changed to positive support for Japan and Allen was recalled, Sands was replaced by an American employee of the Japanese, Durham White Stevens. On a visit to San Francisco Stevens gave several addresses in which he said that the Koreans were not fit to govern themselves and praised the humanity and benevolence of the Japanese. There was by this time a considerable body of well-educated Koreans in San Francisco and their association sent four representatives to meet him and demand an explanation. It ended in a struggle, and the next day, as Stevens was leaving he was shot, and died two days later. His assassins readily gave themselves up as they had only wanted to draw attention to their country's fate; in Seoul, Bethell's papers praised them as patriots, asking how otherwise could they have drawn atten-tion to their country's sufferings?

The distribution of the papers was stopped and the Japanese renewed their demand that Bethell should be expelled. He was brought to trial again, this time with a Marshal, Counsel, Prosecutor and Judge sent over from the British Supreme Court in Shanghai, while the Korean Association in Shanghai provided an English-speaking representative, Kim Kyu-sik, as an interpreter for the defence. The liberal-minded *Japan Chronicle* sent a reporter who described it as a unique event in the history of the Far East, and noted the juxtaposition of British legal wigs, Korean robes, Japanese frockcoats and gold-laced uniforms and the summer dresses of the lady missionaries

Bethell's counsel began by questioning the validity of the trial as there was no jury, but the judge regarded this as unavoidable in view of the shortage of British citizens. The Japanese were represented by Miura Yagoro who was Ito's number two and 'Resident' of Seoul. Bethell's counsel wished to clarify the question of whether he repre-sented the government of Korea or the government of Japan, as they were still legally distinct, though this was in practice ignored, so that Miura was easily tied up and became the victim of laughter in the court. The Judge told the defence to stick to matters of fact rather than politics. Many of the Korean witnesses, whether directly hin-dered or too frightened, did not turn up, but a few distinguished ones testified that the anti-Japanese disturbances dated back to the murder of the Queen in 1895, and the defence threatened to become a prosecution of the Japanese.

The Prosecutor dismissed all this as an attempt to defend terrorism and the Judge ruled that Bethell was guilty of a 'first class misdemeanour' and sentenced him to three weeks' imprisonment, followed by six months' probation. HMS *Clio* was summoned from Yokohama to take him to Shanghai. As Korea was kept financially in debt to Japan, his paper had supported an organization that collected voluntary contributions to repay it. As soon as Bethell had gone Yang was arrested for allegedly misusing this fund and when Bethell's British assistant visited him in prison he looked so near to death that Cockburn appealed to Tokyo and London, as a result of which he was moved to a hospital. From there he escaped to Bethell's office and Cockburn refused to hand him over, despite orders from his superior in Tokyo. After further Japanese protests Cockburn had to give in, and was recalled to London, where he resigned in protest, bringing his 25-year diplomatic career to an end.

Bethell returned to Shanghai in poor health and died of a heart attack shortly afterwards. Cockburn's successor arranged for the newspaper to be sold to the Japanese. Bethell, only 36, was buried in the Foreign Cemetery in May 1909 and his grave has been a place of pilgrimage ever since. Yang Ki-t'ak would live on to defy the Japanese, more often in prison than out of it.

Against the advice of Ito Hirobumi, the Japanese decided to replace their 'protectorate' by direct 'annexation', which while it would preserve Sunjong as a figurehead, would put the country under the direct rule of the Governor General. Ito, now 68, resigned, and in October 1909, on a visit to the Russian provinces, he was assassinated on the railway platform at Harbin by the Ŭibyŏng leader and former Tonghak general, An Chung-gŭn.

The man chosen as Governor General was the Minister of War, and future premier, Terauchi Masatake, and in expectation of public outrage the police presence was greatly increased, including a formidable force of secret police and spies, and even the Japanese-run newspapers were closed down. It so happened that the assassins of both Stevens and Ito had been Christians, and after An Myŏng-gŭn, the brother of Ito's assassin, made an unsuccessful attack on Terauchi in December 1910 the whole Christian movement would come to be treated with increasing suspicion. With generous support from the Methodist and Presbyterian establishments in America the Protestants had numerous schools and hospitals and their followers, already numbering about 200,000, were snowballing under the slogan of 'A Million Souls for Christ'.

The Japanese attempted to pin responsibility for the attack on

Terauchi on the largely Christian 'New People's Association' and arrested about 700 members, of whom 105 were tortured to produce confessions. They included Yun Chi-ho, a distinguished diplomat and former minister who had studied in the United States and had followed Sŏ Chae-p'il as leader of the Independence Club, and Yang Ki-t'ak, both of whom were sentenced to ten years in prison. The trial was fully reported in the American press and aroused so much protest from Western diplomats that an appeal to a higher court was allowed. It enabled the defendants to describe their tortures and resulted in acquittals for most of them, whilst Yun, Yang and four other leaders had their sentences reduced from ten years to six, and would be released after four.

By 1910 large numbers of Koreans had emigrated around the North Pacific basin, notably to Hawaii, where since 1903 displaced farmers had been transported to provide cheap labour, and from there they would move onwards and upwards in the fluid society of the American West coast. Others went to Beijing or Shanghai, but for activists these were dangerous places as they were constantly under Japanese surveillance. Because of the many French priests who had lived, and died, in Korea, the French concession in Shanghai offered a secure refuge. Great numbers moved into Manchuria as migrants or as refugees, but in later times they would go there as the victims of Japanese schemes by which whole village communities would be herded on to trains and transported to empty areas. They would leave behind good rice-land to be exploited by Japanese corporations and become new 'citizens' to justify their occupation of Manchuria, as few, if any, Japanese farmers would show any inclination to go there.

They began a land survey in 1910 which was completed by 1918. Apart from a few patriots who refused to cooperate, the larger landholders were allowed to keep their land, but many smallholders, tenants or squatters were unable to claim any title, and all the hills, forests and other areas that had been regarded as 'the King's land' or held in the name of the court, were transferred to the governor General's department, amounting to about 40 per cent of the total area. From 1904, the Japanese had gained the right to buy land, and large corporations, partially owned by the government, purchased great tracts of farmland. By protecting the interests of the Korean landlords, and providing educational opportunities for their children, they tried to transform the racial antagonism into a class conflict that in the Cold War situation of the 1950s would help to bring about the territorial division into 'North' and 'South'. These divided loyalties were reinforced by recruiting Koreans into the ranks of the police and the bureaucracy, and later into the lower ranks of the teaching profession.

As well as farmland, minerals and timber also found their way into Japanese hands and most of the fish in the surrounding seas into their nets, and stomachs. Their fishermen were encouraged to emigrate to the islands off the coast where their larger boats and superior equipment enabled them to take the greater share of the catch. Korean gold would keep them on the 'Gold Standard' and allow them to purchase from America and elsewhere the oil, machine tools and other materials they needed for the conquest of China just as, later, Korean uranium would enable them to join the race for the atom bomb, in which they would not be far behind.

Although tenant farmers had to hand over about half their crop in rent and taxes, and were often in debt, most of them were probably no worse off than they had been under the old regime. The introduction of improved strains of rice, chemical fertilizers and better methods of farming, the investment in reservoirs, roads, railways, and hydro-electric power, and the cheap products of Japanese factories, would bring them, through the 20s and the 30s, a steady improvement in living standards.

In the period up to the Annexation most of the Western-style schools had been founded by American missionaries, giving many of the country's future leaders a blend of traditional Confucian values with those of small-town America, independent and democratic, but puritan and hostile to socialism. The Japanese aimed to provide universal education up to primary level. They valued the Churches' contribution, but could not countenance their ideology and religious teaching was banned from the curriculum, though it could still be given outside school hours. All teaching was eventually to be in Japanese but Korean or foreign teachers were to be allowed five years in which to learn it.

The wealthier Koreans were encouraged to send their children to high schools and universities in Japan and by 1912 more than 3,000 were studying there. It was hoped that this would hasten assimilation but most of them supported a fervent underground independence movement that had the backing of left-wing groups in Japan, for this was a period when Marxism was gaining ground and liberal and Christian attitudes were still tolerated. Some graduates would go on to Manchuria to join the resistance movement, but the majority would go home to accept positions as teachers or civil servants while remaining resolutely opposed to the occupation.

CHAPTER THIRTY-FOUR

ASIAN CO-PROSPERITY

WITH THE end of World War I, in 1918, the preparations for the Peace Conference, and Woodrow Wilson's Fourteen Points, with their emphasis on rights of self-determination and national autonomy, raised new hopes in Korea. Even the Churches and other organizations that had opposed violent resistance were ready for peaceful demonstrations, and as most of the activists were already in jail or had been forced to flee, further protest became more dependent on their support. The exiles in Shanghai sent agents to help to organize moves in Seoul and Tokyo while those in America were planning to send representatives to the Conference at Versailles.

The deposed Emperor Kojong died on 22 January 1919 and his funeral was set for 3 March. It provided the target date for a national Declaration of Independence that aimed at bringing out the whole population, and all over the country, church ministers, local headmasters, and other leaders rehearsed their flocks. The Japanese knew that something was afoot, for beacon fires frequently appeared on the hills and young people were continually on the move. They were quick to question, torture and intimidate any local gathering, but by using students to take messages, and finally by moving the date forward by two days, the leaders managed to sustain an element of surprise. Copies of the declaration had been printed beforehand and sent out to be stored in provincial centres.

On the eve of 1 March the 33 leaders of the movement met at a restaurant in the centre of Seoul where they signed the declaration, which was read aloud the next day in Pagoda Park to an assembled crowd, mostly students, who then marched through the streets chanting *Tongnip, mansae!* 'Long-live Independence!', and every corner of the country echoed with it. The Japanese forces, taken by surprise and frightened by the numbers, reacted with almost hysterical violence. Thousands of demonstrators were killed, many more injured, and nearly 50,000 arrested, while more than 700 houses and nearly 50 churches were burned. Yu Kwan-sun, a 15-year-old girl from the Methodist Ewha School, who took part in the Pagoda Park demonstration, went on to organize one in her own home area of Ch'onan in which thousands of people participated and hundreds, including her own parents, were shot. She herself was detained and tortured, and in the following year died in prison.

The persecution, both in Korea and in Japan itself, led to a gathering of refugees in Shanghai, and in April, with the addition of representatives from those in Russia and the United States, a Provisional Government in Exile was formed with Syngman Rhee as President, and Kim Kyu-sik, who had interpreted at the trial of Bethell, as Foreign Minister. In May Kim led a delegation to the Peace Conference in Paris, without gaining any recognition, the participants being more concerned with gaining new colonies of their own, but they received a sympathetic hearing at an international socialist congress in Geneva.

The guerrilla forces in Manchuria and Russia were also temporarily united under a single command linked with the new provisional government, though before long local rivalries and ideological differences would split them again. Similar disagreements would plague a Korean Bureau set up in Washington by Syngman Rhee. It was to be directed by Kim Kyu-sik, but his left-wing contacts were not acceptable to Rhee and his American supporters, who belonged to right-wing Christian organizations, and in 1923 the bureau had to close and Kim returned to Shanghai.

A new Japanese government under Hara Kei, chastened by the uprising in Korea, replaced their trigger-happy military administration by *Bunka seiji*, 'civilized rule', and in place of General Hasegawa Yoshimichi came Saito Makoto, a former admiral who was seen by contemporaries as 'an urbane, well-travelled diplomat'. He was given a staff of talented civil servants, and although he was greeted with a bomb when he arrived at the railway station in Seoul, he introduced a relatively benevolent regime that the general public would come to tolerate through the 20s and the early 30s.

In the 1920s in Korea, as also in Japan, there was a strong labour movement amongst workers and tenant farmers, and a great many battles were fought by striking workers and protesting farmers, all of which they lost, and by 1931 the police were so oppressive that public protest was no longer possible. Students helped small Communist groups to survive, but they were constantly being infiltrated and broken up, and hundreds of their members ended up in prison. In 1925 twenty-one students were sent to a special university in Russia, including two who would subsequently rise to prominence,

Cho Pong-am and Pak Hŏn-yŏng. Occasional terrorist activities in Japan itself fostered an extreme hostility towards Koreans that still survives. In the Tokyo earthquake of 1923, in which perhaps 100,000 died, most of them through fires that ran through the close-packed wooden houses, a rumour that the Koreans were responsible for both starting the fires and poisoning the wells set off a pogrom in which an estimated 2,000 were killed.

There was a continual expansion of education, both private and government sponsored, and specialist colleges were set up, chiefly for farmers and teachers, but also for doctors and lawyers, as well as technical schools. Yonhŭi (later Yonsei), founded by the Christian missions, was for many years the only surviving college with liberal arts courses, as a number of earlier ones had been refused government licences. The intention was to limit Korean education to technical and vocational teaching, given entirely in the Japanese language, but a university established for the children of the many thousands of Japanese residents who taught in the schools, manned the police, ran the bureaucracy and managed enterprises of every kind, also took in a quota of favoured Koreans.

Newspapers and magazines were censored but survived, notably the two great dailies, the *Chosŏn Ilbo* and the *Tonga Ilbo*, whose editors and staff would, at great personal cost, never cease to test the limits of free speech, a tradition that they would continue under the repressive governments that would follow the country's 'liberation' in 1945. Although restricted in their political comments, they generated a lively intellectual atmosphere and serialized works by leading novelists and translations of Western authors, and a cursory study of them leaves the impression that their readers were kept as well informed on the trends of European thought as their contemporaries in, say, Australia or Canada.

Much of this Western influence was mediated through Japanese translations, for Japan itself in the 1920s was in an intellectual ferment. Tolstoy, Dostoevsky and Zola were the most popular authors, and although a great deal of English literature was translated, only Thomas Hardy would produce a comparable resonance. Tess, in particular, would become a character perhaps more widely known and loved in Korea than in England itself. Best known among the Korean authors of this period would be Yi Kwang-su, who combined didactic modern themes and patriotic historical ones with a storyteller's talent reminiscent of Victor Hugo.

The women's movement was quite strong in the 20s, a notable pioneer being the artist Na Hye-sŏk, who after studying Western techniques at the Tokyo Women's College of Art returned in 1921 to put on the country's first individual exhibition by a woman artist.

She also wrote stories and poems, including a witty poem based on the heroine of Ibsen's *A Doll's House*, the refrain of which goes, 'Nora-rŭl No-a-ra!' which in Korean means 'Let Nora go!'

Although they were small in comparison with the great Japanese firms, a number of local entrepreneurs were successful in producing clothes, shoes and other items angled towards Korean tastes, and locally owned trading companies and department stores appeared. The growth of these, along with a continual increase in the number of doctors, teachers and civil servants, many of them educated in Japan, built up a middle class sufficient to support, in the 1930s, a considerable range of weekly and monthly magazines and there was a continual increase in the circulation of the daily papers.

Despite the Japanese people's deep conviction of their own divine origins, their racial similarity to the Koreans, their common cultural heritage, and the obvious ability of Korean children to keep up with their Japanese classmates led to a great many friendships, secret loves and affectionate teacher-pupil relationships. The poet Sŏ Chŏng-ju has described his jealousy at the age of ten when on a school picnic an older boy was chosen to carry on his back, because her feet were sore, their pretty young Japanese teacher, and when she was moved to another school the whole class sat on the road to stop her bus from leaving and there was a great flow of tears on both sides.

A few years later, in 1929, a less attractive side of the relationship appeared when at Kwangju, the South Chŏlla capital, the teasing of some Korean high school girls by Japanese boys who travelled daily on the same local train angered one of their brothers and started a student war that escalated day by day with increasing injuries from sticks and stones. It spread to other cities and ended with hundreds of Korean boys being herded into police stations and severely thrashed. Some idea of the degree to which, despite the instinctive attractions, public prejudice kept the two races apart can be judged from the fact that although by 1937 630,000 Japanese would be resident in Korea, many of them born there, only 664 of the men would have married Korean women and only 474 Korean men Japanese women.

The continuing internal unrest in China made the Japanese militarists keen to press on with the occupation of Manchuria. The treaty that followed the war with Russia had allowed them to take over the South Manchurian Railway and to keep a regiment at Port Arthur to protect it, and after the Russian revolution this force, now known as the Guandong Army, was increased to divisional strength and eventually grew to five divisions, a force of about 50,000, with the latest weapons and the most able officers. Regarded as the bridgehead for continental expansion, they kept in practice by attacking the

Korean guerrillas in Manchuria, who were forced further into the mountains, though not without strong resistance. On one occasion in Chilin Province in 1920 a Korean force of 1,800 under Kim Chwa-jin are said to have turned back a whole division of the Guandong Army, after which they had linked up with groups in Siberia to form an army of about 3,500 with their own military academy at Alekseyevsk.

During the same period, on the other side of the Pacific, an emigrant to California, Han Ch'ang-ho, founded in 1920 the Korean National Air Force. Three aircraft were purchased and the crews trained at San Francisco's Redwood Aviation School, the plan being to take them by sea to a spot on the coast of China from which they could bomb Tokyo into submission. A year later a drought in North California ruined the wealthy Korean rice farmer who was providing most of the finance and the project collapsed, but the idea would be successfully exploited by General James Doolittle in his daring raid on Tokyo in April 1942.

The depression in world trade in 1929 served to undermine the popularity of the liberals in Japan and boost the confidence of the generals, and in September 1931, while Zhang Xueliang, the war lord who controlled Manchuria, was away in the south fighting the Communists, the Guandong Army was able to seize Shenyang and the other main towns and present the world with a *fait accompli*, after which their puppet, the former Manchu Emperor, Puyi, was fetched from a safe house in Tianjin to be set up as the ruler of 'Manchuquo'. The population was largely Manchu, but included nearly a million Koreans and from this time the guerrilla forces in the hills would be ruthlessly hunted.

The Japanese now began an intensive exploitation of Manchuria's resources of iron and coal, which with hydro-electric power from the rivers of the Yalu basin would enable their factories in North Korea to produce steel, cement, synthetic oil, bakelite, fertilizers and other chemical products. Gold, tungsten and copper were mined as well as mica, uranium and lead phosphates. Cheap Korean labour was attracted there, and would later be forcibly moved in, as also to the Japanese mainland and later, in the war, all round the Pacific basin, including thousands of Korean girls to provide 'comfort' for the army. The British travel-writer Peter Fleming, who passed through Manchuquo in 1933 noted that 'the first civilians to enter Jehol on the heels of the Japanese army were twenty lorry loads of Korean girls'. One whom he met in a canteen 'looked about seventeen. She had that heavy listlessness which is commonly born of some deep disgust or pain' and gave him 'a feeling of horror and pity difficult to express'.

From 1933 onwards Japan's military ambitions put an ever-increasing strain on the Korean economy and led to a relative decline of living standards. Their demands for rice reduced the Koreans own per capita consumption from 3.5 bushels in 1921 to 1.7 by 1939, the shortage being alleviated by importing Chinese millet and other inferior grains for which the Koreans were charged more than they received for their rice. They were also encouraged to turn over more fields to produce cotton, and there was an unsuccessful attempt to put sheep on the hills made bare by the export of timber.

With the growth of industry in the north, roads, railways and ports were continually improved and extended, with double track lines between Pusan and the centres in Manchuria. In 1927 Japan Air Lines began flights between Fukuoka and Dalian, the headquarters of the Guandong Army, with stops at Ulsan and Seoul, and air links were later extended to other industrial centres such as Hamhŭng, Ŭiju and Wŏnsan in the north and Taegu in the south.

With the development of Manchuria, Korea came to be seen more and more as an integral part of the Japanese heartland, with increased pressure on complete assimilation, though still on the assumption that, as obedient younger brothers, they should be content with menial tasks. The Korean elements in their education were progressively reduced to provide more time for Japanese beliefs and history. The shrines and rituals of Shinto were an essential element of this and an insistence that every public event must begin with worship brought renewed conflict with the churches.

In 1935, in the Pyongyang area, where the Presbyterian church was strong, the provincial governor invited Professor G. S. McCune – best known as the co-author of the 'McCune-Reischauer' system for the romanization of the language, but then head of Chosŏn Christian College – and other educational leaders to a conference, and proposed to open it with a visit to the newly completed Shinto shrine. The Christian representatives insisted that they could not participate in this, and were told to go away and think about it for 60 days.

They called a meeting of 27 local pastors, all but one of whom shared their view, so they again declined to go. The Governor revoked their teachers' licences and put a police guard on their houses to turn away and abuse visitors.

A Foreign Office representative from Seoul, himself a Christian, was sent to assure them that it was merely a form of patriotism, but when asked if he could state that they were not worshipping gods or spirits, he said that he could not, as that was the general belief of the Japanese people. As pressure increased the Churches would be split on this issue. The liberals felt that to close their schools would be a greater evil than a bow to the Emperor, but the majority, being of a more fundamentalist turn of mind, chose to see them closed and even to face imprisonment, torture, and in some cases death. As a result the number of Protestant Christians declined from 700,000 in 1938 to about 250,000 by 1941.

Although the successive Governor-Generals were always men with a naval or military background, Saito, who had introduced 'civilized rule' in 1919, and Ugaki Kazushige, who followed him in 1931, were both liberals. They had been sympathetic towards the *zaibatsu*, the great business empires, ready to encourage Korean entrepreneurs and friendly towards the churches and missionaries, but Minami Jiro, who took over from Ugaki in August 1936, was the former Minister of War involved in the Manchurian coup of 1931, and his arrival was a prelude to the attack on North China that would be launched in the following July.

Assimilation was now pursued with rigour and in 1937 he introduced the 'Pledge of the Emperor's Subjects' which had to be learned by heart by everyone and recited at every public gathering:

> We, subjects of the Emperor, shall serve the Nation with loyalty and faithfulness.
> We, subjects of the Emperor, through faith and love, shall work together to strengthen our unity.
> We, subjects of the Emperor, shall endure hardship and train ourselves to further the Imperial Way.

The enforced settlement in Manchuria of Japanese 'subjects' who were in fact Koreans had alarmed the Russians who now began to see the ethnic Koreans in their own Maritime Provinces as a potential fifth column. In 1937 Stalin decided to move them to his underpopulated nomad territories in Central Asia and over the next few years 180,000 of them would be packed into railway vans and tipped out, with a minimum of support, to establish collective farms in Uzbekistan and Kazakstan. The survivors would eventually flourish and in the next generation provide a few leaders for Kim Il-sung's Stalinist state.

From 1938 onwards Korean boys were invited to volunteer for service in the Japanese Army and it is a measure of the success of their propaganda, as of the country's poverty and lack of alternative employment, that they began by choosing 1,300 from over 15,000 applicants, and by 1943, when it would be replaced by conscription, they would have had more than 800,000 volunteers, from whom about 18,000 had been accepted. A few of the more talented were admitted to the Military Academy in Tokyo and many more to a colonial academy in Manchuria. The 'Name Edict' of 1939 went on to require all Koreans to use Japanese names, which sounded bizarre to Korean ears, accustomed to the monosyllabic names of the Chinese tradition.

These absolute demands for loyalty as 'subjects' were not accompanied by corresponding privileges of 'citizenship', which was rarely granted to anyone of Korean birth, though any fame they might win was credited to Japan. When Son Ki-jŏng, as a member of the Japanese team, with his name given as Ki Tei Sohn, won the marathon at the 1936 Olympics in Berlin, two papers dared to print a photograph of him with the Japanese emblem removed from his singlet, and were suspended for almost 12 months.

By the 1940s, Koreans of all classes, and particularly a younger generation who had spoken Japanese every day at school and been saturated with Japanese cinema, papers and radio, began to accept that they had no choice but to throw in their lot with them and to seek to improve it by campaigning for full citizenship and a full share of the promised 'Asian Co-Prosperity'. Ancient Korean heroes who had charged their foes with lances or commanded galleys could hardly compete with the handsome young men who flew sleek monoplanes in Japanese movies, and boys whose Japanese college mates had gone off proudly to train as pilots could not but envy them. Their fathers, many of them men who had wasted their lives in and out of Japanese prisons, could not but wonder whether they had any right to commit their children to a similar fate, while the cost of Korean patriotism rose ever higher, and the deaths in prison more frequent.

The extension of the war after the Japanese attack on Pearl Harbor in December 1941 meant that the Korean people would now, like those of Japan, be totally subordinated to the needs of the war machine. Households throughout the country were joined in neighbourhood units of ten families each to devote labour, money and, at a later stage, even their metal utensils and their jewellery to the war effort. The children were rewarded with rubber balls to celebrate the acquisition of the Malaysian plantations, but their hours of study were reduced to enable them to do war work and join in patriotic assemblies. From 1943 onwards there was general conscription for young males either as soldiers or slave labourers, those called up in the army being used only for work behind the lines as drivers, orderlies or prison guards. From this time, also, rumours that the Japanese were losing the war became more persistent, and the police, both civil and military, arrested more and more people for having *kiken shiso*, 'dangerous thoughts', an offence which, by its nature, required no visible or audible evidence, and enabled thousands of people to be imprisoned at the whim of the police.

PART V

THE TWO REPUBLICS

CHAPTER THIRTY-FIVE

LIBERATION AND DIVISION

THE SPLIT between the Nationalists and the Communists in China in 1926 had led to a similar division among the members of the Provisional Government in Shanghai, which virtually ceased to function. The moderates under Kim Kyu-sik continued to work for unity, but as fast as a new 'United Front' could be put together fresh rifts appeared and the difficulties of the distances across the Pacific, and across Russia, where the Korean forces were now divided between bases at Khabarovsk, north of Vladivostok and at Irkutsk, on the far side of Lake Baikal, the lack of finance, the multiplicity of double agents and the fanaticism of the political extremes all worked against them. In April 1941 co-ordination between nine separate non-Communist groups was organized into a Provisional Government under Kim Ku and Kim Kyu-sik, and at the same time the non-Communist military forces were brought together under General Yi Pŏm-sŏk, who had served under Kim Chwa-jin.

When Roosevelt and Churchill met at Cairo in 1943 to prepare for their later conference with Stalin, they also invited the leader of the Chinese Nationalists, Jiang Jieshi (Chiang Kai-shek), to discuss future operations against Japan. Jiang, mindful of his Korean allies, ensured that the Cairo declaration included the promise that 'Korea shall become free and independent'. Churchill had 'never heard of the bloody place' but Roosevelt, guided by a department that had once supported Japan's colonial claims, added the prefix 'in due course' as he thought that a trusteeship might be needed for 20 to 30 years before its people were fit to govern themselves.

When the struggle in Europe ended in May 1945, the Soviet Union promised to declare war on Japan within three months, which would prevent the powerful Guandong Army from leaving Manchuria to strengthen the defences of the homeland, but might well involve the whole area coming under Russian influence. The West's best chance of avoiding this lay in launching its atomic bombs in time, which it just managed to do. The first one fell on Hiroshima on 6 August, two days before Stalin declared war. On the tenth the Japanese began to negotiate and by the fifteenth the war would be over.

The Russians made immediate landings on the north-east coast of Korea, while their rivals were still 600 miles away. The Americans drafted a hasty proposal to divide the country into two zones along the 38th parallel, which, to their surprise, the Russians accepted, without informing the Japanese. After the surrender, the Governor-General in Korea, Abe Nobuyuki, realized that to get his 700,000 fellow-countrymen home safely he would need not only the full cooperation of all the landowners, businessmen, bureaucrats and policemen who had connived in their rule, but also the forbearance of those who had not. He appealed, therefore, to the leading moderates, and was able to make an agreement with Yŏ Un-hyŏng, then in prison, who belonged to the political left and had organized a movement known as the Alliance for Independence. He was to be responsible for the safety of the Japanese and their personal property in return for a complete relinquishment of their authority, and the immediate release of all political prisoners. The Japanese, expecting an immediate occupation of the whole peninsula by the Russians, kept out of sight but retained their weapons, while the populace danced in the streets and quickly stitched together national flags.

Yŏ set up a Committee for the Preparation of Independence, followed by People's Committees to take over local government offices and by the end of August they were established in all the main centres and would soon spread downwards until each village had its committee. It was not until 2 September that they learned that their country was to be arbitrarily divided into two zones of military occupation. This was strongly opposed by all shades of opinion, and in an attempt to pre-empt it the Committee called together a national assembly and announced the formation of the Korean People's Republic. Syngman Rhee, the best known of the exiled leaders, although still in America, was named as President, with Yŏ Un-hyŏng as vice-president. Kim Ku, the right-wing leader, and Kim Kyu-sik, both still in China, were also nominated to the cabinet, and the other posts divided fairly equally between left and right.

The XXIV Corps of the US Army, under Lieutenant General John R. Hodge, had taken Okinawa, with heavy losses, and were war-weary and eager to get home when, as the nearest available force, they were ordered to occupy the southern half of Korea. They took three weeks to get there, without receiving much in the way of guidance, and with no one who could speak the language. Hodge, a brave soldier who had risen from the ranks, regarded the Japanese and the Koreans as 'kittens from the same cat' and decided to approach the country as if it were 'an enemy of the United States'.

The Japanese Governor General was told that his forces were responsible for maintaining law and order until they had handed over to the Americans and American aircraft flew over the southern half of the country dropping leaflets that instructed the people to obey their Japanese rulers. They were also told to make no attempt to welcome the Americans, but of course they did. As Hodge's ship approached Inch'ŏn on 6 September it was met by a small boat carrying two members of the Provisional Government, but his instructions were to ignore any such approaches. When the ship berthed the Koreans allowed Abe, escorted by his police, to go aboard while they prepared their own welcoming party of leading citizens, accompanied by children with flags. Abe, assured that his authority would be upheld, used his armed police to keep them away, and when the Koreans surged forward they opened fire, killing two and wounding ten.

With Abe temporarily reinstated as Governor, Hodge set up a Military Government, imposed an 8 p.m. curfew, and sent fully armed units to liaise with the Japanese officials in each provincial centre. Despite this disastrous beginning and their wounding tendency to fraternize with their former enemies rather than with the Koreans, the general goodwill of the Americans and the people's gratitude for their victory eventually produced a calmer atmosphere which enabled the Japanese to be peacefully repatriated, as they were also from the North, where the Russians worked through the local people's committees. At the same time thousands of Koreans who had been conscripted as soldiers or forced labour were flowing in from Japan and other points around the Pacific.

The KPR and its people's committees had too much of a leftist flavour for the Americans so they had no alternative but to use the existing officials and police who had served the Japanese. As soon as this became clear, the non-Communist elements who had been willing to serve under Yŏ Un-hyŏng in the expectation of a Russian occupation now left the KPR to form their own parties, chiefly the KDP, 'Korean Democratic Party', and with the support of the police and the landowners they began to denounce the KPR as Communist-inspired and would soon succeed in having it outlawed in the South.

In the North, the Russians found the KPR under the chairmanship of Cho Man-sik, whose courageous peaceful resistance to the Japanese had won him the title of the 'Gandhi of Korea'. The influence of his party, the Christian Nationalists, reflected the strength of the Presbyterian Church in this area. The Russians accepted the KPR and its local committees, but they encouraged the Communist elements and were consequently resisted and resented by the Nationalists, a reflection of the similar struggle going on in China.

In October a Russian ship arrived at Wŏnsan from Vladivostok with Colonel Kim Il-sung and 66 officers of a special Korean battalion that had been trained in Khabarovsk to form the nucleus of a People's Army. Then in his early thirties, Kim had been a member of the Chinese Party before going to Khabarovsk in 1940. He was highly thought of by his Russian superiors and, though reluctant, was encouraged by Stalin who, evidently knowing as little as Roosevelt or Churchill of the '5,000 years of history', told him 'Korea is a young country, it needs a young leader.'

After a conference in Moscow in December it was announced that the four-power trusteeship would last for five years, whilst a joint Soviet-US Commission would go ahead with arranging nationwide elections, to be followed by the eventual withdrawal of the occupying armies. This was at first violently opposed by all sides, with strikes and mass demonstrations, but soon the Left, confident of winning the elections, began to support the Trusteeship. Consequently, in the North, Cho Man-sik, who led the movement against it, was marginalized and eventually ousted as chairman of the Provisional Government by Kim Il-sung. There were now violent clashes with right-wing groups which paralleled those taking place in the South, but with opposite results, the Communists coming to dominate the local KPR committees and businessmen, landowners and former Japanese collaborators moving southwards in increasing numbers.

In the South, the Right refused to acknowledge the Trusteeship as they knew that with the country in its present mood they had little chance of winning, but trusted in the Americans to support them against the Left. The first meeting of the Soviet-US Committee was held at the Tŏksu Palace in Seoul in January 1946 and some agreement was reached on practical matters such as the movement of goods across the thirty-eighth parallel and the provision of electricity, fertilizers and minerals by the North in exchange for rice from the South, but on political matters the Russians refused to deal with any party that did not accept the Trusteeship itself, while Hodge had not only these parties, but others that refused to recognize his own military government.

In March the North introduced a land reform which not only distributed the land that had been held by the Japanese but reduced that of the larger Korean landowners to a maximum of five *chŏngbo*, a little over 12 acres, which was considered to be as much as one family could be expected to farm. Small and medium businesses were encouraged but the large corporations were nationalized. This was a reasonable reform, originally proposed by the KPR, which the peasant population in the South were still hoping to see. Those who chose to stay in the North, never having had any experience of conflicting political parties, would soon come to accept a one-party Marxist state as the logical path to a better future, and records of the lively debates of their early local committees give no hint of the coming transformation into an oppressive Stalinist state.

In the South, Hodge now tried to set up a 'Democratic Advisory Council' to prepare for the proposed national elections, and to preserve the political balance he wanted to have Yŏ Un-hyŏng as its Chairman, but Yŏ refused on the principle that the Americans were the guests and not the hosts, as did Kim Kyu-sik and the other members of the moderate left. He had to turn therefore to Syngman Rhee, whose status as 'President-elect' had survived the demise of the KPR and enabled him to remain above 'party politics' and also largely beyond the control of General Hodge. Charged with avoiding any kind of confrontation with the North, Hodge tried to censor some of Rhee's anti-Russian radio broadcasts, but Hodge was also determined to suppress any Communist activities in the South.

In October 1945 he shut down three Communist newspapers and arrested many of the party's leaders, forcing Pak Hŏn-yŏng, their chairman, to flee to the North. This was followed by strikes and riots in the main cities, and by more arrests. By this time the military administration had put all the government departments into the hands of Korean nominees, with American advisers, and an election was held for one half of a Legislative Assembly of which the other half would be appointed by the Americans. As the Left either boycotted it or were intimidated, only right-wing representatives were elected and Hodge attempted to restore the balance by appointing a few from the moderate left, including Yŏ and Kim Kyu-sik, who became chairman.

In this way both the North and the South now had their separate and distinctive administrations and became increasingly intolerant of their political opponents. In the North, those opposed to Communism continued to move to the South, where the police were increasingly active in rounding up members of labour unions and any other leftist organizations, forcing hundreds of young males either to flee to the North or face imprisonment. Cornelius Osgood, Professor of Anthropology at Yale, was at that time sharing the life of a southern village and in his classic *The Koreans and their Culture* he describes how in 1947 he witnessed young married farmers, members of village committees that supported land reform, being rounded up and carried away in truck-loads.

At the same time the North was infiltrating guerrillas into the mountain areas of the South, where with their backing Communist sympathizers came to control the hamlets scattered through the hills, dividing families and setting the scene for many small-scale tragedies. In the outside world, also, Cold War attitudes were hardening. The so-called 'Truman Doctrine' of active resistance to Soviet pressure was affecting American policy everywhere, while the Russians were not prepared to see an unfriendly government set up on their borders. Their delegates to the Joint Commission protested at the wholesale arrests in the South, but it would appear that very similar things were happening in the North.

In September 1947 the American government submitted the problem to the General Assembly of the United Nations, where the Russians proposed that all foreign troops should withdraw. A poll in Korea showed that this was favoured by a majority on both sides of the parallel, but the Assembly supported an American proposal for elections to be held under UN supervision. The Russians refused to cooperate but eventually, in February 1948, it was resolved that in May the UN would hold elections in such parts of Korea as were accessible to them.

The moderates in the Southern Assembly under Kim Kyu-sik, supported by Kim Ku, opposed it, and the North threatened to cut off the electricity supply, and did so two weeks later, causing a temporary collapse of much of the industry in the South. There followed a series of violent insurrections in the South, and an armed rebellion on Cheju Island in April 1948, followed by a mutiny of the troops from Chŏlla Province that were to be sent there to quell it, and the island would be in Communist hands for more than a year. In the wake of further insurrections Rhee persuaded the National Assembly to pass a National Security Law that virtually legalized his supression of the left and by the spring of 1950 the country's prisons would hold about 60,000 people, most of them held on political charges.

For the majority of the population who were small farmers paying up to 50 per cent of their crop in rent, land reform had been the most popular item in the KPR programme, but only in the North had it happened. It had already been implemented in Japan, by MacArthur, but Hodge did not have the same dictatorial powers. He did, however, have at his disposal the great areas of land formerly owned by the Japanese, which amounted to about 20 per cent of the total, and in March 1948 it was finally agreed that it would be offered to the tenants, who would pay by contributing 20 per cent of their crop for the next 15 years, one man's holding being limited to a maximum of two *chŏngbo*, about five acres. It more than doubled the number of farmers who owned their own land but did nothing for the others. The Military Government had attempted to reduce rents to 30 per cent of the crop, but as this was accompanied by removing all controls on the price of rice, it led to hoarding, price rises and foot shortages, so that less-educated members of the public came to think that the Americans, like the Japanese before them, were taking away their rice, though in fact they were attempting to mitigate the shortage with aid at the level of about $1 million a year.

The elections took place on 10 May, with a large turnout, and in a relatively free atmosphere. But as Kim Ku's right-wing Independence Party boycotted them, Yŏ Un-hyŏng had been assassinated and the Communists were banned, it was easily dominated by Syngman Rhee, who was returned unopposed in his Seoul constituency and became the President. By this time 73, he was a strong decisive character who saw himself as the 'Father of the Country'. His master's degree in political science from Harvard and his doctorate from Princeton, where Woodrow Wilson had been his supervisor, earned him respect, and although the Western media would demonize him, it is arguable that anyone less obstinate would have been forced simply to abandon the country to the Communists.

The new assembly allotted a proportional number of empty seats to be taken up by representatives from the North when they had been duly elected, expressing their claim to be the country's legitimate government. Rhee had gained the backing of the powerful men in the KDP by promising them places in his cabinet, but when the time came he gave the vice-presidency to a supporter of his chief rival, Kim Ku, and the premiership to Yi Bŏm-sŏk, the hero of the Manchurian resistance, whose right-wing 'Youth Corps' had won only six seats, while as evidence of his intention to bring in the land reform, he gave the Ministry of Agriculture to the progressive leader, Cho Pong-am, who was a former Communist. It left only two places for the KDP, who felt betrayed and united with some of the smaller groups to form the Democratic National Party and oppose him.

The North conducted their own elections for a 'People's Assembly' with Kim Il-sung as premier and Pak Hŏn-yŏng, former chairman of the Workers' Party in the South, as vice-premier, and in addition to the 212 delegates from the North they also elected 360 refugees from the South to represent its greater population. They were recognized by the Soviet Union and the socialist states of East Europe, so that the line of demarcation on the thirty-eighth parallel now became the frontier between two states each of which claimed the whole peninsula as its legitimate territory.

CHAPTER THIRTY-SIX

DRAWING THE LINE

THE ARBITRARY division along the thirty-eighth parallel gave the North about 50,000 square miles of territory, considerably larger than the South, but mountainous, with little rice land and only about one-third of the total population. It inherited the hydro-electric turbines that provided power for the whole country, and almost all of its heavy industry, including the great chemical complex at Hŭngnam on which the country depended for fertilizer and cement.

In military terms, it had an industrial base for the eventual manu-facture of its own weapons and could welcome back groups from the Maritime Provinces who had served in the Russian armed services, including technicians and pilots. Although Mao was still fighting the Nationalists he allowed the Korean partisans based at Yan'an to go home, in return for which, when Lin Piao's forces in Manchuria were defeated by the Nationalists in 1946, the North Koreans pro-vided them with bases and aid, which Mao would later remember with gratitude.

The introduction of conscription meant that by 1948 the North had an army of about 20,000, and this was greatly increased in 1949 when Lin Piao turned the tide, Beijing was taken, and about 22,000 Manchurian Koreans who had been fighting the American-backed forces of Jiang Jieshi were released, many of them ready to volunteer for service against the American 'puppets' in the south of the penin-sula. The Soviet forces had been withdrawn by 1949 but they had left a core of advisers and handed over all their weapons together with a large armoury collected from the departing Japanese.

By the spring of 1950, with their number now built up to more than 100,000, they had about 1,000 pieces of artillery, a few naval vessels, 258 T-34 tanks, and nearly 200 aircraft. The Americans were slower to withdraw, and Syngman Rhee fought desperately to retain them, or at least gain some promise of their return if the North attacked them, but without success. They assisted in the building up of a regular army, but organized, in General MacArthur's words, 'to indicate clearly its peaceful purpose and to provide no plausible basis for allegations of being a threat to North Korea'.

To control the internal unrest the Southern police were provided with firearms, jeeps and radios. Aided by the innate conservatism of the farming community who had been alienated by the violence of the insurrections and encouraged by hopes of land reform, they were able to isolate the guerillas into a few remote mountain areas, of which the most dangerous was that around Mt Chiri on the border between South Chŏlla and South Kyŏngsang.

Within the limits of its anti-Communist consensus the Southern Assembly could still raise issues of reform and social justice, of which the most pressing were land reform and the ousting of officials who had collaborated with the Japanese. Both had been promised by Rhee but it seemed that the right wing could always muster enough votes in the assembly to have them delayed or watered down. In the North the Japanese collaborators had been dealt with quickly and spontaneously, and in the South, also, some of the worst offenders had suffered at the hands of the People's Committees, but many able and honest members of the army, police, hospitals and schools had in some way or other cooperated with the Japanese, and now after three years it was a painful subject that generated charges and counter-charges and much resentment.

Cho Pong-am, Rhee's Minister of Agriculture and Forestry, had a strong following among the farmers, but his years in Russia and his record as a former agent of the Comintern made him an easy target for the Right and Rhee would eventually be forced to dismiss him. Even so, his radical Land Reform Bill was passed in May 1949, though it was slightly watered down before it became law in June. The aim was to put the land into the hands of those who worked it. Landlords were paid one and a half times the value of the annual crop by the government, who then distributed it to the tenants at a 30 per cent discount to be paid in instalments over 15 years, no one person being allowed to hold more than seven and a half acres.

Along with the earlier distribution of former Japanese holdings, it changed the South from a land of impoverished peasants to a land of struggling small farmers. It gave them just enough money to send their children to high school, after which they borrowed more, or even sold the land, to get them through college. This measure, along with the massive expansion of the education industry that followed, was Rhee's one great achievement, and served both to undermine the political left and to ensure his enduring popularity with the farming community. Most of the larger landholders had already transferred their resources into industrial concerns, so that this period saw also the establishment, in embryo, of what would become the *chaebŏl*, the great family corporations of the 1970s.

The rival Cold War powers were preoccupied with Europe and neither wanted a confrontation in Korea. Rhee's apparent confidence that his lightly armed forces, which were building up to about 100,000, could, with a few better weapons, defeat the North without directly involving the Americans, did not convince them, but a similar bid by Kim Il-sung had the active support of Terenti Shtykov, the Soviet Ambassador in Pyongyang. He accompanied Kim on a secret visit to Moscow in April 1950, along with Pak Hŏn-yŏng, the former leader in the South. Pak assured Stalin that they had 200,000 supporters in the South ready to rise, and a guerrilla army hidden on Mt Chiri, and it would all be over in three days. On his way home Kim visited Beijing, where Mao, recently reconciled with Stalin, could not oppose the move but was desperately anxious not to provoke the Americans into a renewed attack from Taiwan.

Further weapons began to arrive from Russia by sea, thus avoiding any involvement with the Chinese in Manchuria, and a team of Soviet experts set to work on a battle plan which was from the outset labelled as a 'counter-attack', as there were always enough provocations on the frontier to justify the claim. After the establishment of separate governments in 1948 the border had been closed, with armed patrols on both sides, and there were hundreds of incidents, sometimes local battles involving two or three thousand men, and lasting for days or even weeks. There was high tension there in the spring of 1950, but as the summer monsoon approached it quietened down. From the end of 1949 the American headquarters in Tokyo had been receiving reports of an invasion planned for June, but the Supreme Commander, Douglas MacArthur, was convinced that they would continue to rely on guerrilla warfare as he, also, overestimated Kim's underground support in the South. Even when reports came in of large-scale troop movements, they were held to be no more than manœuvres.

Thus, the South was taken by surprise when, on Sunday, 25 June 1950 what was at first thought to be no more than another border incident developed into a full-scale invasion. In the United States it was still Saturday 24, and a meeting of the Security Council was called for the next day. The Russians were currently boycotting the Council over its refusal to recognize Communist China, and were probably glad to avoid having to use their veto as in any case they expected the whole thing to be over within a few days.

That evening Truman conferred with his top military and foreign

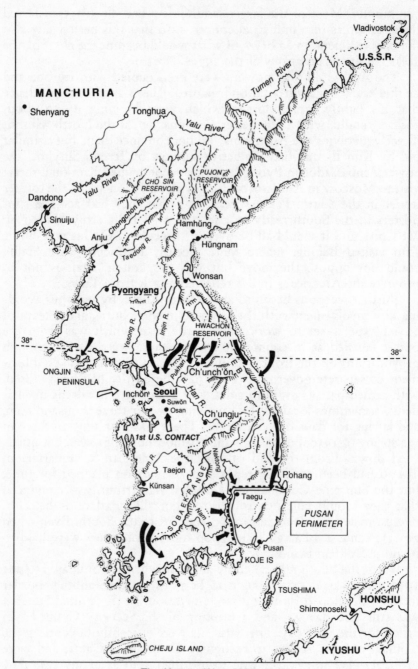

The Korean War, 1950–1952

policy advisers. They saw Kim Il-sung simply as a puppet, so this had to be Stalin's next step in his plan to conquer the world, and they had to stop it. According to the official minutes, General Omar Bradley said, 'We must draw the line somewhere', to which the President agreed and Bradley went on to say that as the Russians were not yet ready for war, Korea was as good a place as anywhere to draw it.

In Tokyo, General MacArthur, obsessed with China, believed that the North Korean move was merely to mask an invasion of Taiwan and persuaded Truman to send the Seventh Fleet to the straits of Formosa, which the Chinese saw as a direct American threat. In Britain, Attlee's cabinet, meeting on 27 June, saw it rather as a North Korean adventure from which the Russians and the Chinese might well wish to dissociate themselves, but as the Anglo-American 'special relationship' was their only safeguard against Russian advance in Europe, they ordered the Far Eastern Fleet to sail immediately to join the Americans off the Korean coast.

The South Korean forces had been kept alert by the repeated border incidents and in many places resisted with great courage and some temporary success, but they were thinly scattered along the line and had no heavy artillery or anti-tank guns. The main attack was directed towards Seoul, and the Imjin River, traditionally its last line of defence, was crossed before the bridges had been blown. By the evening of the 27th the Northern Army was approaching its outskirts and a flood of refugees began to pour southwards. The bridges across the Han were mistakenly blown too early, killing many who were crossing, and bottling up half of the Southern Army.

After taking Seoul, the Northern forces, apparently confident that the war was won, stayed on the north bank for a week while they regrouped. What remained of the Southern army set up their headquarters 20 miles to the south, at Suwŏn, and MacArthur flew in from Tokyo escorted by four Australian Mustangs which chased off a North Korean Yak as he came in to land. He was greeted calmly by Rhee who had flown in from Taejŏn with John Muccio, the US Ambassador, in two light planes that had escaped an attack from a fighter by hedge-hopping. MacArthur then drove north to look at the line on the Han River, and his presence, as a guarantee of American aid, did something to restore their morale.

They were unable to hold the river for long and Suwŏn was taken on 2 July, after which the Northern army again paused for a couple of days. By this time the first American troops of the 24th Infantry Division were moving up from Pusan. They were ill-prepared and poorly armed, mostly 18-year-old conscripts who had been having an easy time in Japan. On the night of 4 July they dug in on hills either side of the road a few miles south of Suwǒn. It was the time of the *changma*, 'long rain', not cold, but wet. They woke early in the morning to the sound of approaching tanks. Their anti-tank rifles and small bazookas had no effect on them, truck-loads of infantry began to outflank them, and before long the survivors were splashing away through the paddies. It was a pattern that would be constantly repeated as the Northern Army moved steadily southwards, pushing a great flock of refugees in front of them. The only seemingly triumphant elements were the British and American Navies which pounded the coastline and their Air Forces which would pour down thousands of pounds of bombs with a reckless disregard of the indigenous population.

As the defending armies were pushed back the UN Commander, Walton H. Walker, made a siege line along the high ground to the west of the Naktong River, where Silla had held out against its enemies. With mountains to the north and the sea on the other two sides, it was known as the 'Pusan Perimeter'. It was a large area to hold but reinforcements were pouring in, including two British battalions from Hong Kong, so that they soon outnumbered the attackers, who by the beginning of September had reached the point of exhaustion and began to falter.

Two weeks later MacArthur arrived off Inch'ǒn with a division of Marines, an Infantry Division, and about 9,000 Koreans, altogether about 70,000. The marines climbed down into 250 rusty landing craft, many of them borrowed back from the Japanese fishermen to whom they had been sold, and in the face of concrete walls, 30-foot tides, the opposition of all the experts in amphibious warfare and the experience of his Chinese predecessor, Xue Rengui, who in 674 had failed in a similar attempt from the northern side, they clawed their way into the town. Four days later the 7th Infantry Division, which followed them ashore, reached the outskirts of Seoul. The Northern Army held out there for days under continuous bombardment and it was 29 September before MacArthur, at a lavish ceremony that was said to have been more carefully planned than the landing, handed over the ruined city to Syngman Rhee.

Cut off from the rear and outnumbered by two to one, it was now the turn of the North to make a costly and disorganized retreat which did not halt until they had recrossed the line, leaving behind them thousands of prisoners who had surrendered on the way. The UN had not authorized its armies to pursue them any further, but the Americans, with reluctant British consent, had already decided to occupy the North. On 2 October the Chinese Foreign Minister, Zhou Enlai, warned the Indian Ambassador in Beijing that if American, as distinct from South Korean, troops crossed the line, they would have to intervene, but Truman dismissed this as an attempt at blackmail and on 7 October the UN Assembly adopted a British resolution calling for a united Korean government to be elected under UN supervision.

On 9 October the US Eighth Army swept across the border near Kaesŏng and up the West coast towards Pyongyang, South Korean forces moved up the centre and the Marines were sent round by sea to land at Wŏnsan on the east coast, but the South Koreans had taken it before they arrived and by 25 October tank crews of their 6th Division were triumphantly pissing in the Yalu. They thought the war was over: they did not know that for the past two weeks the Chinese had been silently crossing the river, the first of 130,000, under Peng Dehuai.

The war that had begun in an almost tropical summer would now be fought amongst northern mountains already frosty and snowbound, conditions for which neither side was adequately equipped. The highly mechanized UN forces were dependent on the few narrow roads which often became so jammed with vehicles that under massive Chinese attacks the panic-stricken troops had to abandon them to fight in beleaguered corrals or simply flee. On 5 December Pyongyang was abandoned by the Eighth Army, which had suffered 11,000 casualties and had completely lost its nerve. Vast supply dumps were set on fire and by 15 December they were back in the South.

Those on the east side had no such easy escape. About 10,000 Marines who had reached the northern end of the great Chosin Reservoir and were preparing to link up with the forces to the west were attacked by 30,000 Chinese and looked like being cut off before they could get back to their base at the southern tip of the lake, which was itself soon attacked and cut off. In isolated garrisons, under freezing conditions that reached -20° at night, they were defending themselves against 12 Chinese divisions. When they finally decided to break out for the coast they were ordered to leave everything behind, but insisted, against the Corps commander's orders, on taking with them the trucks loaded with their frozen dead, reminiscent of the frozen bodies in the account of Silla's retreat from the north under Kim Yu-sin in 661. By 10 December they began to trickle into the port of Hŭngnam where by the end of December nearly 200 ships had rescued 105,000 UN troops.

On 30 November, as the full force of the Chinese onslaught became apparent, Truman declared that he would take whatever steps were necessary to meet it, and when asked whether that included the atomic bomb, he said that it included 'every weapon we have'. This produced such a furore in the House of Commons that Attlee flew to Washington to be given a quotable, but unwritten, promise that the bomb would not be used without consultation.

At the end of the year the Eighth Army commander, Walton H. Walker, was killed when his jeep hit an army truck and he was replaced by Matthew B. Ridgway, one of the great generals of World War II. His force, which now numbered 365,000, included several Korean divisions, the British Division, and thousands of 'Katusas' and 'Katcoms', Koreans integrated into the American or Common-wealth forces at the rate of a hundred men per company. As well as the Commonwealth countries of Australia, Canada, India, New Zealand and South Africa there were units from Belgium-Luxem-bourg, Colombia, Denmark, Ethiopia, France, Greece, Italy, Nether-lands, Norway, Philippines, Sweden, Thailand, and Turkey. In the first days of 1951 the Communist forces were on the outskirts of Seoul and those who had returned there were beginning once more to flee, this time across the frozen river in the bitterest period of the winter, but the Chinese had had terrible losses, by frostbite as well as by bullets and bombs, and the offensive was losing its impetus.

Ridgway restored the Eighth Army's morale and once again the flow was reversed. The North Korean Tenth Division was cut off deep within the South, South Korean troops recrossed the line on 27 March and the UN established 'Line Utah' just to the north of it, but it was known that the Chinese were preparing for a spring offensive. Faced with the alternative of risking an all-out war with China or accepting a stalemate and looking for a settlement, MacAr-thur was determined on the former and Truman on the latter. MacArthur had such strong support from the Republicans, the press and the public that Truman did not dare to forewarn him of his dismissal – he heard about it on the news, and Ridgway took over as supreme commander.

The UN ground forces, now under James Van Fleet, continued to advance, but this was a Chinese feint while they also changed generals and brought in large-scale reinforcements for an offensive which took them south again. It was here that the British made their most notable contribution. 29 Brigade, made up of the Northumber-land Fusiliers, the Ulster Rifles and the Gloucesters, with the tanks of the 8th Hussars and the infantry of the 1st Belgian Battalion, were spread out over seven miles of hills looking down on the Imjin River when the Chinese, against expectations, decided to make this the centre of their thrust on Seoul. In wave after wave two divisions of infantry were thrown against the artillery and heavy mortars of the defenders and even cavalry charges, in the manner of Crimea. The Chinese eventually forced their way between the hill-top positions of the Fusiliers and the Gloucesters, to reach high ground behind them and from this point the Gloucesters were doomed. With more than 100 dead and 200 wounded, about half of them were taken prisoner. Van Fleet later described it as 'the most outstanding example of unit bravery in modern warfare.'

It helped to blunt the Chinese offensive which failed to reach Seoul and by the end of May they had been forced back across the Imjin, while the ceaseless bombing of Pyongyang and other northern cities made civilian life intolerable. Behind-the-scenes negotiations for peace began in May and peace talks in July, but both sides were convinced of their own moral superiority, and felt they had won, each expecting the other to make concessions. The North Koreans began to dig in along their line and established a deeply fortified belt while the United States persisted with its bombing of civilians in the North and made continual forays along the cease-fire line intended, in Van Fleet's words, to 'sustain morale and demonstrate the Army's continuing will to fight'.

There would now be two long years of bickering in which every day dozens of lives were lost in the taking and retaking of small bare hills. Van Fleet, a disciple of MacArthur, may have still had the 'will to fight' but the American public were weary of it and Eisenhower, in his 1952 election campaign, promised to end it. He stepped up the bombing and threatened the North with atomic weapons. They had made tremendous efforts to move their munition works underground and were prepared to endure, but in March 1953, under pressure from the Chinese, they agreed to begin an exchange of the wounded, to be followed by a general return of prisoners.

Much of the argument concerned their repatriation as many from the North wished to be freed in the South, or in the case of the Chinese, to go to Taiwan. The largest of the Southern camps was on Kŏje Island near Pusan, where nearly 100,000 were held in a series of wired compounds, in some of which Party activists drilled them with improvised weapons, and on one occasion seized the American commandant as a hostage to demand better conditions.

In other camps Protestant clergy, with aid organized by missionaries, were able to forestall the Communists in gaining the upper hand. Here there was daily Bible study instead of lectures on Marxism, thousands of converts were made, and some hundreds of them would eventually be ordained as pastors, one of the factors that contributed to making Protestantism the dominant religion in the South. Many of them did not wish to return to the North, and Rhee pre-empted the argument by giving his troops orders to open the gates on the night of 18 June and the UN forces were unable to prevent them from flooding out, clutching leaflets with instructions as to where to go next, altogether about 25,000.

It was finally agreed that all prisoners should be given a choice, and 70,000 North Koreans went home, some of them demonstrating their anti-American feelings by stripping off the uniforms and boots they had been given and returning in their underpants. Of about 8,000 Southerners held by the North, 325 elected to stay, while of the 4,000 American or UN prisoners one or two chose to go to China and about 20 were 'turned around', including George Blake, the British vice-consul in Seoul, whose arrest as a Soviet agent in 1962 would be followed by the flight of Kim Philby and his own escape from Wormwood Scrubs. In subsequent years interviews with former British prisoners indicate that a great many of them would never lose a certain sympathy for the Northern point of view.

CHAPTER THIRTY-SEVEN

STUDENTS AND SOLDIERS

EARLY in the war the southern government had moved to Pusan, and for a time all political activity was suspended, but early in 1951 two scandals brought the opposition to life again. One was the burning of houses and the slaughter of about 600 villagers in the Kŏch'ang area, north of Mt Chiri, when they resisted an attempt by the army to evacuate them because they were believed to be providing sustenance for the Communist guerrillas, followed by an attack on the team sent by the National Assembly to investigate the incident. The three ministers responsible for the army, home affairs and justice in Rhee's cabinet resigned, and the officers responsible were punished, but Rhee later gave their commander, 'Tiger' Kim, a special pardon and put him in charge of the national police. The other was the embezzlement of millions of dollars worth of defence funds and supplies by officers in charge of the National Defence Corps, a militia many of whose members were found dying of cold and starvation. The commander and five others were condemned to death.

Having lost his majority in the Assembly, Rhee abandoned his claim to be above party politics and at the end of 1951 he united his followers in a new party to be known as the Liberals. Rhee's original choice for premier, Yi Pŏm-sŏk, had been replaced by the less amenable Chang Myŏn and it seemed unlikely that in 1952 the Assembly would re-elect him as president, so he proposed that in future the president should be chosen directly by the people. There was no chance that this would be passed by the Assembly, so he declared a state of emergency and used the police to put enough of the opposition in prison to get it through.

When the election came, there were nearly 600,000 votes for Cho Pyŏng-ok, the American-educated leader of the Democratic Party, 800,000 for Cho Pong-am, leader of the small and perpetually persecuted Progressive Party, and 5,000,000 for Rhee, helped, maybe, by corruption and intimidation, but largely because, to the inheritors of a Confucian past, he was the legitimate ruler, the 'Father of the Country'.

In the North, there was generous financial aid from the Soviet Union with contributions also from China, East Germany and Mongolia, and a three-year plan for industrial development would be completed ahead of time by 1956. Kim Il-sung seems to have put his trust in a number of Stalinist hardliners, some of them from the communities in Uzbekistan and Kazakstan as well as the Maritime Provinces. Under Hŏ Ka-i, from Tashkent, the Workers' Party was built up on lines of mass-membership, rather than the élitist style of the Chinese Party, growing in 1946 from 20,000 to nearly 300,000, and Pak Hak-se, who had worked for the secret police, the NKVD, would build up a similar system. Thus, although Kim had been faced originally with the leaders of four other Communist groups based respectively on the two halves of the peninsula and the Russian and Chinese (Yan'an) expatriates, by the end of the War he had eliminated all but two, Pak Hŏn-yŏng, former leader in the South and Kim Tu-bong, of the 'Yan'an faction'.

As the leader of the numerous refugees from the South, Pak Hŏn-yŏng had a considerable following, but his assurances of a popular uprising there had proved to be highly misleading, perhaps fatally so, and this, followed by his opposition to the cease-fire in 1953, led to his being convicted as an American agent. It left only Kim Tu-bong, who also had a large following, including many of the better educated. He tended to play down the class-war aspects and in 1956, when Krushchev made his attack on Stalinism and called for collective leadership, he dared to criticize Kim Il-sung's Stalinist style, as a result of which he was executed and his followers purged, to free them from 'the ugly historical phenomenon of factionalism'.

There now remained only the 'Kapsan Faction', those who had accompanied Kim Il-sung from Russia. They took their name from a remote and sparsely populated plateau in the Long White Mountains that had been the base for his legendary exploits as a partisan, an area so isolated that it has its own endemic diseases. They, with their associates and descendants, would eventually form a new 'Meritorious Élite' under a hereditary ruler, for here, even more than in the South, would the ingrained social habits of Yi-dynasty Confucianism prevail.

After the demise of Stalinism economic aid from Russia would continue but Kim could no longer look to them for fatherly support and despite his gratitude to the Chinese, he saw them as backward and incompetent. He now began to develop the doctrine of *Juche*,

(Chuch'e) 'self-reliance'. It may once have meant little more than, 'Pay no attention to what they do in Russia, or anywhere else!', but over the years it would grow into a complete Post-Confucian system providing rules and rituals for every aspect of human life. Under the four-year plan begun in 1956 tower blocks sprang up, tractors were mass-produced, and by 1960 the GNP would be $140 per head compared with less than $100 in the South. There was also a steady collectivization of farm land and eradication of small private businesses.

In the South, Rhee's opponents had taken comfort from the clause in the constitution that did not allow the president a third term but once again he had it changed in his favour. This time he was opposed not only by Cho Pong-am, but also by Sin Ik-hŭi who had been foreign minister in the Provisional Government in China under Kim Kyu-sik, a highly respected figure who so far had avoided directly opposing Rhee. He would almost certainly have won had he not died of a cerebral haemorrhage on the eve of the election, and his running mate for vice-president, Chang Myŏn, defeated Rhee's nominee. For the presidency, Cho Pong-am, on the left, despite oppressive intimidation, won 30 per cent of the vote and a majority in five major cities.

Elections for the National Assembly came midway between those for President, and by 1958 both the electorate and the candidates were becoming more sophisticated. Instead of an influential local man standing as an Independent and then selling his support, there would now be two influential men representing the two major parties. Rhee's Liberals were backed by a powerful network of national organizations for 'Youth' and for 'Farmers', which, with police support, largely controlled the countryside, while the Democrats had the support of the intelligentsia and the urban workers. The intimidation reached a new level in 1958, when Rhee added new crimes of 'disturbing people's minds' and 'impairing the prestige of constitutional organs'. It virtually brought to an end political meetings or any public gathering not sponsored by the government, and the press was sporadically censored.

As part of its enforcement, Cho Pong-am was put in prison, and soon afterwards, as the 1960 election approached, executed! The election was due in May, but when Cho Pyŏng-ok, the leader of the Democrats, went to America for a stomach operation, Rhee's party moved it forward to get it over before he came back. As it happened, Cho died of a heart attack and again Rhee avoided a contest that he would almost certainly have lost. The choice of vice-president was between the existing incumbent, Chang Myŏn, who had now inherited the leadership of the Democrats, and Rhee's previous running mate, Yi Ki-bung.

Rhee, now 85, led an isolated life with his Austrian wife and a credible anecdote of the time tells of a hatter in the Myŏngdong shopping area receiving a visit from a functionary who unwrapped a smart imported felt hat and said, 'Tomorrow morning the President will come here to buy a hat. This is the one he will buy. It will be labelled as made in Korea and it will cost 5,000 hwan' – about one-quarter of the market value. He was probably equally ignorant of his party's plans, which required local government and police chiefs to offer formal resignations which would take effect unless their areas voted correctly, and they were recommended to put 40 per cent of the ballot papers in the boxes beforehand. They were successful far beyond the bounds of credibility – ten million votes for Rhee, eight million for Yi Ki-bung and fewer than two million for Chang Myŏn.

There were election-day riots, the worst being in Masan, where seven were killed, and when it was subsequently discovered that the body of a student who had been killed by a tear gas canister had been dumped in the harbour, public protests increased. On 18 April a rally led by students from Koryŏ University was attacked by police and thugs of the 'Anti-Communist League'. The next day they were joined by other colleges and by the public in a march on the presidential mansion. This was met by gunfire, casualties, and censure from America. The army was called in, but the demonstrations continued, and on 25 April the students were joined by their professors, the army refused to fire on them, and Rhee resigned. The vice-president, Yi Ki-bung, was thought to be primarily responsible for the rigged election and after his house had been besieged by a hostile crowd for a couple of days his elder son, who had been adopted by the childless Rhee, shot the family and then himself. Rhee returned to Hawaii, but before dying there in 1965 he would be reconciled with his countrymen and affectionately received on a last visit.

An interim government under Hŏ Chŏng, an acceptable moderate who had earlier been a minister under Rhee, revised the constitution to provide for an advisory upper house, a figure-head president, and a Prime Minister. At the elections in July the Democrats had a large majority and Chang Myŏn, a quiet and cautious Catholic layman, who had once been Rhee's first ambassador to the United States, and in 1952 the first premier to oppose him, became Prime Minister. The upper house elected as president Yun Po-sun, an elderly Presbyterian graduate of Edinburgh University. Their party was already divided into warring factions of 'New' and 'Old' and it seemed that the disappearance of Rhee had left a gap that these two mild-mannered gentlemen were not large enough to fill. They had no distinctive policies and the generals with their 600,000 men, the industrialists with their rapidly growing wealth, and the Americans on whose aid the country was still to some degree dependent, were all forces over which they had little control. A chastened police force no longer opposed demonstrations and radical left-wing elements had plenty to protest about, their calls for a purge of Rhee supporters and reunion with the North raising fears of new insurrections that would invite another invasion.

The generals who had supported Rhee, mostly educated in Japanese military institutions, were increasingly at odds with younger men from the Military Academy founded by the Americans in 1949, who were just as resolute in their opposition to Communism, but angry at the rigged elections and the misuse of the army's generous American supplies. The highest-ranking member of this group was Park Chung Hee (Pak Chŏng-hŭi), who spanned the generations. A small, intense man with a taste for Buddhist asceticism and the reading of history, he had, despite service in two wars, spent most of his life in study. He had attended successively a teachers' training college in Taegu, the Military Academy in Manchuria from which as the top graduate of 1942 he went to the Imperial Military Academy in Tokyo, followed by a year in the Guandong Army, then the American-run South Korean Military Academy, followed after the war by a year as a Brigadier at the US Army Artillery School, and after a spell as a divisional commander he finally emerged from the Korean Staff College in 1957 as a 40-year-old major general.

In January 1960 he was sent to reorganize the Army's main supply base at Pusan, 'a sea of corruption' that was connected with high places in Seoul, and he soon made plenty of enemies. He took to wearing dark glasses and acting with increasing insolence towards those of his superiors whom he regarded as corrupt, and they were hesitant and divided on how to deal with him. His group had already been planning a coup before the student uprising. After it, they looked to the Democrats for a purge of the 'corrupt' generals, but this was unrealistic. Soldiers were poorly paid, army supplies flowed freely from America, and it was commonly said that 'privates stole on foot, officers stole with jeeps and generals stole with trucks'. Colonel Kim Chŏng-p'il, married to Park's niece, became the group's spokesman in appeals to the government and the army chiefs, as a result of which he was dismissed, but about 250 senior officers, including the Commander of the Marine Corps, supported their views.

On 16 May 1961 their units, in a quick and bloodless coup, occupied the Broadcasting Station and other key points in the capital and set up their headquarters behind the walls of the Tŏksu Palace beside the City Square. The Prime Minister took refuge in a Convent, the CIA sent an agent up the tower of the Anglican Cathedral with a pair of binoculars to see what was happening in the Tŏksu grounds, and General Magruder, the UN Commander, asked the President whether they should retake the city. The Americans suspected that Park was a crypto-Communist but he quickly persuaded the Army Chief of Staff, Chang To-yŏng, to join them as Chairman, and they issued an immediate declaration of their support for the USA and the UN, and for Yun Po-sun as President.

Park ruled through a junta known as the Supreme Council, operating with an austere authoritarianism that presumably stemmed from his days in the Imperial Military Academy. For almost two decades the country would be run very much as Japan was in the 1930s, and with rather similar results – it would hatch the 'economic miracle'. His trusted assistant Kim Chŏng-p'il became the head of a Korean 'CIA' which, while it took its name from the American organization, was more oriental in its methods. It had a long reach – on one occasion some dissidents in West Germany were packed into crates and sent home on a scheduled flight, to be tried and executed.

He promised civilian rule by 1963 but all former members of the Assembly were banned from political activities for six years. At the end of 1962 a referendum approved a new constitution with a president to be elected by the public and an assembly chosen by a form of proportional representation that multiplied the number of seats awarded to the parties that had won the most, ensuring final results not unlike those of the British system of 'first past the post'. Two days after the referendum Park announced that the junta would resign from their military duties so that they could play their full part in the new government. The public protest it aroused he attributed to Communist subversion, which required him to ban all political activities and extend military rule for a further four years.

This raised a storm of protest in the United States, where the heavy losses in the war and the large numbers of war brides, adopted orphans and sponsored students had built up a strong commitment to the country. Kennedy threatened to withdraw all aid, forcing Park to lift the censorship and promise elections. Kim Chŏng-p'il was withdrawn from the KCIA and charged with founding a Party, which in view of its intention to fulfil the roles of both of America's, was appropriately named the Democratic Republican Party. In the presidential election Yun Po-sun, the incumbent president, was narrowly beaten and in the subsequent election for the Assembly Park's DRP gained 32 per cent of the vote, but because of the levered system had an overall majority.

Park was determined to normalize relations with Japan, which was an emotional issue on which the opposition found it easy to arouse public indignation. When a form of agreement was published it was opposed by a majority in the Assembly, including Ch'oe Tusŏn, the German-educated chief of the Korean Red Cross whom Park had chosen as Premier, and accompanied by student demonstrations, as a result of which Park reimposed martial law and censorship and went ahead with the treaty. Its provisions included an indemnity of $300 million from Japan and a long-term loan of a similar sum which gave a great impetus to the country's economic development.

Occasional acts of terrorism by North Korean agents and tales of oppression in the North provided some justification for Park's dictatorial rule, and the USA, while active in trying to restrain its excesses, was grateful for the South's contribution to the war in Vietnam, where between 1965 and 1973 they provided 300,000 well-trained men. The war also brought them large contracts for the supply of goods and services, which by 1966 accounted for 40 per cent of their foreign exchange. It also helped them to establish sea and air transport services that would soon span the globe and gave them experience of construction work that would enable them to move into the Middle East and earn the oil they needed for continuing industrial expansion.

The South was now developing more rapidly than the North, where under the claustrophobic cult of the Great Leader and a time-serving bureaucracy there had been little technological advance since the 1950s. In sport, at least, they were still competitive and in 1966 their footballers reached the World Cup Finals in England where with noisy support from the crowd at Middlesbrough they knocked out Italy to reach the quarter-finals, and led Portugal three-nil until a failure of nerve and the skill of Eusebio turned the game round. Twenty years later, in 1986, Italy would face South Korea with some apprehension, but scraped past them at three-two. The foundations for the Far East's two best football teams had been laid by a sergeant of the marines from the British consulate and a lay brother of the Anglican Church's Society of the Sacred Mission who were coaching them at the Royal English School in Seoul in the 1890s.

A new North Korean Six-year Plan in 1971 involved the updating of their technology by importing machinery from Japan and Western Europe, but this built up heavy debts, made worse by the hike in the price of oil. Tension between North and South was probably at its highest in 1968 when a commando team from the North hijacked a Southern bus and set off to assassinate the President, almost reaching his doorstep before they were mown down. Two days later they grabbed the *Pueblo*, an American 'spy-ship' that was carrying out electronic surveillance just off the shore at Wŏnsan, and soon after a similarly equipped Naval aircraft was shot down over the Sea of Japan. These events served only to strengthen Park's authoritarian grip on the South and after further purges the constitution was altered in 1969 to allow him to stand for the third time in the election due early in 1971.

The main opposition parties united to form a New Democratic Party under 'The Two Kims', Kim Dae Jung (Kim Tae-jung) and Kim Young Sam (Kim Yŏng-sam), of whom the former became their presidential candidate. He won more than half of the votes in the cities and at the Assembly elections in the following month the DRP was reduced to 113 seats against 89 for the NDP. The deteriorating situation in Vietnam, the change in America's attitude to China after Kissinger's visit in July, and talk of an American withdrawal, along with opposition support for peace talks, backed by student demonstrations, combined to engender in Park something close to panic. On 6 December 1971 he declared a state of emergency, put the country under martial law, suspended the constitution, dissolved the Assembly, closed the universities and closely controlled the press.

His Japanese education may have impressed him with the importance of the Meiji 'Restoration', the great nineteenth-century upheaval that had begun with a 'National Council', as he used the same two ideograms *Yu, Sin*, 'making all things new', as the title for an extraordinary constitution which was enforced on the country by a 'referendum' for which 92 per cent of the public were said to have voted. The President would in future be elected by a National Council for Unification, a body of 2,359 worthy people from all parts of the country who had no political commitments, and he would nominate a third of the Assembly, so that under the guise of preparing for reunification, he imposed on the South a thinly veiled dictatorship that was virtually a mirror image of that in the North. Kim Dae Jung, who was on a visit to the USA, faced arrest if he returned, so he remained in Japan.

Park carried with him the Army, the Police and the heads of the Civil Service, as the years of KCIA purges had ensured their docility, while the industrialists and their technicians were not averse to a 'non-political' regime that fostered growth, managed the unions and outlawed strikes. He also kept the support of the naturally conservative farmers, with whom he liked to fraternize, and for whom his Saemaŭl or 'New Village Movement' had improved their efficiency and helped their income to catch up with the 'salary men', though a mass migration to the cities meant a constant decline in village life.

While the college students continued to be the main strength of the protest movement, the trade unions became increasingly active. In

1971 Ch'ŏn T'ae-il, prevented from organizing a union for clothing workers, had set himself on fire, a martyrdom that gave the movement a strong impetus but also provoked more forcible suppression of it. In 1973 the KCIA, now led by Yi Hu-rak, kidnapped Kim Dae Jung from Japan, injuring him in the process, and arousing worldwide condemnation. Kim, though released from prison, was kept under house arrest.

Continued unrest led to harsher laws and more arrests and in 1974 nine dissidents were sentenced to death, including the internationally known Catholic poet Kim Chi-ha, who had already been arrested and tortured several times. His sentence produced such an outcry around the world that it was commuted to a life sentence. Numerous Christians were arrested for taking part in protest marches, including American priests, and even Yun Po-sun, the aged former president, was given a suspended prison sentence. Twenty others were given life sentences.

In August 1974, while Park was addressing a rally to mark the anniversary of the liberation, a marksman from a Korean organization in Japan attempted to assassinate him and killed his wife, Yuk Yŏng-su. It aroused much sympathy for Park, along with revived hostility to Japan, but seemed to increase his paranoia. He turned against Kim Chŏng-p'il, who had been regarded as his successor, but was now perceived as a rival. He even distanced himself from the KCIA, which was now headed by Kim Chae-gyu, and dealt with the outside world only through the chief of his bodyguards, Ch'a Chi-ch'ŏl, and Ch'oe Kyu-ha, a colourless bureaucrat whom he had nominated as premier.

Meanwhile, President Carter's concern about human rights and proposals to withdraw US troops were followed in 1975 by 'Koreagate', which revealed a KCIA network to harass and exploit the Korean community in America and to bribe politicians involved in Korean issues. There was also increasing discontent within the country itself. Its industrial achievements, reflected in the attractive and well-made goods they were exporting to every corner of the earth, had been accompanied by the growth of a large and sophisticated middle class whose lifestyle made Park's primitive politics look increasingly anachronistic.

He survived largely because of the powerful threat of invasion from the North, which peaked every year in the spring, and was kept alive by border incidents and commando raids. Despite its industrial failures, the North was active in international politics. The Conference of Non-aligned Nations held in Sri Lanka in 1976 adopted a resolution supporting their demands for the removal of foreign troops and nuclear weapons from the South and by the end of the year they had ambassadorial relations with 138 countries, only four fewer than the South.

In October 1979, in the South, Kim Young Sam, now the leader of the opposition, was expelled from an increasingly restive Assembly and protests in the Pusan and Masan areas, which he represented, spread to Seoul, where they were more violent than at any time since 1960. Park berated the KCIA chief, Kim Chae-gyu, for failing to control them and was determined to call out the Army, but Kim was bitterly opposed to this as he knew its sympathies would be divided, creating an uncontrollable situation that might easily encourage intervention from the North. On the evening of 26 October he invited Park and Ch'a Chi-ch'ŏl to a cabaret supper at the restaurant in the KCIA compound, adjacent to Park's house, where, having failed to persuade them, he shot and killed them.

CHAPTER THIRTY-EIGHT

AWAITING REUNION

THE COUNTRY was stunned by Park's sudden death, for despite the paranoia of his last days and the ruthlessness of his dealings with the opposition, he had been for 18 years a father-figure and many felt that without him the South itself might not have survived. As always, they felt themselves to be under threat from the North, which had from 1957 onwards operated a system of conscription that kept young men in the Army between the ages of 20 and 25. Its size had grown from 420,000 in 1955 to 678,000 by 1979, equipped with about 2,500 tanks, whilst the Air Force had 700 Chinese or Russian-built aircraft, the Navy had 450 ships, including ten Russian submarines and six supplied by China between 1973 and 1975.

They had also acquired some Scud missiles from Egypt which they copied and improved to balance the American missiles based in the South, and by 1990 they would be themselves exporting them to Egypt, and elsewhere. The Japanese nuclear installation at Hŭngnam had been dismantled by the Russians, but once the North Koreans had their own nuclear powerplants they had the basic requirements for making atomic warheads, and despite their economic problems they were still the world's fourth largest military power. In 1974 the South discovered that they had built a tunnel of generous proportions under the demilitarised zone and later several more were unearthed at critical points along the line. As the fifth largest power, the South were not far behind them, with an army of 520,000 and about 3 million reservists. They had been generously supplied with American ships, tanks, aircraft and missiles and by 1978 most of their weapons were being built, and increasingly, designed, at home.

After the assassination there were strong hopes that the South's advanced technology might now be matched with some political progress, and when Ch'oe Kyu-ha, who had been premier under Park, took control, he promised eventual reform but his first act was to impose martial law for an interim period, during which the Yusin constitution would remain in place. It meant that the National Council would elect the next president regardless of the wishes of the National Assembly, and the Council's members were mostly the sort of people to whom the very idea of a political 'opposition' was tainted with suspicions of disloyalty and Communist influence.

Such views were shared by Major General Chun Doo Hwan (Chŏn Tu-hwan), who as the head of the Army Security Command was in charge of investigating Park's death. He believed that Park had been right to demand intervention by the Army and that General Chŏng Sŭng-hwa, the Army Chief of Staff, and several other generals who had been reluctant to intervene, were guilty of complicity in the crime, and that even the heads of the KCIA could no longer be trusted. From this time onwards Chun, along with two other Major Generals who had been his classmates at the Military Academy in the class of 1955, Roh Tae Woo (No T'ae-u) and Chŏng Ho-yong, began to plan a repeat of Park's coup of 1961 in order to sustain the full-blooded anti-Communist cause for which he had died.

The National Council met on 6 December and elected Ch'oe Kyu-ha as President for the remainder of Park's term. He promised reform of the constitution before the next election, in a year's time, and released many of the political prisoners, including Kim Dae Jung. It implied an eventual return to democracy but there was a great deal of dissension in the Assembly, where the right-wing DRP was split between the rival factions of the two former heads of the KCIA, Kim Chŏng-p'il and Yi Hu-rak, whilst in the NDP there was a feud between the old leader Kim Dae Jung, with support based on his native province of Chŏlla, and Kim Young Sam, based on the Pusan area.

Under these conditions, rumours of troop movements north of the border could always create a climate of fear, and on 12 December, just six days after Ch'oe's election, they provided the context in which Chun Doo Hwan launched his coup. He began by capturing the Army Chief of Staff, Chŏng Sŭng-hwa, at his home, and other senior officers, but units of the Seoul garrison moved quickly to protect the Ministry of Defence and the nearby Army Headquarters. They were attacked by armoured units from Roh's Ninth Division, which had been responsible for guarding the approaches to the capital, and there was a bitter battle for about seven hours before Chun's forces prevailed.

Chun was content to leave the government under the nominal control of Ch'oe Kyu-ha, but he ensured that the main cabinet posts and the army high command went to men whose 'purity' met his standards, while he himself took control of the KCIA. There were more student demonstrations in May, accompanied by a miners' strike and widespread unrest, to which Chun replied with a further extension of martial law, arresting the leaders of all the three main parties in the Assembly – Kim Chŏng-p'il of the right-wing DRP as well as the two Kims of the NDP. Trade union leaders and any other public figures with even the slightest taint of leftist thought were labelled as 'communists' and given spells of internment in which they were to be 're-educated'.

The strongest opposition came from the South Chŏlla capital of Kwangju, which had a tradition of resisting oppression and was also the home base of the imprisoned Kim Dae Jung. For three days from 19 May, with up to 200,000 people on the streets, the police and the army units lost control. Paratroops were sent in to restore order, but despite bloody battles failed to quell them. The Citizens' Council tried to negotiate with the troops and appealed to the United States to mediate, but the American UN Commander only freed more frontline troops for Chun to send in. The number of casualties has never been revealed, but the deaths recorded in the city in May 1980 were 2,300 above the monthly average, most of them young. It was not reported in the press either at home or abroad, other than in Korean periodicals in Japan, but the story spread throughout the land and would haunt Chun to the end of his career.

This 'incident', as he called it, allowed him to accuse Kim Dae Jung of being its instigator and have him once more condemned to death, but pressure from Democratic congressmen in America eventually forced him to commute it to a 20-year sentence. Chun became the chairman of a new Special Committee for National Security, which replaced the cabinet, largely with generals, and began an intimidatory purge in which, in the name of 'social purification', hundreds of officials were dismissed, though by this time, after their long experience under Park, the bureaucracy knew how to reinstate them under different titles. After the resignation of Ch'oe Kyu-ha in August, Chun promoted himself to four-star rank, the Special Committee elected him as President, and the newly elected Ronald Reagan invited him to Washington for mutual congratulations.

Chun lacked the integrity and purposefulness of Park, but his rule followed very much the same pattern, seeking again to ban the 'old' politicians and replace them with 'purer' ones of his own. They were known as the Democratic Justice Party (DJP) and under the same system of proportional representation 30 per cent of the vote was enough to give them a majority. He had promised to hand over to an elected successor, but not until the end of a seven-year term.

The country's continual increase in wealth and sophistication stimulated the desire for political freedom, whilst an increasing gap between rich and poor led to uneasy consciences among the children of the rich and growing resentment among the poor, so that students and workers found themselves as allies. These issues were both sharpened and confused by the longing for reunification, resentment against the Americans for their support of the junta, and the resurfacing of a socialist underground whose activities seemed sinister and dangerous to many of the older generation.

The liberal newspapers, despite censorship and persecution, persisted in their endeavour to tell the truth, but the junta controlled the television channels and made constant use of the army to clear the streets. Regular church attendance by the large Christian population gave their leaders considerable influence, the Catholics being, as in the past, mainly supporters of the opposition, whilst the Protestants, brought up in a fundamentalist tradition and closely associated with the business community, were generally more reluctant to be politically involved, but provided some influential campaigning groups.

Like Park, Chun had the sense to listen to the technocrats, so that the very real threat from the North along with the risk of throwing away their newly won affluence would be enough, for a while, to persuade most of the country, apart from the college students, to shrug their shoulders and carry on raising the GNP. Typical of the quiet, talented men on whom Chun depended was Ham P'yŏng-chun, then 48. After graduating in economics he had studied international law at Harvard, become a professor at Yŏnsei, interrupted it for a few years to be an ambassador-at-large for the Foreign Ministry under Park, and in 1982, under Chun, became Chief Secretary at the President's Office. He was not uncritical of American policies but he recognized that for its very survival the South needed their friendship. In 1985 he would accompany Chun on a visit to Rangoon, where North Korean agents were planning to plant a bomb. Ham and Chun were both slim, with shiny balding heads, and it was probably this that led the agent to press the plunger too soon and kill the Professor rather than the President.

The choice of Seoul for the 1988 Olympics was a critical factor in the unrest, uniting the South in a determination to show the world what they could do, but with the majority equally concerned that it should be under democratic rule, whereas the junta tried to use it as an excuse for postponing it. The opposition, renamed as the New Korea Democratic Party in 1985, campaigned for a new constitution with a presidential election in the year before the Games and in support of it the students began to escalate their protests. The Junta responded by recruiting high-tech riot police, young men in deep-blue designer jeans, with staves, armour and shields, trained in the martial arts and provided with a fleet of armoured buses to carry mayhem from one college campus to the next.

Early in 1986 the demonstration of 'People Power' in Manila that ousted Marcos inspired those in Seoul and encouraged the Catholic hierarchy to give them similar support, so that the Catholic and Anglican Cathedrals would become rallying points and refuges for urban warriors. By April Chun had been persuaded to change his mind and begin discussions on a new constitution, but early in 1987 he changed it back again and reversed the decision. Protests intensified in May and June, spreading to all the main cities, with more of the public supporting the students. The spectacular street battles that appeared on TV screens all round the world seemed to threaten the success of the Olympics, and something had to give.

At the end of June Chun's accomplice, Roh Tae Woo, who had been nominated as his successor and chosen as their candidate by the DJP, realized that his chances of election depended on distancing himself from Chun, and he threatened to resign unless the President accepted a whole package of reforms that included direct elections for the presidency, the release of political prisoners, freedom for the press, and the return of Kim Dae Jung, and under American pressure, Chun agreed. In October a new constitution was approved by a national referendum, and the presidential election was held in December. Roh was a more relaxed and personable figure than Chun, whilst the two Kims failed to unite their regional interests or agree on a common policy and stood against each other, with the result that Roh won with 37 per cent of the vote.

The new constitution was designed to limit Presidential powers, exclude the army from politics, and embody basic human rights, and its acceptance enabled the Olympic Games to be carried off in 1988 with complete success, bringing the country to the attention of a wider world in the same way as the 1964 Olympics had for Japan. Another, perhaps more fateful, portent was the opening, in 1987, at the south-eastern industrial port of P'ohang, centre of the steel industry, of a new technological institute with a physics laboratory sufficiently advanced to provide a synchroton with a particle energy of two GeV. It was enough to bring home from Britain, Canada and the USA a number of internationally recognized physicists, including Kim Ho-gil and Saewoong Oh (O Se-ung). Their students are encouraged by plinths with busts of Newton, Edison, Maxwell and Einstein along with a space for the next one.

The *chaebŏl*, the great industrial octopuses like Hanjin, Hyundai, Samsung, Daewoo or Goldstar, continued their close and confidential relationship with a government which, while allowing them financial privileges, strictly controlled their activities in the overall interests

of the economy. The legalization of union activity from 1987 was
followed by widespread strikes and a rapid improvement in wages
which encouraged the *chaebŏl* to build plants in less-developed areas
of south-west Asia, a policy which, to counter increasing protection-
ism, they have since extended to Europe and the USA. Along with
many smaller entrepreneurs, they have also moved into China, where,
by 1992, the South was able to develop its so-called *Nordpolitik*,
which, unlike the eighteenth-century importation of Northern
Learning from China, was a flow of ideas and investment in the
opposite direction which after 1990 would be extended also to Russia
and Eastern Europe.

Elections for the first Assembly under Roh's presidency left his
party still the largest but with no overall majority, a recipe for
frustration. But it came to a surprising conclusion in 1992 when Roh,
nearing the end of his term, did a deal with Kim Young Sam on
the left and Kim Jong Pil on the right to create a new party, the
Democratic Liberals. It would involve some factional infighting but
it represented a general recognition of the fact that there were no
deep divisions among the country's moderate majority and at the
end of the year Kim Young Sam was elected as president. Perhaps
the most reassuring aspect of his rule was the publication in 1994 of
The Incorrigible YS, a best-selling collection of irreverent jokes about
him.

The real division was, as always since 1945, between North and
South. The strong momentum towards reunion in the 80s seemed to
lose pace in the early 90s, and even the death of Kim Il-sung in 1994
produced no immediate changes, but discreet commercial exchanges
continued and the people's longing to walk the length of their land
again as one family remained as strong and as persistent as ever.
United, they have the resources, the talents and the energy to be
among the leaders of Asia Pacific, and with the combined footballing
talent of North and South even the World Cup may be within their
reach!

Koryŏ (Wang)

(918–1392)

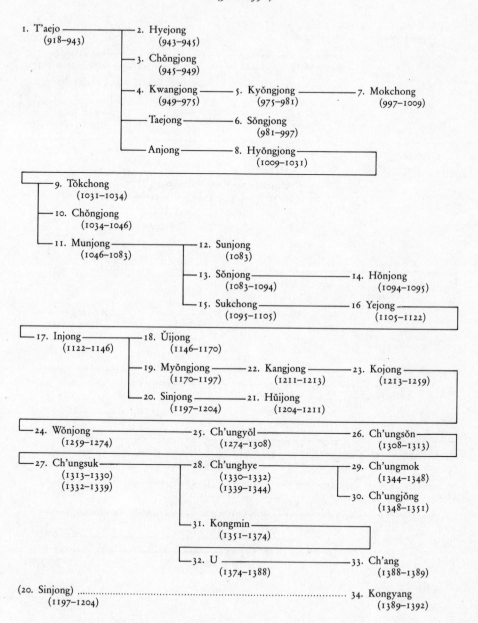

1. T'aejo —— 2. Hyejong
(918–943)   (943–945)

—— 3. Chŏngjong
(945–949)

—— 4. Kwangjong —— 5. Kyŏngjong —— 7. Mokchong
(949–975)   (975–981)   (997–1009)

—— Taejong —— 6. Sŏngjong
(981–997)

—— Anjong —— 8. Hyŏngjong
(1009–1031)

9. Tŏkchong
(1031–1034)

—— 10. Chŏngjong
(1034–1046)

—— 11. Munjong —— 12. Sunjong
(1046–1083)   (1083)

—— 13. Sŏnjong —— 14. Hŏnjong
(1083–1094)   (1094–1095)

—— 15. Sukchong —— 16 Yejong
(1095–1105)   (1105–1122)

17. Injong —— 18. Ŭijong
(1122–1146)   (1146–1170)

—— 19. Myŏngjong —— 22. Kangjong —— 23. Kojong
(1170–1197)   (1211–1213)   (1213–1259)

—— 20. Sinjong —— 21. Hŭijong
(1197–1204)   (1204–1211)

24. Wŏnjong —— 25. Ch'ungyŏl —— 26. Ch'ungsŏn
(1259–1274)   (1274–1308)   (1308–1313)

27. Ch'ungsuk —— 28. Ch'unghye —— 29. Ch'ungmok
(1313–1330)   (1330–1332)   (1344–1348)
(1332–1339)   (1339–1344)

—— 30. Ch'ungjŏng
(1348–1351)

—— 31. Kongmin
(1351–1374)

—— 32. U —— 33. Ch'ang
(1374–1388)   (1388–1389)

(20. Sinjong) .... 34. Kongyang
(1197–1204)   (1389–1392)

289

Chosŏn (Yi)

(1392–1910)

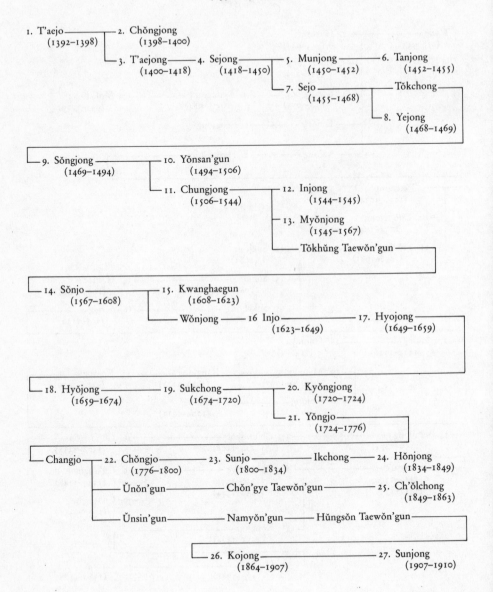

NOTES

As this book is based mainly on modern Korean textbooks that will be readily available to those familiar with the language I have limited the notes to a brief summary of the primary sources for each section with a few further suggestions from the available works in English.

PART I. THE THREE KINGDOMS

The court records of the Three Kingdoms, Koguryŏ, Silla and Paekche, have survived only in the form in which they were edited by the Koryŏ historian Kim Pu-sik for his *Samguksagi* (History of the Three Kingdoms), first published in 1145. As well as Chinese histories he used other books such as those of the early eighth-century scholar Kim Tae-mun, who is known to have written about the achievements of the Hwarang, the lives of famous monks, and so on, but none of them has survived. Some essays and poems by Koreans employed by the Tang have been preserved in China, but apart from a few poems, memorial inscriptions and scraps of paper, the *Samguksagi* provides the only reliable Korean source for this period.

The edition I have used gives the Chinese text, edited with a Korean translation by Kim Chong-sik (2 vols. Myŏngmundang, Seoul, 1988).

For the general archaeological background:

Barnes, Gina L. (ed.) *Hoabinhian, Jomon, Yayoi, Early Korean States* (Oxbow Books, Oxford, 1990).
Dr Barnes' essay in this book provides a critical review of various historical interpretations of the archaeological evidence between 500 BC and AD 500, with an extensive bibliography.

Nelson, Sarah M., *The Archeology of Korea* (Cambridge University Press, Cambridge, 1992).

PART II. KORYŎ

The official *Koryŏsa* (History of Koryŏ), based on the edited versions of the court records produced after the death of each of its successive Kings, was completed, on revisionist lines, by Yi dynasty scholars over the period between 1395 and 1451, and runs to 140 volumes in Chinese. They are available in Korean. I have relied heavily on the guidance of Professor Pak Yong-ŭn's *Koryŏsidaesa* (History of the Koryŏ Era) (Ilchisa, Seoul, 1988), so the primary sources for most of what I have written for this period can be found in his footnotes. Richard Rutt's footnotes to Gale will also be of value.

For the early Mongol period (Chaps 12 and 13):

Henthorn, William E., *Korea: The Mongol Invasions* (Brill, Leiden, 1963).

PART III. CHOSŎN

The official history of the dynasty, *Chosŏn Wangcho Sillok*, based on edited records, in Chinese, of each reign from the days of its founder in 1392 to the Japanese annexation in 1910, runs to 2,077 volumes, the master copies of which are preserved in an annexe of Seoul National University. An edition in 48 volumes was printed by the National History Editorial Committee between 1955 and 1958.

The total literature relating to the period is vast, and the list of items available in Western languages is continually expanding. The following suggestions for further reading are in the chronological order of the periods they deal with:

FOURTEENTH TO SEVENTEENTH CENTURIES
Deuchler, Martina, *The Confucian Transformation of Korea: A Study of Society and Ideology* (Harvard University Press, Cambridge, Mass. and London, 1992).

A richly detailed study of how, over this period, laws and customs were changed by Neo-Confucian ideology.

FIFTEENTH CENTURY
Meskill, John (tr.), *Ch'oe Pu's Diary: A Record of Drifting across the Sea* (University of Arizona Press, Tucson, 1965).

Wagner, Edward W., *The Literati Purges: Political Conflict in Early Yi Korea* (Harvard University Press, Cambridge, Mass., 1974).

SIXTEENTH CENTURY
Park Yune-Hee, *Admiral Yi Sun Sin and his Turtleboat Armada* (Hanjin, Seoul, 1978).

Ha Tae-hung (tr.) and Sohn Pow-key (ed.), *Nanjung Ilgi: War Diary of Yi Sun Sin* (Yonsei, Seoul, 1977).

Ha Tae-hung (tr.) and Lee Chong-young (ed.), *Imjin Changch'o: Admiral Yi Sun Sin's Memorials to the Court* (Yonsei, Seoul, 1981).

SEVENTEENTH CENTURY
Ledyard, Gari, *The Dutch Come to Korea* (includes the English text of Hendrik Hamel's *Narrative* of 1668) (Royal Asiatic Society, Korea Branch, Seoul, 1971).

EIGHTEENTH CENTURY
Choe-Wall, Yang-hi (ed.), *Memoirs of a Korean Queen* (KPI, London, 1985). A translation of *Hanjungnok*, the story of the 'Rice Box King' by his widow.

NINETEENTH CENTURY

Choe, Ching Young, *The Rule of the Taewŏn'gun, 1864–1873: Restoration in Yi Korea* (Harvard University Press, Cambridge, Mass., 1972).

Cook, Harold F., *Korea's 1884 Incident: Its Background and Kim Ok-Kyun's Elusive Dream* (Royal Asiatic Society, Korea Branch, Seoul, 1972). The story of the Young Reformers.

Deuchler, Martina, *Confucian Gentlemen and Barbarian Envoys: The Opening of Korea, 1875–1885* (University of Washington Press, Seattle, 1977).

Hall, Captain Basil, *A Voyage of Discovery to the West Coast of Corea and the Great Loo-choo Island* (John Murray, London, 1818; reprinted Royal Asiatic Society, Korea Branch, Seoul, 1975).

Harrington, Fred Harvey, *God, Mammon, and the Japanese: Dr Horace N. Allen and Korean-American Relations, 1884–1905* (University of Wisconsin Press, Madison, 1944).

PART IV. THE EMPIRE OF THE SUN

Chong, Chin-Sok, *The Korean Problem in Anglo-Japanese Relations 1904–1910* (Nanam, Seoul, 1987). The story of E. T. Bethell and his newspapers.

Fisher, James Ernest, *Democracy and Mission Education in Korea* (Columbia University Press, New York, 1928; reprinted by Yonsei University, Seoul, 1970). An objective and irenic study of Japanese and American methods of education in Korea in the 1920s.

McKenzie, Frederick, A., *The Tragedy of Korea* (Hodder and Stoughton, London, 1908; reprinted by Yonsei University, Seoul, 1969). A British journalist with the 'Righteous Army' in 1907.

—— *Korea's Fight for Freedom* (Revell, New York, 1920; reprinted by Yonsei University, Seoul, 1969).

PART V. THE TWO REPUBLICS

Pak Chi-Young, *Political Opposition in Korea, 1945–1960* (Seoul National Press, Seoul, 1980).

Hastings, Max, *The Korean War* (Michael Joseph, London, 1987).

Whelan, Richard, *Drawing the Line: The Korean War 1950–1953* (Faber, London, 1990).

Goncharov, Sergei with John Lewis and Xue Litai, *Uncertain Partners: Stalin, Mao, and the Korean War* (Stanford University Press, Stanford, Calif., 1994).

Declassified documents from Russia and the USA enable Whelan, from the UN side, and Goncharov, Lewis and Litai from the other, to clarify the misunderstandings that almost turned a local rivalry into a third World War.

SUGGESTIONS FOR FURTHER READING

GENERAL HISTORY

Lee Ki-baik, *A New History of Korea*, trans. Edward W. Wagner with Edward J. Shultz (Ilchokak, Seoul, 1984). Outstanding, detailed, one-volume history. Intended originally for Korean readers, it assumes some general background knowledge of the country. English-language bibliography and glossary. Takes the story as far as 1960. An abridged version, from the same publisher, with no bibliography, but with new material by other writers, bringing the story up to 1989, appeared in 1990 with the title, *Korea Old and New: A History*.

Nahm, Andrew C., *Korea: Tradition and Transformation* (Hollym, Elizabeth, NJ and Seoul, 1988). Provides a summary of the early history up to 1850 and then a detailed account of the modern period up to 1980, including a close survey of events in both North and South since 1945.

Rutt, Richard (ed.), *A Biography of James Scarth Gale and a New Edition of his History of the Korean People (1927)* (Royal Asiatic Society, Korea Branch, Seoul, 1972). Both the biography of the great Canadian missionary pioneer and his scholarly but idiosyncratic history make fascinating reading.

EARLY WESTERN VISITORS

Bishop, Isabella Bird, *Korea and her Neighbours* (John Murray, London, 1897; reprinted Yonsei University, Seoul, 1970 and KPI, London, 1985). One of the great travel writers of the nineteenth century who happened to be in Korea during the most dramatic period of its overthrow.

Hamilton, Angus, *Korea* (Heinemann, London, 1904). The travels of an observant and intolerant Scotsman who hated Americans and Catholics, but made friends with palace dancing girls and Buddhist abbots.

Underwood, Lillias H., *Fifteen Years among the Topknots* (American Tract Society, Boston, Mass., 1904; reprinted Royal Asiatic Society, Korea Branch, Seoul, 1977). The author went to Korea as a missionary doctor in 1884, became physician to the Queen, married the most adventurous of the Protestant missionaries, Horace Underwood, and set off with him on a long and hazardous journey to the North.

CLASSICAL LITERATURE

Chung Chong-wha (tr.), *Love in Mid-Winter Night: Korean Sijo Poetry* (KPI, London, 1985).

Kim Jong-gil (tr.), *Slow Chrysanthemums: Classical Korean Poems in Chinese* (Anvil Press Poetry, London, 1987).

Rutt, Richard (tr.), *The Bamboo Grove: An Introduction to Sijo* (University of Los Angeles Press, Berkeley, Calif., 1971).

Rutt, Richard (tr.), *Virtuous Women: Three Masterpieces of Traditional Korean Fiction* (Unesco, Seoul, 1974). (*Kuŭnmong* by Kim Man-jung, *Inhyŏn wango chŏn* and *Ch'unhyang ka*).

Skillend, W. E., *Kodae Sosŏl: A Survey of Traditional Korean Popular Novels* (SOAS, University of London, London, 1968).

ANTHOLOGIES

Chung Chong-wha (ed.), *Korean Classical Literature: An Anthology* (KPI, London, 1989).

Lee, Peter H. (ed.), *Anthology of Korean Literature from Early Times to the Nineteenth Century* (University of Hawaii Press, Honolulu, 1981).

VILLAGE LIFE

Kang, Younghill, *The Grass Roof* (Follett Publishing Company, Chicago, 1968; originally published in 1931).

Li, Mirok, *The Yalu Flows: A Korean Childhood* (Michigan State University Press, East Lansing, Mich., 1956). Translation of *Der Yalu Fliesst* (Munich, 1946).

Kang in America and Li in Germany were both émigrés who wrote highly acclaimed accounts of their turn-of-the-century childhood in North Korea.

Osgood, Cornelius, *The Koreans and their Culture* (Ronald Press, New York, 1951). A detailed study by a professor of anthropology from Harvard who spent the summer of 1947 sharing the life of a typical village.

Rutt, Richard, *Korean Works and Days: Notes from the Diary of a Country Priest* (Royal Asiatic Society, Korea Branch, Seoul, 1964).

RELIGION

Grayson, J. H., *Korea: A Religious History* (Clarendon Press, Oxford, 1989).

Iryŏn, *Samguk Yusa: Legends and History of the Three Kingdoms of Ancient Korea*, trans. T. H. Ha and G. K. Mintz (Yonsei University, Seoul, 1972).

Lee, Peter H., *Lives of Eminent Korean Monks: The Haedong Kosŭng Chŏn* (Harvard University Press, Cambridge, Mass., 1969).

Paik, Lak-Geoon George, *The History of Protestant Missions in Korea, 1832–1910* (Union Christian College Press, Pyongyang, 1927; rev. edn. reprinted by Yonsei University Press, Seoul, 1970).

INDEX